Y0-ABQ-712

WITHDRAWN
UTSA LIBRARIES

SUCCESSION IN THE MUSLIM FAMILY

Succession in the Muslim Family

N. J. COULSON

Professor of Oriental Laws, University of London

CAMBRIDGE

AT THE UNIVERSITY PRESS 1971

Published by the Syndics of the Cambridge University Press
Bentley House, 200 Euston Road, London N.W.1
American Branch: 32 East 57th Street, New York, N.Y.10022

© Cambridge University Press 1971

Library of Congress Catalogue Card Number: 78-130907

ISBN: 0 521 07852 0

Printed in Great Britain
at the University Printing House, Cambridge
(Brooke Crutchley, University Printer)

CONTENTS

INTRODUCTION

In any legal system of succession the fundamental consideration is the extent to which an individual has the personal right to determine the devolution of his property after his death. Such power was commonly denied in those early forms of society where the individual was wholly subordinate to the group. Instead, the law imposed compulsory rules of succession of general application; for the security of the group required that property should, on the decease of its owner, be transmitted in a foreseeable way to those held by the law as best entitled to it rather than to those whom the deceased might personally prefer. By contrast, most modern systems of succession rest firmly upon the freedom of the individual to determine the devolution of his property upon his decease. Under English law, for example, the wishes of the deceased as expressed in his will are paramount, and basically the law only intervenes to specify the manner in which the property shall devolve when a person has died wholly or partially intestate – that is to say, when he has not made a valid will, or when such testamentary dispositions as he has made do not exhaust the whole of his estate.

1. The general nature of the Islamic law of succession

It is from the way in which it resolves this fundamental question that the Islamic law of succession derives its most distinctive characteristics. The supreme purpose of the Islamic system is material provision for surviving dependants and relatives, for the family group bound to the deceased by the mutual ties and responsibilities which stem from blood relationship. The manner in which this provision is to be made is prescribed by the law in rigid and uncompromising terms. Relatives are marshalled into a strict and comprehensive order of priorities and the amount, or *quantum*, of their entitlement is meticulously defined. "Legal heir", in the Islamic context, is a term which is properly applied only to those relatives upon whom property devolves, after the decease of its owner, by operation of law; and it is the rights of the legal heirs which are the keynote of the whole system of succession, for they are fundamentally indefeasible. The power of the deceased to dispose of his property by will is recognised but is basically restricted to one-third of his net assets. Only where the legal heirs are prepared voluntarily to forgo their rights will testamentary disposition in excess of this limit be operative. Accordingly, the transmission of property by way of bequest, or in accordance with the wishes of the deceased, is of secondary importance, and the central core of the system of succession is formed by the compulsory rules of inheritance designed for the material benefit of the family group.

This approach stands in sharp contrast, for example, with that of English law, where it is only under the comparatively recent and limited terms of the Inheritance (Family Provisions) Act, 1938, that the court may vary or override the will of the deceased in order to make reasonable provision for the maintenance of family dependents. "Intestacy" may be used as a term of convenience to describe the Islamic law of inheritance, but it should certainly not carry with it any notion of a necessary recourse to a scheme of succession invoked only because the deceased has failed in his duty personally to arrange the devolution of his property. In Islamic legal philosophy the rules of inheritance propound the ideal way for the deceased to fulfil his duty to his surviving family.

2. The heirs' rights in the estate

For the purposes of the law of succession the estate of a deceased Muslim comprises all the property that he owns, whether his ownership is of the substance or corpus of a thing or merely of its usufruct or income. Nor is any distinction made, as regards the rights of the different legal heirs, between the various types of property. Moveables and immoveables, realty and personalty, make up the single entity of the estate in which each entitled heir is given a quantitative or fractional share. The right of a legal heir, therefore, is that of a defined quota share in each and every item of property that comprises the estate. Settlement or composition between the heirs, of whom there will normally be a considerable number, may result in the distribution of the various properties among them in accordance with the value of their quantitative entitlement. But in practice the system must inevitably produce, particularly in regard to land, either an extensive incidence of joint ownership or an excessive fragmentation of property, according as to whether the heirs insist upon division or not.

3. The importance of succession law in Islam

Within the framework of the Islamic legal system as a whole the laws of succession occupy a particularly prominent and important position. Historically they provide an excellent example of the general process of legal development in Islam, under which new standards and precepts introduced by the religion were superimposed upon existing customary law and the two heterogenous elements gradually fused and welded together into a composite and cohesive system. From a sociological standpoint, the laws of inheritance reflect the structure of family ties and the accepted social values and responsibilities within the Islamic community. For in the eyes of the law rights of inheritance are generally regarded as the consideration for duties of protection and support owed to the deceased during his lifetime; so that the stronger the family bond, the greater the right of inheritance. There is also the particular rule that the duty of a person to maintain his needy collateral relative is dependent upon, and proportionate to, his right to inherit from that relative. Juristically, the law of succession is a solid technical achievement, and Muslim scholarship takes a justifiable pride in the mathematical precision with which the rights of the various heirs, in any given situation, can be calculated.

Above all, however, the great esteem which this branch of legal science enjoys among Muslim peoples stems from its particularly strong religious significance. True knowledge, or *'ilm*, in the Islamic view, stems from divine revelation, and in a statement attributed to the Prophet Muḥammad the laws of inheritance are said to constitute "half the sum of *'ilm*". Nowhere is the fundamental Islamic ideology of law as the manifestation of the divine will more clearly demonstrated than in the laws of inheritance. The skeleton scheme of priorities and, in particular, the fixed fractional shares of the estate to which various relatives are entitled were laid down in the Qur'ān itself. Thus the system is firmly based on what is, to the Muslim, the very word of Allāh himself, and this is reflected in the terminology of the law.[1] "*Farḍ*" is the root Arabic term for a duty imposed by divine command, but the word is also used both in the singular and in one of its plural forms, "*farā'iḍ*", specifically to denote the shares of inheritance allotted to various relatives by the Qur'ān; so that the phrase *'ilm al-farā'iḍ*, or "science of the *farā'iḍ*", which is commonly used to describe the system of inheritance as a whole, epitomises the notion of religious obligation. In providing for the continuity of the family group as one cell of the universal Islamic community, the laws of inheritance appear as a vital aspect of the individual's supreme duty to the religion of Islam. In

[1] For the non-Arabist the transliteration of the Arabic terms and proper names which appear in the text may be briefly explained. An opening quotation mark represents the Arabic consonant *'ain*, which is a hard glottal stop. In the term *farā'iḍ*, the closing quotation mark represents the Arabic *hamza*, which is a soft glottal stop; the point under the letter ḍ indicates that it is a hard consonant, and the line over the ā indicates a long vowel.

many modern Muslim states whole spheres of traditional Islamic law have been abandoned and replaced by laws of European origin. But the law of succession still continues to be generally applied in practice throughout the world of Islam largely because it constitutes such an integral and deep-rooted part of the religious ethic.

4. The various schools of Islamic law

In order to explain the scope and nature of this book it is necessary to remark briefly upon two particular features of the Islamic legal system. Firstly, traditional Islamic law is not a single uniform legal code. Islamic jurisprudence originated as the attempt to define, in terms of concrete legal provisions, the will of Allāh for Muslim society. It was, in essence, a process of discovery of Allāh's law, or the Sharīʿa, by speculative reasoning on the part of scholar-jurists. From their work of interpreting, expanding and supplementing the basic precepts of divine revelation embodied in the Qur'ān and the precedents, or *sunna*, set by the Prophet Muḥammad, there gradually emerged a comprehensive corpus of legal doctrine. And this corpus, as it is recorded in a succession of manuals dating from early mediaeval times onwards, forms the traditional or classical expression of Sharīʿa law. But such a process of growth inevitably produced considerable diversity of doctrine. Variant rules arose not only because of controversy on intrinsically juristic issues – such as the authenticity of an alleged text of divine revelation, the canons of interpretation and construction, or the methods of legal reasoning – but also because of the external influences which naturally conditioned the thought and approach of the jurists, as individuals or as groups. Social standards and practices current in a particular locality, different political affiliations and schism on fundamental theological questions were among the factors which helped to shape divergent legal doctrines.

As a result there eventually came into existence several different schools or versions of Sharīʿa law, each of which possessed its own authoritative legal manuals and each of which represented, for its own exponents and followers, the true interpretation of the Sharīʿa. Today no less than eight such separate versions of the Sharīʿa are important from the standpoint of the practical application of law in Islam. The vast majority of Muslims, known from their basically common religious dogma as Sunnīs, are divided among the four schools of the Ḥanafīs, Mālikīs, Shāfiʿīs and Ḥanbalīs, while there are two sectarian minorities who stand apart from the Sunnīs on fundamental theological issues – the Ibāḍīs and the numerically infinitely larger group of the Shī'a, which is itself split into the three distinct branches of Ithnā 'Asharīs, Ismā'īlīs and Zaidīs.

In principle it is the duty of the court to apply that school of law to which the individual litigants concerned have personally chosen to give allegiance. Rules exist to regulate cases of conflict between the different schools, and in matters of succession it will generally be the school of the praepositus which will apply. In practice, however, owing to factors connected with the historical spread of Islam and political developments, the populations in fairly well-defined geographical areas of the Muslim world have embraced a particular school and the courts in that area have become wedded to the application of the doctrine of that school. Thus, throughout the Middle East and the Indian sub-continent, it is the Ḥanafī school which is generally applied by the courts administering Sharī'a law. In North, West and Central Africa Mālikī law prevails. Shāfi'ī law obtains in South Yemen, in the Muslim communities of East Africa and in Ceylon, Malaysia and Indonesia. The courts of Saudi Arabia apply the Ḥanbalī doctrine. Iran is the stronghold of Ithnā 'Asharī law and the Yemen of Zaidī law. The communities of Ismā'īlīs in East Africa observe their own version of the Sharī'a. Finally, Ibāḍī law is today confined to Uman and small groups of Muslims in Algeria, although until very recent times it had official status in Zanzibar.

In substantive law generally, and certainly in the law of succession at death, the differences between these various schools are often not merely variations in detail but matters of a fundamentally different approach. Furthermore, the authoritative texts of each particular school embody variant shades of opinion as between individual jurists subscribing to that school. From all this it will be apparent that diversity of doctrine is of the essence of traditional Sharī'a law. As a doctrinal system which is constantly searching through the various accepted criteria of juristic method to ascertain the most proper definition of Allāh's law, the Sharī'a appears, on a universal plane, as a comparative system in its own right.

5. Modern reform of Sharī'a law

The second feature of the Islamic legal system which must command attention is the process of modern reform of the law which has taken root in many Muslim countries and communities over the last few decades. Because of the problems of principle inherent in the reform of a religious law, the far-reaching changes which have been introduced into the terms of the traditional law – in the field of family law in general and succession law in particular – have been effected in a variety of ways. In the Indian sub-continent, for example, statute law has in many respects directly superceded the traditional Ḥanafī doctrine and become an integral part of the body of succession law applied by the courts. In the Ḥanafī countries of the Middle East, on the other hand, there has been a particular concern to ensure that reforms should rest on a juristic basis for which support can be found in the principles of traditional Islamic jurisprudence. Thus, for example, the codification of parts of the family law, including the law of succession, which have recently appeared in the Middle East include rules and doctrines which are derived from schools other than the Ḥanafī school – on the principle that all are equally legitimate expressions of the Sharī'a. This is a process which has naturally accentuated the comparative aspect of Sharī'a law and led to a breaking down of the barriers between the different schools. In more extreme cases reforms are openly based on what is claimed to be a novel and valid interpretation of the basic precepts of the Qur'ān or the *sunna* of the Prophet.

But whatever the principles upon which reforms have been based, their purpose is clear enough. It is to align the terms of Islamic law to the present needs and circumstances of Muslim society. This constitutes a radical break with past tradition under which Sharī'a law, as the eternally valid and immutable will of Allāh, was regarded as a rigid and static system. Today Islamic law is a living and developing system which, within the accepted limits imposed by the divine command, is conditioned by and grows out of the phenomena of social change.

6. The scope of this book

Because, therefore, of the existence of the different schools of law and the further variations which have been introduced into the traditional legal practice of a given area under the recent process of reform, modern Islamic law, when viewed on a world-wide basis, is an extremely complex and variegated phenomenon.

Taking, for example, the simple case of a deceased who dies intestate, survived by his daughter, the daughter of his predeceased son and his brother, the distribution of the inheritance will vary according as to whether the deceased is a Pakistani, Egyptian, Tunisian or Iranian Muslim as shown on page 7. Such diversity poses considerable problems as regards the composition of a text book on the subject.

Ideally, perhaps, the legal practitioner whose purpose is to ascertain current law would require a comprehensive account of the law of succession as it is actually applied today, country by country and community by community, throughout Islam. But this would entail innumerable volumes and a great deal of unnecessary repetition; it would unduly emphasise the diversity in a system which is basically and fundamentally a unity, and it would in any case be a somewhat barren and superficial exercise as far as the study of Islamic law is concerned. For the study of law generally, if it is to be a discipline of depth and significance, is not confined to a grasp of technical rules and principles, but involves the understanding of the place that those rules occupy, in terms of their genesis and purpose, within the society which supports them. And such an understanding of Islamic law, as a whole, necessarily includes an appreciation of both the phenomenon of diversity of doctrine and the process of modern reform.

	Pakistan	Egypt	Tunisia	Iran
Daughter	$\frac{1}{3}$	$\frac{1}{2}$	$\frac{3}{4}$	All
Granddaughter	$\frac{2}{3}$	$\frac{1}{6}$	$\frac{1}{4}$	—
Brother	—	$\frac{1}{3}$	—	—

Within the limits of a single volume, therefore, perhaps the scheme adopted in this book is the best way to achieve these various purposes. In each major division of the subject the traditional Sharī'a law will first be described with an explanation of the principal divergencies among the several schools, although for reasons of space Ibāḍī law will be omitted and only the Ithnā 'Asharī version of Shī'ī law will be dealt with in any detail. This will be followed by a consideration of the outstanding changes introduced into the law in modern times in the two principal areas of the Indian sub-continent and the Middle East. In most other parts of the Muslim world the traditional law of the school applicable in the area remains of general validity.

As regards the scope of its subject matter this book is confined to the substantive law of inheritance, bequests and ancillary matters. It deals only with solvent estates, taking up the law from the point where funeral expenses and debts have been paid and a net estate is available for succession. For all the preliminary issues which form the subject of the administration of estates the student is referred to the excellent book of Dr I. Mahmud, *Muslim Law of Succession and Administration* (Karachi, 1958).

The arrangement of the subject matter of the book is as follows. As preliminary and essential background, the first chapter deals with the principal institutions of Islamic family law, traditional and modern, which are relevant to rights of succession. Chapters 2–7, pp. 29–107, are concerned with the traditional Sunnī law of inheritance, and Chapter 8, pp. 108–34, with the fundamentally different scheme of intestate succession adopted by traditional Shī'ī law. This is followed, in Chapter 9, pp. 135–63, by a consolidated review of the major reforms which have recently been introduced in the law of inheritance in various Muslim countries. Chapter 10, pp. 164–71, is devoted to the particular problem of the rights of inheritance of persons who have a dual relationship with the deceased. Impediments to inheritance (i.e. the circumstances in which a surviving relative is disqualified from inheritance) are the subject of Chapter 11, pp. 172–94, and the conditions of inheritance (i.e. the establishment of the death of the praepositus and the survival of the heir) the subject of Chapter 12, pp. 195–212. Chapter 13, pp. 213–34, considers the legal incidents of the transaction of bequest. Finally, Chapters 14 and 15, pp. 235–79, are devoted to the subject of the protection afforded by the law to the rights of the legal heirs through the *ultra vires* doctrine, which imposes limits upon the power of the praepositus to dispose of his property by will or to interfere with the due devolution of his estate by transactions undertaken during his death sickness.

This order of topics is dictated primarily by the consideration that a comprehension of the various aspects of Islamic succession law requires as its basis a knowledge of the rights of the legal heirs, in terms of the priorities that obtain among them and the quantum of their individual entitlement. It may appear, in fact, that the arrangement of this book is almost precisely the opposite of the chronological sequence of events and problems involved in the actual administration of an estate. For the first step is to ascertain the gross estate, upon which funeral expenses and debts are a first charge, and this involves the application of the *ultra vires* rule to the deceased's acts and transactions during his death sickness. The next step is to give such effect out of the net estate to bequests as the *ultra vires* doctrine and the rules relating to the validity of bequests allow; then to ascertain who are potentially the heirs of the praepositus by taking into account the circumstances upon which the rights of the heirs depend – i.e. applying the rules regarding the conditions of, and impediments to, inheritance; and finally to distribute the inheritance among the entitled claimants. At the same time, a knowledge of who the entitled legal heirs are and what the *quantum* of their entitlement is must be the practical starting point for the administrator, since it is the legal heirs who, by their consent or otherwise, determine the effect of any *ultra vires* disposition of the praepositus.

I have endeavoured throughout to deal with the subject as a living aspect of contemporary jurisprudence and in a manner which will be intelligible to the modern student of law. For this reason I have omitted almost completely any reference to the institution of slavery, which is no longer relevant to present day Muslim society but which is the subject of a massive corpus of law in the traditional authorities. It gives rise there, for example, to such complex problems as the effect of a testamentary gift of freedom to a slave who becomes the legal heir of the testator upon his emancipation. Similarly, I have not included in the text any discussion of some of the rather extraordinary situations which attracted the attention of the mediaeval scholars, such as the case of the deceased whose sole surviving relatives are his thirty-two great-great grandparents, or the problem as to whether a person with two heads counts as one or two persons for the purpose of inheritance. (The solution proposed for this last problem is that the two-headed person, when asleep, should be touched on one of his heads. If both heads wake up together he is to be counted as one, but if only the head touched awakes he is to be counted as two.) Nor have I followed the particular techniques and methods of exposition adopted by the traditional Arabic authorities where these appear to place an unnecessary strain upon the powers of comprehension of the modern lawyer who is not also an Arabist. This is the case, for example, with the whole subject of the fractional shares in the estate which are the entitlement of certain relatives. While the Arabic texts deal with this topic essentially as an arithmetical discipline, I have tried as far as possible to consider the problem in terms of the legal principles involved. There are sufficient complexities for the lawyer here without him being also required to don the mantle of the mathematician.

No doubt this approach loses something of the spirit in which the mediaeval jurists worked and expounded the law. But today Sharī'a doctrine – in the spheres of family law in general and succession law in particular – is more and more coming to be applied, not in the manner visualised by the traditional authorities, but as part of a modern legal system. The modern Muslim legal system is in fact an amalgamation of aspects of the Sharī'a and other laws which follow Western models in their form and substance. And the proper integration of Sharī'a law within this system requires the revision of the techniques and methodology of education in the law no less than of the application of the law through the courts. The aim of this book is simply to present, in a spirit which is in conformity with the present trends of legal education, a subject which Muslim jurists of the past and the present have fashioned into one of the most illuminating and distinctive features of the Islamic legal system.

1. FAMILY TIES AS GROUNDS OF INHERITANCE

Rights of inheritance rest upon the two principal grounds of marriage and blood relationship with the praepositus.[1] In both cases, obviously, the tie with the praepositus must be a legal tie, that is to say the marriage must be one which is valid, and the blood relationship must be one which is legitimate, in the eyes of the law. The primary purpose of this first chapter, then, is to deal with these preliminary issues of precisely what constitutes a marital or a blood-tie for the purposes of inheritance. At the same time, the broad review of the basic institutions of Islamic family law which this entails will provide the general background necessary for a proper understanding of the scheme of succession law as a whole.

1. Marriage (*nikāḥ*)

A spouse relict in succession law is one whose marriage with the praepositus is (i) valid, and (ii) existing, actually or constructively, at the time of the decease.

1.1. The validity of marriage

For a marriage to be valid, the two principal requirements are the proper conclusion of the marriage contract and the absence of any impediment to marriage between the parties.

1.1.1. Proper conclusion of the marriage contract

1.1.1.1. Formalities

Like any other private contract, a marriage under traditional Sharīʿa law is validly concluded simply by the mutual agreement, oral or written, of the parties – the bride and bridegroom or their respective representatives. The only formality required by the law is the presence of two witnesses at the conclusion of the contract to ensure its due publication, and even this is not necessary under Shīʿī law. Further, Mālikī law does not insist upon

[1] Under traditional Sharīʿa law a third ground for rights of inheritance lay in the institution of patronage (*walāʾ*), or the relationship between a freed slave and his former master. By virtue of his act of manumission, the master acquired the right to inherit from his freedman if the latter died without any heirs by blood.

witnesses to the contract if due publicity is given to the commencement of married life. Those formalities which are usually attendant upon a Muslim marriage, such as the performance of the ceremony in the presence of a religious official like the Imam of the mosque, are matters of customary practice and in no sense legal essentials.

1.1.1.2. Capacity to conclude marriage contract

Sanity and majority are the two essential ingredients of the legal capacity to contract. It is a general principle of traditional Sharī'a law that legal majority comes with physical puberty. Hence, in theory, capacity to conclude a marriage contract depends basically upon proof of sexual maturity established under the normal rules of evidence rather than upon the attainment of a specific age. In practice, however, majority or minority is more usually determined by legal presumptions. There is an irrebuttable presumption of law that a girl below the age of nine and a boy below the age of twelve have not reached puberty and are therefore minors, and an equally conclusive presumption that puberty, and therefore majority, is attained for both sexes with the completion of the fifteenth year.

1.1.1.3. Capacity of women

Only in Ḥanafī and Shī'ī law, however, has an adult woman the legal capacity to contract her own marriage. According to the other schools her marriage guardian must conclude the contract on her behalf, and any marriage contracted without his intervention, in person or through his agent, is a complete nullity. This is a quite separate issue from that of whether or not the bride's consent to the marriage is necessary. This latter question is determined by the extent of the guardian's powers over his ward.

1.1.1.4. The powers of marriage guardians

All schools recognise, in principle, that a power of "matrimonial constraint", termed *ijbār*, is vested in a marriage guardian, who may validly contract his ward in marriage at his discretion and regardless of the ward's wishes in the matter. But the precise extent of the power varies between the schools.

In Ḥanafī law the power of *ijbār* vests in any "proper" marriage guardian – i.e. the person so qualified to act under the rules of priority in marriage guardianship. The right belongs first to male agnate relatives in accordance with a system of priorities broadly parallel to that of priorities in inheritance – the father precedes the paternal grandfather, who is followed in turn by the agnatic brothers, nephews, uncles and cousins – and failing them to females and non-agnate relatives. Only minor wards are subject to *ijbār* in Ḥanafī law, and the power is absolute only when exercised by the father or paternal grandfather. In all other cases the ward may repudiate the marriage on attaining puberty, although until that time the marriage is, of course, perfectly valid.

Under the law of the other Sunnī schools only certain "close" guardians possess the power of *ijbār* – in Mālikī law the father or his appointed executor; in Shāfi'ī and Ḥanbalī law the father or the paternal grandfather. But their power is absolute, inasmuch as the ward has no right to repudiate the marriage on attaining puberty, and furthermore the power may be exercised over any adult woman who has not been married before, at least as long as she is of child bearing age. Shī'ī law recognises an absolute power of *ijbār* only in favour of the father or paternal grandfather and only over minor wards.

1.1.1.5. Modern reforms: registration

Registration of marriages has now become a necessary legal formality in most Muslim countries. As a general rule, however, a marriage which is not registered is not invalid, although the parties may be liable to statutory penalties. In Pakistan, for example, under the terms of the Muslim Family Laws Ordinance, 1961, failure to register a marriage in the prescribed way renders the celebrant of the marriage and the parties thereto liable to three months imprisonment or a fine of 1,000 rupees or both. Generally, too, a marriage may be proved by means other than the official registration. But in Egypt since 1931, and in Tunisia since 1957, a marriage can be proved only by the official certificate of registration. In both these countries, therefore, the effect of the procedural regulation is to deny judicial relief to the parties to an unregistered marriage which is disputed; and this may result in an inability to establish a claim of inheritance as a spouse relict.

1.1.1.6. Modern reforms: marriageable age

In Egypt the same expedient was used to modify the law relating to the marriageable age. A law of 1923 provided that a marriage where the bridegroom was below the age of eighteen or the bride below the age of sixteen could not be registered and therefore could not, if disputed, be the subject of judicial relief. By contrast with this approach, legislation concerning the marriageable age in other Middle-Eastern countries has directly affected the validity of marriage. Full competence to marry is acquired, not with the advent of puberty as under traditional Sharī'a law, but on attaining a specified age. This age is almost everywhere eighteen for males, and for females varies between eighteen (Iraq), seventeen (Syria and Jordan) and fifteen (Tunisia and Morocco). Marriage below these ages, however, is permissible on proof of sexual maturity. Generally the Middle-Eastern codes specify ages below which no claim of sexual maturity will be heard and which therefore represent the minimum ages for marriage. The lower limit of puberty laid down in this regard by traditional Sharī'a law – the age of nine for girls and twelve for boys – has been raised in Syria, for example, to fifteen for males and thirteen for females; in Jordan to fifteen for both sexes, and in Iraq to sixteen for both sexes. Young persons who have reached these ages, but not yet the age of full competence to marry, may marry subject in most cases to the consent of the marriage guardian and in all cases to the permission of the court.

Failure to obtain the necessary permissions will, of course, preclude registration of the marriage and may render the parties liable to statutory penalties, but it will not invalidate the marriage. It is clear, however, that the modern legislation relating to marriageable age has almost completely abolished the right of the marriage guardian to contract a valid marriage by constraint, or *ijbār*. In the Middle East generally no legal recognition is any longer afforded to the marriage of a minor who is not physically mature.

In India and Pakistan a guardian may still validly contract his minor ward in marriage by *ijbār*, notwithstanding the punitive sanctions attached to the marriage of minors (boys below eighteen and girls below sixteen) by the Indian Child Marriage Restraint Act, 1929 (as confirmed by the Pakistani Muslim Family Laws Ordinance, 1961). However, a girl so contracted in marriage during minority may now repudiate the marriage even if it was contracted by her father or paternal grandfather. Under the terms of the Pakistani Ordinance she may do this by satisfying the court that she was contracted in marriage by her father or other guardian before she was sixteen; that she repudiated the marriage before she was eighteen, and that the marriage had not been consummated.

1.1.1.7. Modern reforms: the woman's capacity

Finally, on the matter of the conclusion of the contract, the traditional Mālikī rule that an adult woman must be given in marriage by her proper guardian still obtains in the Sudan and Morocco, although the woman's consent to the marriage is now, as a general rule, essential for its validity. In Tunisia, however, a Mālikī woman no longer suffers from this incapacity and may now validly conclude her own marriage contract. It is also noteworthy in this regard that a series of recent judicial decisions in India and

Malaya have ratified marriages contracted by Shāfi'ī girls without their guardian's consent on the broad ground that it was admissible to apply the more liberal Ḥanafī doctrine in these cases.

1.1.2. Impediments to marriage

Impediments to a valid marriage lie in personal attributes or circumstances which prevent an individual from being a proper subject for marriage in general or for marriage with a particular person. For present purposes the principal impediments may be listed under six heads.

1.1.2.1. Relationship by blood, affinity or fosterage

Relationship by blood, affinity or fosterage creates a bar to marriage. As regards blood relatives, a person is prohibited from marrying any lineal descendant, any lineal ascendant, any descendant of his or her parents, and the immediate child of any grandparent. Relationship through marriage, or affinity, raises the bar to marriage between a person and the spouse of any ascendant, the spouse of any descendant, any ascendant of his or her spouse and any descendant of his or her spouse. Foster relationship arises when a woman breast-feeds someone else's child. It creates a bar to marriage not only between foster brothers and sisters but also between the foster mother and all her relatives on the one side and her foster children, their spouses and their descendants on the other side.

1.1.2.2. Married women and women observing *'idda*

Since Islam does not permit polyandry, a man may not validly marry a woman who is already married or who is observing *'idda*. *'Idda* is a period of waiting imposed upon a wife after the termination of her marriage. Its primary purpose is to determine whether or not she is pregnant as a result of the marriage, and therefore she is not allowed to remarry during this time. Following divorce the *'idda* lasts until the completion of three menstrual cycles or, where the wife proves to be pregnant, until the birth of the child. In cases of widowhood the *'idda* also serves as a mark of mourning for a deceased husband and lasts for a prescribed period of four months and ten days, or until the birth of the child in cases of pregnancy.

1.1.2.3. Married men

Polygyny is permitted under traditional Sharī'a law subject to two principal restrictions. First, the maximum number of wives that a man may have concurrently is four. A marriage to a fifth wife is therefore invalid. Second, a man is not allowed to have as co-wives two women so closely related that, if either one of them were a male, they would themselves be within the prohibited degrees of marriage. This is usually known as the bar of "unlawful conjunction", and means that a man may not validly marry, for example, the sister or the niece of his existing wife.

1.1.2.4 Modern reforms relating to polygyny

Modern legislation has sought to set strict limits to the practice of polygyny, if not eliminate it altogether. At the one extreme of the process of reform is the Tunisian Law of 1956, which prohibits polygamy outright. At the other is the Moroccan Law of 1958, which enacts: "If any injustice is to be feared between co-wives, polygamy is not permitted", but only allows the court to intervene retrospectively by granting judicial divorce to a wife who complains of injury suffered as a result of her husband contracting a further marriage. Syria, Iraq and Pakistan have adopted a middle course by requiring official permission for a polygamous marriage. In Syria the court may refuse such permission where it is established that the husband is not in a position properly to maintain and support a plurality of wives. To this criterion the Iraqi Law adds the proviso that there must be "some lawful benefit involved" in the proposed union, and gives the court a discretion to refuse permission "if any failure of equal treatment between co-wives is feared". In Pakistan the necessary permission is to be given by an arbitration council, consisting of the chairman of the local union council, a representative of the husband and a representative of the existing wife, on the basis as to whether or not it is "satisfied that the proposed marriage is necessary and just" and "subject to such conditions, if any, as may be deemed fit".

In Tunisia, after a great deal of hesitation, the view gradually prevailed in the courts that a polygamous marriage was invalid; and this was expressly stated to be so by subsequent legislation of 1964. Elsewhere, however, a polygamous marriage contracted in defiance of the various provisions is not invalid *per se*. This reflects the strength of traditionalist opposition to the reforms, particularly in Iraq where the Code of 1959 dealt with polygamous unions improperly contracted in the context of impediments to a valid marriage. But an amendment of 1963 to the Iraqi Code deliberately removed "marriage with more than one wife without the permission of the court" from the list of impediments to a valid marriage. In all cases, however, infringement of the provisions entails statutory penalties. In Pakistan a second marriage without the permission of the Arbitration Council entails a threefold sanction. The husband becomes liable to imprisonment for up to one year, or a fine of up to 5,000 rupees, or both;

he is obliged to pay forthwith the entire dower of his existing wife, even though it had been agreed that the payment of a portion thereof was to be deferred; and finally the existing wife has a right to judicial dissolution of her marriage.

1.1.2.5. Difference of religion

A Muslim woman is allowed to marry only a Muslim, while a Muslim male may marry either a Muslim or a *kitābiyya* – i.e. a woman belonging to a religion which has a revealed scripture (*kitāb*), such as Judaism or Christianity. A difference of religion between a man and a woman outside these limits renders their marriage invalid.

1.1.2.6. Divorcees

In two particular circumstances a bar to marriage exists between a divorcee and her former husband. The first is the case of a couple divorced by the procedure of *li'ān* (p. 25 below), where the bar to remarriage is absolute and perpetual. The second is the case of a woman divorced from the same husband three times. Here, however, the bar to remarriage between the couple will be removed by the divorcee's marriage to someone else, the consummation of this marriage and, of course, its termination.

1.1.2.7. Pilgrimage

In Shāfi'ī and Shī'ī law it is unlawful for a person who is in the course of performing the rite of pilgrimage to contract a marriage.

1.1.3. Any invalidating element bars inheritance

Muslim jurisprudence, naturally enough, does distinguish between these various causes of invalidity of marriage on the general ground of their comparative gravity. Lack of proper mutual agreement, for example, or a defect in the legal capacity of a party, goes to the essence of the contract and makes it a total nullity, whereas the absence of the requisite two witnesses at the contract is regarded merely as an irregularity in the attributes of the contract. So, too, an impediment to marriage may be of a permanent and absolute nature, like blood relationship, or a temporary and partial bar which may be removed by the act of a party, like difference of religion, or simply by the passage of time, like the *'idda* period. These distinctions are very relevant to the general question of the legal effects of an invalid marriage and to the particular question of the status of any children of the union (p. 25 below). But they have no relevance to the matter of rights of inheritance. A spouse relict inherits only if the marriage is valid in every respect.

1.1.4. Consummation of marriage not required

A spouse relict's right of inheritance arises from the marriage contract itself and does not depend upon consummation of the marriage. Even minors, who have been validly contracted in marriage by their guardians, have mutual rights of inheritance although they have not reached the age at which marital cohabitation normally begins.

1.1.5. Temporary marriage in Shīʿī law

In the contemplation of Sharīʿa law, and notwithstanding the comparative ease of divorce, marriage, or *nikāḥ*, must be intended to be a life long union. Hence, in Sunnī law, any condition or stipulation by which the parties seek to set a time limit to their union renders the whole contract a nullity, since it is an agreement contrary to the essence of marriage. Shīʿī law, however, recognises another legal form of sexual union in the institution of *mutʿa*. This is a contract whereby a woman agrees to cohabit with a man for a specified period of time in return for a fixed remuneration. A temporary marriage of this kind does not of itself give rise to mutual rights of inheritance between the partners, although such rights may be created, according to traditional Shīʿī doctrine, by stipulation. It seems, however, that under the current Civil Code of Iran (article 940) such a stipulation will be void.

1.2. Subsistence of the marriage at the time of decease

Mutual rights of inheritance between spouses cease as soon as their marriage is finally terminated, but following divorce a marriage may be deemed to be in existence constructively, *inter alia* for purposes of succession, for as long as the wife remains in her *ʿidda*. This depends upon the nature of the divorce.

A divorce under Sharīʿa law may be classified either as revocable (*rajʿī*), or absolute and irrevocable (*bāʾin*). A divorce is revocable when the husband is entitled to retract it during the wife's *ʿidda*, the main purpose of this rule being to afford an opportunity for reconciliation. In these circumstances the marriage is not dead during the *ʿidda*, but merely dormant and capable of being revived. Hence, a substantial enough ground for mutual rights of inheritance between the parties continues to exist during the *ʿidda*. An irrevocable divorce, on the other hand, is a final severance of the marital tie. Rights of inheritance cease immediately upon this type of divorce and do not persist during the wife's *ʿidda*. The primary purpose of the following pages, therefore, is to indicate to which of these two categories the various forms of divorce known to Sharī'a law belong.

Three principal modes of divorce are recognised by traditional Sharī'a law – unilateral repudiation of the wife by the husband, or *ṭalāq*; divorce by mutual consent, and dissolution of marriage by judicial decree.

1.2.1. Divorce by *ṭalāq*

A Muslim husband has the power to terminate his marriage unilaterally at his absolute discretion. No intervention by a court or any other official body is required, not even for the formal recognition of the divorce. *Ṭalāq* is an extra-judicial proceeding, validly effected simply by the husband pronouncing the appropriate words of repudiation at such time and in such place as he sees fit.

1.2.1.1. Revocable and irrevocable *ṭalāq*

Basically a *ṭalāq* does not constitute a final severance of the marital tie since the husband may retract the repudiation at will during the wife's *'idda*. A husband, however, is not allowed to withdraw a repudiation against the same wife more than twice. Hence a third *ṭalāq* is final and irrevocable. From this rule derived the institution of the irrevocable "triple" *ṭalāq*, a term used here to cover cases of three repudiations pronounced on the same occasion, or repudiations coupled with words or signs indicative of three pronouncements (e.g. "I repudiate you three times"). It was also held to be possible for a husband to effect an immediate and irrevocable divorce by adding to a single repudiation an oath or other solemn expression of finality. These two latter types of repudiation were regarded by Sunnī jurisprudence as particularly "blameworthy" from a moral standpoint but nonetheless legally valid and effective. Shī'ī law, however, held them to be null and void, or at least to constitute only a single and revocable *ṭalāq*.

When a marriage has not been consummated and no presumption of consummation arises in law through the spouses having been together in circumstances of privacy, no *'idda* is incumbent upon the wife when the marriage ends by divorce. In these circumstances, therefore, a single and simple *ṭalāq* in fact constitutes an immediate and final divorce, since there is no period during which the husband may revoke it. There is also one circumstance in which an ostensibly final type of *ṭalāq* does not have the effect of immediately cutting off the wife's right of inheritance, namely, a final *ṭalāq* pronounced by a husband during his death sickness (pp. 276–7 below).

1.2.2. Divorce by mutual consent

Divorce by agreement may take the form either of *khul'*, where the wife secures her release from the marital tie by offering some kind of financial consideration, commonly the return of the dower, which is accepted by the husband, or of *mubāra'a*, which represents a dissolution of marriage on the basis of the mutual release of the spouses from any outstanding financial commitments arising from the marriage. In both cases the divorce is extra-judicial and effected simply by the mutual agreement of the parties.

1.2.2.1. Divorce by agreement final and irrevocable

Following the normal principle that a contract becomes binding as soon as an offer is accepted, the divorce takes place the moment mutual agreement is reached and is not deferred until, for example, the payment by the wife of the agreed consideration. Such a divorce is always final, on the basis that a bilateral agreement cannot be unilaterally broken. Accordingly there are no rights of inheritance if either spouse dies during the *'idda*.

1.2.3. Divorce by judicial decree

Traditional Ḥanafī law knows no doctrine of dissolution of marriage by judicial decree. On the petition of a wife, a Ḥanafī court may annul her marriage on the ground that the husband has proved totally unable to consummate it, or, where the husband is a missing person, it may declare her marriage to have ended after such a period of time (in effect ninety years from the date of his birth) as enables the court to presume her to be a widow. But these are not cases of judicial divorce in the accepted sense.

1.2.3.1. The Mālikī law of judicial *ṭalāq*

To varying degrees, however, the other schools recognise the right of a wife to petition for judicial divorce on the broad ground of the husband's failure to fulfil his marital duties. Mālikī law is the most liberal in this respect and allows judicial divorce under the following four major heads.

(i) Physical or mental disease: in broad terms this covers all cases of the husband's serious disease of body or mind where the continuation of the marital relationship would jeopardise the wife's health.

(ii) Failure to maintain: a decree will issue on this ground whether the husband's failure to provide maintenance at the proper standard is the result of a wilful refusal or a simple inability to do so.

(iii) Desertion: even where property of the husband is available to provide the wife with maintenance and support, she is entitled to dissolution where the husband has absented himself without lawful reason and thus deprived her of the right of *consortium.*

(iv) Prejudice: *ḍarar* is the Arabic term usually used in this context and there is no precisely equivalent English term. This almost residual ground for a wife's petition certainly includes the husband's physical or mental cruelty, but also covers cases of incompatibility which in effect amount to a decree of divorce based on the established breakdown of the marriage.

1.2.3.2. Judicial divorce is final except in cases of failure to maintain

In point of procedure, when a ground for divorce is established under Mālikī law, the court invites the husband to pronounce a *ṭalāq* against his wife, and if he fails to do so the court will pronounce it on his behalf. This always takes the form of a final (*bā'in*) *ṭalāq* except in the case of a petition based on the ground of the husband's failure to provide proper maintenance. Here, the court pronounces a *ṭalāq* which is revocable (*raj'ī*) and will be withdrawn at the instance of the husband if he satisfies the court during the wife's *'idda* that he is now both able and willing to maintain her. In this one case, therefore, mutual rights of inheritance between the spouses continue during the *'idda.*

1.2.4. Modern reforms in divorce law

Modern reforms of divorce law in the Ḥanafī areas of the Middle East and the Indian sub-continent have been directed towards the two principal objectives of increasing the remedies available to the wife in cases of marital injury on the one hand and restricting the husband's power of *ṭalāq* on the other.

1.2.4.1. The modern law of judicial dissolution

As regards a wife's petition for judicial divorce, it is broadly the Mālikī law which now applies in the Middle East, although there is considerable variation on minor details from country to country. Substantially the same grounds for judicial divorce were made available under the Indian Dissolution of Muslim Marriages Act, 1939, which now applies in India and Pakistan. But since this Act was not as conscious or direct an application of Mālikī principles as was the legislation in the Middle East, there are significant variations in both the substantive and procedural aspects of the law. In particular, as far as rights of inheritance are concerned, a judicial decree granted under the Indian Act is always final and absolute,[1] so that rights

[1] Final and absolute also is a judicial decree of divorce granted on the two fresh grounds recently established in Pakistan in addition to those available under the Dissolution of Muslim Marriages Act. Under the Pakistani Muslim Family Laws Ordinance, 1961,

of inheritance between the spouses do not continue during the *'idda* following divorce for failure to maintain as is the case in the Middle East.

1.2.4.2. Abolition of the irrevocable forms of *ṭalāq*

One of the principal features of modern reform in the law of *ṭalāq* has been the progressive restriction of the husband's power to terminate his marriage immediately by pronouncing a final and irrevocable repudiation. The various steps taken in this regard were, of course, primarily designed to afford greater opportunity for reconciliation between an estranged couple, but they also have the effect of prolonging the spouses' mutual rights of inheritance until such time as their divorce becomes absolute.

In Egypt, the Sudan, Jordan, Syria, Morocco and Iraq, the traditional institutions of the triple repudiation and the single but final repudiation have been abolished by the rule that every pronouncement of *ṭalāq* which is not the third in a series of separate pronouncements shall take effect only as a revocable divorce.

Under the Pakistani Muslim Family Laws Ordinance, 1961, a husband is required to give written notice of his having pronounced a *ṭalāq* both to his wife and to the Chairman of the Arbitration Council set up under the Ordinance. A *ṭalāq* pronounced "in any form whatsoever" will not be absolute (and therefore the spouses' rights of inheritance will not terminate) until ninety days after delivery of this written notice to the chairman, or, where the repudiated wife is pregnant, until delivery of the child, whichever period be longer. It seems, therefore, that even if a husband gives notice of a third repudiation, this will no longer constitute an immediate and final divorce. Furthermore, the same procedure is to apply "where any of the parties to a marriage wishes to dissolve the marriage otherwise than by *ṭalāq*". This clearly covers the case of extra-judicial divorce by mutual agreement, which will accordingly no longer constitute a final and irrevocable divorce as it does under traditional Sharī'a law. On the other hand, where a husband does not give the requisite notice of his *ṭalāq*, or the spouses do not give notice of divorce by agreement, the divorce will apparently be valid and effective under the terms of traditional Sharī'a law, since the sanction for failure to comply with the provisions of the Ordinance is purely punitive – the offender being liable to imprisonment for a term of up to one year, or a fine of up to 5,000 rupees, or both.

a wife has a ground for divorce if her husband has taken a second wife without the necessary permission of the Arbitration Council. Under the doctrine laid down by the Supreme Court of Pakistan in *Khurshid Bibi* v. *Mohammed Amin*, P.L.D. (1967), S.C. 97, a wife's petition for divorce may be granted when the court is satisfied that the marriage is irretrievably broken down.

It is the Tunisian Law of Personal Status, 1956, however, which provides the most radical and systematic reform of Sharī'a law in this regard. The essence of the Tunisian Law lies in the complete abolition of extra-judicial divorce, whether by *ṭalāq* or mutual consent, and the placing of a wife on a footing of absolute equality with her husband.

In detail, section 31 of the Law provides that a decree of divorce will be granted: (i) on a petition by the husband or wife based on any of the grounds specified in the Law (broadly the grounds known to traditional Mālikī law); (ii) in cases of mutual consent; (iii) when either husband or wife insists on ending the marriage, in which case the court will determine "what financial indemnity the wife shall be granted by way of compensation for the damage she has sustained, or what compensation she shall pay to her husband".

Section 32 of the Law then provides that "A decree of divorce shall not be given until the court has first exerted itself to the utmost in investigating the causes of dissension between the spouses and has failed to reconcile them."

The Tunisian Law, then, entirely sweeps away the traditional distinction between a revocable and an irrevocable form of divorce. In all cases the marriage continues to exist, and with it mutual rights of inheritance, until the court issues a decree of divorce; and since the decree is final in all cases, there are no rights of inheritance if either of the parties dies during the wife's *'idda*.

2. Blood relationship (*nasab*)

Rights of inheritance arise only from blood relationship, and not from relationship by affinity or by fosterage. In the contemplation of traditional Sunnī law, the family group knitted together by the web of social rights and obligations was the extended agnatic family of males linked through males to a common ancestor. Hence, although maternal relatives do have rights of inheritance, the main emphasis lies on the paternal connection; and indeed the primary significance of the word *nasab* is that of paternity.

2.1. Legitimacy is the basis of rights of inheritance

Legitimacy of birth is the legal postulate for admission to the family group. No legal paternity, or *nasab*, exists between a father and his illegitimate child, and illegitimacy precludes the existence of any legal bond between the blood relatives of the father on the one hand and the illegitimate child and its issue on the other. Possibly, although somewhat paradoxically, it was because the maternal connection was not so important socially that Sunnī law was prepared to recognise the existence of legal duties and rights, including those of inheritance, between a mother and her illegitimate child and between their respective relatives. In the eyes of Shīʿī law, however, as will be explained in greater detail below (Chapter 8), the maternal and the paternal connection are of equal standing. Hence the criteria of what constitutes a legal tie are the same in both cases, and an illegitimate child has no legal relationship with either its father or its mother.

Except for maternal relatives in Sunnī law, therefore, rights of inheritance depend upon the relationship between the praepositus and the claimant heir, whether immediate or through any number of intermediate links, being a legitimate relationship. Accordingly, there follows a summary of the Islamic law of legitimacy in both its traditional and modern expressions.

2.2. Traditional Sharīʿa law

Under traditional Sharīʿa law a child is illegitimate if it is the product of *zinā*, i.e. the criminal offence of extra-marital sex relations. There is no process by which such a child can be legitimised, for example by the subsequent marriage of its parents, and the law does not recognise any institution of adoptive paternity. Broadly, therefore, the fundamental criterion of legitimacy is the conception of the child during the lawful wedlock of its parents. The evidential rules which implement this substantive doctrine may be conveniently summarised under the two heads of legal presumption of paternity and acknowledgment of paternity.

2.2.1. Presumption of paternity arising from marriage

The legal presumption that a child born to a married woman is the legitimate child of her husband is expressed in the Arabic maxim: *al-walad li'l-firāsh*, or "the child belongs to the marriage bed". Since, however, the decisive determinant of legitimacy is the date of the child's conception and not its birth, the presumption operates only within the limits of what the law recognises to be the minimum and maximum duration of the gestation period.

The minimum period of gestation according to all schools of law is six months. The maximum period varies between nine or ten months (Shīʿī law), two years (Ḥanafī law), four years (Shāfiʿī and Ḥanbalī law), five to seven years (Mālikī law). Basically, therefore, the law attributes to the husband the paternity of a child born to his wife after not less than six months of marriage and within not more than two years (in terms of

Ḥanafī law) of the termination of the marriage, provided, of course, that in the latter case the birth of the child represents the end of the wife's *'idda* period.

Contemporary medical science, of course, generally regards one year as the absolute limit of pregnancy. But in the more conservative areas of Islam, such as Nigeria and Saudi Arabia, the excessively long periods of gestation recognised as possible under traditional Sharī'a law are still very much of a reality both in popular belief and in judicial practice. In 1948, for example, the High Court of Mecca held that a pregnancy had lasted for almost six years. The case appears as No. 328 in Vol. 5 (1368 A.H.) at pp. 15–17 of the handwritten Record of cases heard by the High Court. One Khadija had been finally divorced by her husband Salih four months after the birth of a child. Five years and nine months after this divorce Khadija gave birth to another child. She claimed that she had been pregnant at the time of the divorce and that she had continued in her *'idda* until the birth of the child. Accepting this claim, the Court adjudged the child to be the legitimate child of Salih. In this case the Court held that the traditional Ḥanbalī rule which sets the maximum period of gestation at four years was not applicable, on the ground that the fact of Khadija's pregnancy at the time of her divorce was established. Events subsequent to this case are of some interest. Khadija had remarried and asserted that she had been pregnant by her husband Sulayman for more than nine months. Sulayman agreed that this was so and the Court issued a decree of prospective paternity, attributing Khadija's child, whenever it should be born, to Sulayman. In 1959 Khadija's married sister, Ruqayya, also claimed to have been pregnant for much longer than nine months. This was supported by the evidence of a midwife and accepted to be so by Ruqayya's husband. The High Court of Mecca again issued a decree of prospective paternity, attributing Ruqayya's child, whenever it might be born, to her husband. This case appears on the Record of the High Court as No. 1144, Vol. 16 (1379 A.H.) at p. 36.

In Ḥanafī law this presumption of legitimacy begins to run six months after the contract of marriage itself, but in the law of the other three Sunnī schools it only begins to run six months after the consummation of the marriage, whether the consummation is acknowledged by the parties or presumed by the law because the parties have been together in circumstances of privacy which present no legal, moral or physical impediment to sexual intercourse. According to the Shī'a the presumption applies throughout marriage only if the spouses had physical access to each other at any possible time of conception.

2.2.2. Rebuttal of the presumption by *li'ān*

Except in Shī'ī law, proof of non-access between the spouses at any possible time of conception does not serve to rebut the presumption of legitimacy. A husband's repudiation of his wife's child creates a particular problem in Sharī'a law because it is in effect an accusation that she has committed the crime of *zinā*. An unproved accusation of *zinā* is itself a criminal form of defamation termed *qadhf*, which carries a penalty of eighty lashes, and *zinā* can be proved, apart from the accused's confession, only by the testimony of four eye witnesses to the very act of sexual intercourse. Hence, the only means under traditional Sunnī law for a husband to effectively repudiate the paternity of a child born to his wife is the formal procedure of *li'ān*. The husband must swear four oaths (taking the place of the four witnesses required to prove *zinā*) that the child is not his and then invoke the curse of Allāh upon himself if he is lying. This operates as an immediate and final divorce. The wife may then take four contradictory oaths and also invoke the curse of Allāh upon herself if she is lying. But whether she does so or not only affects the question of her punishment for *zinā*. In any event the child has been successfully disowned by the husband. Finally, a husband cannot invoke this procedure if he has ever expressly or impliedly accepted the child as his. In practical terms this means that he must repudiate the child during the wife's pregnancy or within a short time of his knowledge of the birth.

2.2.3. Invalid marriages

The legal effects of an invalid marriage, particularly as regards the status of any children of the union, depend essentially upon whether the parties are deemed in law to be guilty of *zinā* or not. If their sexual relationship is one of *zinā*, any children are illegitimate; if it is not *zinā*, the same presumption of legitimacy will operate as in the case of a valid marriage. Determination of this issue involves two principal considerations. First, under the general criteria of criminal responsibility, ignorance or mistake of fact provides a complete defence to a criminal charge. Hence, if the parties to an invalid marriage are ignorant of the vitiating element, even if it is an absolute and permanent impediment of relationship, they cannot be guilty of *zinā* and the presumption of legitimacy will operate in favour of any children of the union. Second, assuming the parties to be aware of all relevant facts, the marital tie, though admittedly invalid, may yet be deemed substantial enough to justify a sexual relationship. This depends on whether the contract is held to be vitiated in its essence or merely in its attributes. Generally a marriage contract is held to be sound in its essence if there is proper mutual agreement between parties who have a legal capacity to contract and who are not permanently prohibited in marriage to each other through, for example, relationship by blood, affinity or fosterage. If these essential requirements are met, then even if the contract is vitiated in some attribute, such as a difference of religion between the spouses or the absence of the required two witnesses at the conclusion of the contract, there is still a substantial enough contract to legalise the sexual union of the parties. In the terminology of Ḥanafī law, a marriage contract which is vitiated in its essence is *bāṭil*, or wholly null and void, while one which is vitiated only in its attributes is *fāsid*, or irregular.

In sum, then, the practical effect of these considerations is that the children of an invalid marriage are presumed legitimate unless the marriage contract is vitiated by a fundamental defect in mutual agreement or by an absolute and permanent impediment which was known to the parties.

Some difficulty arises over the question of the rebuttal of the presumption of legitimacy in these cases since for technical reasons the procedure of *li'ān* cannot apply to parties who are not validly married. The position seems to be simply that the presumption is rebutted by the "husband's" refusal to accept the child as his.

2.2.4. Acknowledgment of paternity

In theory an acknowledgment (*iqrār*) of paternity is not a process of legitimation but the formal recognition of a status of legitimacy which exists in fact. It is evidence which establishes the fact of legitimacy in cases where the legal presumption of legitimacy does not apply. A corner-stone of the Islamic law of evidence, however, is the rule that an acknowledgment by a sane, adult person against his own material interests effectively establishes the facts acknowledged unless and until those who contest the acknowledgment prove it to be false. An acknowledgment of paternity falls into this category because of the financial obligations it entails. Accordingly, an acknowledged child will be held to be the legitimate child of the acknowledgor unless those who contest the acknowledgment can prove the impossibility of legal paternity. To do this they must show either that the physical fact of paternity itself is impossible (because of the respective ages of acknowledgor and acknowledgee), or that the child cannot be the legitimate child of the acknowledgor (because he is known to be the child, legitimate or otherwise, of someone else, or because he cannot have been conceived in lawful wedlock between the mother and the acknowledgor).

Taking into account the general rules of procedure and evidence under

Sharī'a law and the fact that traditionally there was no system of registration of marriages, the burden of proving a negative of this kind would often be an impossible one. In practice, therefore, an acknowledgment might well amount to the legitimation of a child conceived out of wedlock. Normally, for example, an acknowledgment by a husband of a child born to his wife within six months of their known marriage could not be effectively contested.

An acknowledgment of paternity need not be in express words but may be implied by the deliberate conduct of a person who treats a child as his legitimate child. Subject to repudiation by an acknowledgee who is adult and sane, an acknowledgment of paternity is binding for all purposes and irrevocable.

2.3. Modern reforms in the law of paternity

2.3.1. The Middle East

Egyptian legislation of 1920 and 1929 set the pattern for reform of this branch of the traditional Ḥanafī law in the countries of the Middle East. The Explanatory Memorandum accompanying the legislation indicated the social need for reform by pointing out that the bulk of a deceased husband's estate would be inherited by a child who was deemed his legitimate offspring; and this might be a child born to his wife when "their marriage had been concluded while each continued to live in his and her own locality and they had never met, from the time of the marriage until the birth of the child, in any way which could give them access to each other". It might also be a child born to his wife nearly two years after their divorce or his death. In short, the Memorandum asserted, the application of the traditional Ḥanafī rules "encouraged people to allege the legitimate paternity of illegitimate children – a fact about which there have been many complaints".

Accordingly, the Egyptian legislation provided: (*a*) that one solar year was to be regarded as the maximum period of gestation, in the sense that no claim of legitimacy on behalf of a child born more than one year after the termination of the marriage between the mother and the alleged father would be entertained by the courts; (*b*) that proof of non-access between the spouses since marriage or for a year or more preceding the birth of a child to the wife would debar a claim of the legitimacy of such a child.

With some variations the Syrian, Tunisian and Moroccan legislation follows these rules. In all countries one year is adopted as the maximum period of gestation, though as a rule of substantive law rather than as a procedural requirement in the manner of the Egyptian legislation. The

Moroccan Law, however, provides that "If, at the end of the year, a doubt persists regarding pregnancy, the interested party shall bring the matter to the attention of the court so that the assistance of medical experts may be invoked for a solution". In Tunisia proof of non-access to rebut a claim of legitimacy is not restricted, as under the Egyptian and Syrian Laws, to the spouses' separation for a year or more prior to the birth of the child. The relevant provision enacts that a claim of paternity will not be established "in regard to a child born to a wife in circumstances in which it can be proved that the husband had no access to her, nor one born to a woman more than a year after her husband had left her". It would appear that the traditional procedure of *li'ān*, though almost obsolete in practice, is still in law available to a husband in order to disown a child when he cannot establish non-access within the above limits. The Tunisian Law, in fact, embodies a modern and streamlined version of *li'ān*.

If a husband disowns the child with which his wife is pregnant, or the child which is presumed to be his, this repudiation will not be effective without a decree of court – and in such a matter all legal means of proof may be used...If the court confirms the repudiation of paternity...it shall pass a decree of illegitimacy and of physical separation between the spouses.

It is noteworthy, however, that the Jordanian Law of 1951 and the Iraqi Law of 1959 do not prescribe any new maximum period of gestation, and allow proof of non-access by the husband to rebut a claim of paternity only where it is a case of the spouses never having physically come together since the time of the contract of marriage.

2.3.2. India and Pakistan

The law currently applicable in India and Pakistan in this regard (as a result of the Evidence Act, 1872) is distinguished by the fact that the presumption of legitimacy arises in favour of a child "born during the continuance of a valid marriage". This means that the paternity of a child born a matter of weeks or even days after marriage will be attributed to the husband. Thus the six months' rule of traditional Sharī'a law, which is still observed throughout the Middle East, is no longer applicable in India and Pakistan. Under the Indian Evidence Act a child born more than 280 days after the termination of a marriage will not be presumed to be the legitimate child of the husband – although this does not preclude the court from adjudging such a child to be legitimate on the basis of medical or other evidence adduced by the party who seeks to establish legitimacy. Finally, under the Evidence Act, a claim of paternity may be rebutted by proof of non-access at any possible time of conception of the child.

2. PRIORITIES IN INHERITANCE

I. The dual basis of entitlement

The wife of Sa'd b. al-Rabī' came to the Prophet with her two daughters and said: "O Prophet, these are the daughters of Sa'd b. al-Rabī'. Their father died a martyr's death beside you in battle. But their uncle has taken Sa'd's estate and they cannot marry unless they have property." After this the verse of inheritance was revealed and the Prophet sent for the uncle and said to him: "Give the two daughters of Sa'd two-thirds of the estate, give their mother one-eighth and keep the remainder yourself."[1]

Sa'd's case embodies the essence of the changes introduced under Islam into the customary Arabian law of inheritance. In the tribal society of pre-Islamic Arabia the system of inheritance was designed to keep property within the individual tribe and maintain its strength as a fighting force. The tribe was patriarchal and patrilineal. Women occupied a subordinate and subjugated position within the group whose bond of allegiance was that of *'aṣabiyya* – descent through male links from a common ancestor. A woman who married into another tribe belonged henceforth, along with her children, to the tribe of the husband. The maternal or uterine relationship, therefore, lay outside the structure of tribal ties and responsibilities. In these circumstances the proper exploitation and preservation of the tribal patrimony meant, *inter alia*, the exclusion of females and non-agnate relatives from inheritance and the enjoyment of a monopoly of rights of succession by the male agnate relatives, or *'aṣaba*, of the deceased. Hence the initial appropriation of Sa'd's estate by his brother, as his nearest male agnate, to the exclusion of the wife and daughters.

Under Islam, however, the political and social scheme which had supported this customary system of succession was transformed. Politically, the bond of a common religious faith, with allegiance to the Prophet as the head of the community, transcended tribal ties and within the brotherhood of Muslims there was no place, in theory at any rate, for inter-tribal hostility or warfare. Socially, Islam emphasised the more immediate family tie existing between a husband, his wife and their children, and aimed at elevating the status of the female within this group. These changes are mirrored in the novel rules of succession introduced by Islam. Briefly, the Qur'ān establishes rights of inheritance between husband and wife and in favour of certain close female blood relatives – the mother, the daughter

[1] This version of the Prophet's decision appears in *al-Mughnī* of Ibn Qudāma, VI, 166.

and the sisters – by prescribing fixed fractional parts (*farāʾiḍ*) of the deceased's estate as their entitlement. Clearly, however, these rules in themselves do not form a complete system of succession. In the Sunnī view they do not altogether abrogate but merely modify the customary system of succession by superimposing upon it a new class of legal heirs. The male agnates still inherit, but now after the satisfaction of the claims of those relatives nominated by the Qur'ān. Hence, in Sa'd's case, the brother inherited the residue after the Qur'anic heirs – the wife and the daughters – had taken their prescribed portions of one-eighth and two-thirds respectively.

Thus the Islamic law of inheritance rests basically upon the recognition of two distinct categories of legal heirs – the male agnates or *'aṣaba*, the heirs of the tribal customary law, and the new Qur'anic heirs, who are called *ahl al-farāʾiḍ* ("those entitled to prescribed portions"). Through the work of the early Muslim jurists these two distinct basic elements were gradually fused together into a cohesive system. But this process of amalgamation was not a simple one, and almost all the major complexities of the law stem from its dual basis and the attempt to harmonise the claims of these two categories of legal heirs.

2. General classification of legal heirs

2.1. Terminology and classification

Taken together, the relatives nominated in the Qur'ān and the male agnates are the ordinary legal heirs of the Islamic system in the sense that the praepositus will usually be survived by a member or members of this group upon whom succession will devolve. But in the extraordinary situation where no blood relative of this group survives, the inheritance belongs, in the view of the great majority, to the other relatives of the praepositus. This gives rise to difficulties of terminology and classification.

In the first place the Arabic texts, in the context of succession, refer to those relatives who are neither Qur'anic nor male agnate heirs as *dhawū'l-arḥām* (lit. "the possessors of a uterine relationship") and this is usually rendered in English as "uterine heirs" or "distant kindred". Neither of these terms is satisfactory: "uterine heirs" because the group contains female agnates such as the paternal aunt and because the uterine brother and sister are in fact Qur'anic heirs; "distant kindred" because certain relatives in the group are no more "distant", in point of degree of removal from the deceased, than Qur'anic or male agnate heirs. For example, the daughter's son and the maternal grandfather belong to this group while the son's son and the paternal grandfather are male agnates.

In the second place, most authors writing in English on this subject adopt a threefold classification of heirs: Qur'anic heirs (*ahl al-farā'iḍ*), male agnates (*'aṣaba*) and "distant kindred" (*dhawū'l-arḥām*). The objection to this classification is that it confuses two separate issues – the rules of priority or exclusion on the one hand, and the principles of distribution on the other. For while the Qur'anic heirs and male agnates, as a composite class, have priority over the *dhawū'l-arḥām*, the distinction between the Qur'anic heirs and the male agnates is not a matter of priority, in the sense that one excludes the other, but a matter of distribution of inheritance among entitled heirs: it is the distinction between a specific or fractional entitlement and a residual entitlement. Moreover this same distinction can apply within the group of the *dhawū'l-arḥām* when they are entitled to inherit.

2.2. The inner and the outer family

It would seem that these difficulties can be avoided by dividing all relatives, on the broad ground of precedence in succession, into two groups, which may be called respectively "the inner family" and "the outer family" – terminology which at least will be familiar to members of the English Bar. The inner family is made up of all male agnates, whatever their degree of removal from the praepositus, along with those particular relatives nominated by the Qur'ān. All other relatives constitute the outer family, which is only called to succession when there is no surviving blood relative of the inner family. Within each group a system of priorities operates to exclude certain relatives and the subsequent distribution of the estate among the actual heirs may involve the distinction between a specific and a residual entitlement.

3. Priorities within the inner family

3.1. Priorities are the fundamental issue in succession

The case of the estate of Sa'd discussed above lays down what may fairly be called the golden rule of Islamic inheritance – namely, that the Qur'anic heirs first take their allotted portions and the male agnate relatives then succeed to the residue of the estate. But this golden rule comes into operation only at a secondary stage in the solution of any problem of intestacy. It determines the *quantum* of the inheritance which the heirs take after the issue of which of the surviving relatives are in fact entitled heirs has been decided in accordance with the rules of priority.

This is not to say that the distinction between Qur'anic and *'aṣaba* heirs has no bearing on the question of priorities. In the first place, as will be seen shortly, it is a basic characteristic of Qur'anic heirs that they do not exclude other relatives. In the second place, certain female relatives may inherit either as Qur'anic or as residuary heirs. And as far as two of these females are concerned – the germane sister and the consanguine sister – the fact that they succeed in one capacity or the other determines whether certain other relatives are excluded from succession or not. In these particular cases, therefore, the question as to whether the sister is a Qur'anic or residuary heir cannot be divorced from, and is in fact preliminary to, the issue of priorities. As a general rule, however, the distinction between Qur'anic and residuary heirs is best considered as a separate and subsequent question which goes primarily to the *quantum* of entitlement. The first and fundamental issue is that of the priority which is to be given by virtue of the nature of the claimant's relationship with the praepositus. And it is the manner in which such priority is determined that is the subject of the remainder of this chapter.

3.2. *De jure* and *de facto* exclusion

Priority in succession is a term strictly used in the present context to distinguish between those surviving relatives of the praepositus who are legal heirs and those who are not, in the sense that a relative who has priority over another totally excludes the latter from any rights of inheritance. When it comes to the subsequent issue of the distribution of the estate among the legal heirs, the Qur'anic heirs may be said to have priority over the male agnates insofar as the satisfaction of their allotted portions is the first charge upon the estate. Indeed, the result of this golden rule of distribution may be that in certain circumstances the satisfaction of the Qur'anic portions completely exhausts the estate so that nothing of the inheritance remains for the male agnates as residuary heirs. In these cases the residuary heirs are excluded from inheritance not directly by any rule of law which declares their relationship with the praepositus to be inferior to that of the other claimants, but indirectly by the fact that a certain number of other heirs happen to have survived. These cases are, therefore, perhaps best regarded as cases of *de facto* exclusion, to distinguish them from the cases of *de jure* exclusion where one relative is deemed by law to have a superior tie of relationship and thereby excludes other relatives from inheritance. It is the principles of such *de jure* exclusion that provide the logical starting point of the law of inheritance.

3.3. The system of mitigated agnatic succession

The system of priorities rests basically upon the principles of agnatic succession recognised by the customary tribal law in pre-Islamic Arabia. As has been observed above, the Qur'ān did not formulate an entirely novel law of inheritance – or, more precisely, it did not do so in the view of Sunnī jurisprudence. It merely modified the existing customary law by adding thereto as supernumerary heirs a number of relatives who would normally have had no rights of succession under the customary law. As a result of this approach the essential character of the developed Sunnī law of inheritance is that of an agnatic system of succession mitigated by the Qur'anic provisions. Male agnate relatives generally remain in a dominant position, and the consolidated system of priorities covering the members of the inner family as a whole was achieved by absorbing the new Qur'anic heirs within the framework of the customary rules of priority operating among male agnates.

3.3.1. The male agnates: al-Jabarī's rule

Of the surviving male agnates, or *'aṣaba*, the "nearest" relative or relatives alone succeeds. Priority is determined by three criteria which are collectively known as al-Jabarī's rule.

3.3.1.1. The rule of class

All male agnates are divided into classes which, in order of priority, are: I. the son and his descendants (the son of a son how low soever); II. the father and his ascendants (the father's father how high soever); III. the descendants of the father (the brothers of the deceased and their issue, the nephews of the deceased, how low soever); IV. the descendants of the paternal grandfather (the deceased's uncles and cousins and their issue how low soever); V. the lines of descendants of the great paternal grandfather and higher grandfathers in ascending order (the deceased's great uncles and their issue).

Any member of a higher class totally excludes any member of a lower class, the one exception to this rule being the doctrine of the Sunnī majority that the brothers of the deceased are not excluded from succession by the grandfather.

3.3.1.2. The rule of degree

Among relatives of the same class the nearer in degree to the praepositus excludes the more remote. This fundamental rule of priority means that a relative at the second or more distant degree of removal from the praepositus will be totally excluded from succession not only by the relative through whom he is directly connected with the praepositus but also by any nearer relative of the same class. In Class III, for example, a nephew of the deceased will be excluded by the deceased's brother, whether the latter be his own father or his uncle. Similarly, in Class IV a cousin will be excluded by any agnatic uncle of the praepositus.

The rule of priority by degree clearly precludes outright, as far as agnate relatives are concerned, any genuine form of succession by representation – the principle that a more remote relative may represent a predeceased nearer relative through whom he is connected with the praepositus by stepping into the shoes of this nearer relative and inheriting precisely as he would have done had he survived.

For example, the sole surviving relatives of the praepositus are two sons, A and B, and a grandson, G, the son of C, a third predeceased son of the praepositus.

G does not represent his father C, so as to take one-third of the inheritance as C would have done had he survived, but is totally excluded from succession by the nearer descendants, his uncles A and B.

3.3.1.3. The rule of strength of blood-tie

This final determinant of priority applies only to the collateral relatives who fall within Classes III, IV and V of the *'aṣaba* – the descendants of the father or grandfather how high soever of the praepositus. The "root" collateral relationship which is the starting point of each of these three classes – that between the praepositus himself and his brother, or that between the father of the praepositus and his brother, or that between the grandfather of the praepositus and his brother – may be one of the full or the half blood. Brothers of the full blood, having the same father and mother, are germane relatives, while those of the half blood, having the same father but different mothers, are consanguine relatives. The remaining type of half blood connection – the uterine relationship of brothers who have the same mother but different fathers – lies, of course, outside the bounds of the agnatic tie. But it may be observed that both these types of half blood relationship are common in Islamic society and therefore of considerable significance in the laws of succession. The relatively high incidence of the consanguine relationship is primarily due to the institution of polygamy; and that of the uterine relationship to the comparative ease and frequency of divorce and the remarriage of divorcees.

Among agnate relatives of the same class and the same degree, germanes have priority over consanguines and the issue of germanes have priority over the issue of consanguines. Thus, for example, the germane brother of the deceased totally excludes from succession the consanguine brother, and a cousin who is the son of a germane paternal uncle (the germane brother of the deceased's father) excludes a cousin who is the son of a consanguine paternal uncle (the consanguine brother of the deceased's father).

Priorities among the *'aṣaba* are determined exclusively by the tripartite al-Jabarī's rule. There are no further criteria – such as any doctrine of primogeniture – governing *de jure* exclusion. Any number of relatives who are of the same class, the same degree and, where applicable, the same strength of blood-tie rank as equally entitled legal heirs.

3.3.2. The Qur'anic heirs

The Qur'anic heirs, or the *ahl al-farā'iḍ*, are twelve in number according to Sunnī law. They are: the husband, wife, daughter, agnatic granddaughter (the daughter of a son how low soever), father, agnatic grandfather (father's father how high soever), mother, grandmother (maternal and paternal how high soever),[1] germane sister, consanguine sister, uterine brother and uterine sister.

Three of these relatives – the granddaughter, grandfather and grandmother – were not in fact specifically designated by the Qur'ān as legal heirs; but Sunnī jurisprudence added them to the list of *ahl al-farā'iḍ* through the doctrine of analogy (*qiyās*). The presence of two *'aṣaba* relatives in the group – the father and the grandfather – is explained by the fact that their inclusion was designed to enable them to share in the inheritance when they would otherwise be excluded, through the rule of class as applied in the pure agnatic system, by a son or grandson of the praepositus. The remainder of the *ahl al-farā'iḍ* – the husband, uterine brother and eight females – are, of course, relatives who did not rank as legal heirs at all under the customary tribal law. And these are the only female and non-agnatic relatives who inherit as members of the inner family under Sunnī law.

Systematic analysis of the priorities affecting Qur'anic heirs, whether within the group itself or in relation to the *'aṣaba*, is a difficult matter inasmuch as any rule formulated in this regard is subject to significant exceptions. However, the broad principles that do emerge are as follows.

[1] The question of which grandmothers at the third and more remote degrees of removal from the praepositus are to rank as Qur'anic heirs is a matter of controversy between the different schools and is dealt with in detail below (pp. 60–1).

3.3.2.1. Priorities among Qur'anic heirs

Basically, the Qur'anic provisions as extended by juristic interpretation increase the number of legal heirs recognised by the customary law by (*a*) creating an altogether new class of heirs by marriage – the spouse relict, and (*b*) adding other blood relatives to the existing classes – the daughter and agnatic granddaughter to the class of descendants, the mother and grandmother to the class of ascendants, and the three sisters, along with the uterine brother, to the class of descendants of the parents. It was obviously not the intention of the Qur'anic legislation that the heirs it nominated should inherit their allotted portions in all circumstances. On the one hand, the spouse relict, the parents and the daughter were given an unqualified right of succession in the sense that they are not subject to exclusion by any other relative. On the other hand, the Qur'ān expressly states that the rights of succession of brothers and sisters are subject to the absence of a child of the praepositus. As for the granddaughter and the grandparents, their rights are clearly subject to the rule of priority by degree; for the purpose of adding them to the list of the *ahl al-farā'iḍ* by way of analogy was to put them in the position of the respective relatives of the first degree in the latters' absence.

3.3.2.2. Relative priorities of Qur'anic and male agnate heirs

Within the group of the Qur'anic heirs themselves, therefore, criteria of priority are recognised which are parallel to those of al-Jabarī's rule. But the two categories of the Qur'anic and the male agnate heirs were not merged together to the extent that the Qur'anic heirs were given precisely the same position, according to their class and degree of relationship, as that of the corresponding male agnates in al-Jabarī's scheme. One major effect of the Qur'anic provisions, of course, was to put the ascendants of the deceased in a position which cuts through the established rule of priority by class. Neither the father nor the mother, nor in their absence the grandfather and the grandmother, are excluded by any descendant of the deceased. But apart from this the system of priorities among the male agnates remained virtually undisturbed.

3.3.2.3. Qur'anic heirs are not excluders

The fundamental reason for this was the assumption of Sunnī jurisprudence that a Qur'anic heir does not exclude other relatives of the inner family. The father and the grandfather clearly fall outside this principle. They are indeed Qur'anic heirs, in the sense that they are allotted fixed portions of the estate when in competition with a descendant of the deceased, but basically they are to be regarded for purposes of succession as male agnates who have, as such, the power to exclude other relatives.[1] A husband or a wife does not exclude, and is not excluded by, any other relative – the fact that they inherit on the ground of the marital tie setting them apart from the other heirs. The remaining Qur'anic heirs do not, as a general principle, exclude any other relative of the inner family, notwithstanding the superiority of their relationship with the deceased in terms of the three criteria of al-Jabarī's rule.

Thus, no rule of priority by class applies to the Qur'anic heirs. A daughter or granddaughter does not exclude any ascendant nor any agnatic collateral relative, male or female, although she does exclude uterine brothers and sisters. The mother or grandmother does not exclude any brother or sister – not even the uterines whose sole connection with the praepositus is through herself – or any more remote male agnate. Nor does any sister or the uterine brother, as a Qur'anic heir, exclude any relative of the inner family. Similarly, the rule of priority by degree in its strict sense does not apply to the Qur'anic heirs. A daughter, at the first degree of descent, does not *de jure* exclude any agnatic grandson or granddaughter. A mother excludes a grandmother, maternal or paternal, but does not exclude any agnatic grandfather how high soever. Nor does a sister exclude any male agnatic nephew of the deceased. Finally, a germane sister excludes neither a consanguine nor a uterine brother or sister by virtue of the superior strength of her blood-tie.

It must be emphasised, again, that the sole question here is that of which relatives totally exclude others from succession as a matter of law. Certain Qur'anic heirs do have priority over others, and over male agnates, to the extent that they will receive a greater share in the inheritance. In some cases, as will be seen, the satisfaction of the allotted Qur'anic portions will result in the total *de facto* exclusion of other relatives, both Qur'anic heirs and male agnates. And, of course, any Qur'anic heir, with the exception of the spouse relict, does, as a matter of law, exclude from succession any relative of the outer family.

But in regard to inheritance by the inner family the Qur'anic heirs are simply superimposed upon the system of succession by male agnates rather than integrated within it. They take their allotted portions when they are entitled to them and thus reduce the *quantum* of inheritance available for

[1] Systematically, it may be argued that even the father and the grandfather, as Qur'anic heirs, do not exclude others. For when they inherit solely in this capacity – in the presence of a son or agnatic grandson of the praepositus – it is then in fact the son or the grandson who excludes other relatives.

the male agnates; but otherwise they remain outside the established system of *de jure* priorities. The power to exclude other relatives from succession remains essentially the prerogative of the male agnates. To the rule that a Qur'anic heir excludes no other relative of the inner family, the two solitary exceptions are (*a*) the exclusion of the uterine brothers and sisters by the daughter or granddaughter, and (*b*) the exclusion of the grandmother by the mother. There is no exception at all to the rule that a Qur'anic heir does not exclude any male agnate.

3.3.3. Consolidated system of priorities

As a result of the principles outlined in the two preceding sections, members of the inner family may be marshalled into three groups for the purposes of priority in succession.

3.3.3.1. Primary heirs

There are six primary heirs who are never excluded from succession by any other relative of the praepositus. They are the husband, wife, son, daughter, father and mother. Among the children of the praepositus there is no priority by virtue of age or any other factor. All sons stand on a parity, as do all daughters.

3.3.3.2. Substitute heirs

For the four blood relatives who are primary heirs there are four substitute heirs – so-called because they generally take the place of the respective primary heir in the latter's absence. The agnatic grandson, how low soever, is a substitute heir for the son; the agnatic granddaughter, how low soever, for the daughter; the agnatic grandfather, how high soever, for the father; the grandmother, maternal and paternal how high soever, for the mother.

As a general rule, a substitute heir is excluded from succession by the respective primary heir, on the principle that the nearer in degree excludes the more remote, but is not excluded by any other relative. To this rule there are two exceptions. (*a*) An agnatic granddaughter is not *de jure* excluded from succession by the daughter but is so excluded by the son. In other words, the rule of degree operates within the class of agnatic descendants as a whole on the basis that a male always excludes any more remote descendants, male or female, but a female does not. (*b*) According to the doctrine of the Sunnī majority, a paternal grandmother is excluded by the father as well as by the mother of the praepositus. Again, this doctrine rests upon the rule of priority by degree.

Cases of succession by granddaughters and grandmothers are, admittedly, some of the more complex aspects of the law of inheritance. They involve special considerations which are dealt with in detail below (pp. 54–64).

3.3.3.3. Secondary heirs

This group is made up of the brothers and sisters of the praepositus and all other male agnate relatives.

As a whole group the secondary heirs are totally excluded from succession by any male blood relative who is a primary or a substitute heir – i.e. by a male agnatic descendant or ascendant – but not by any female. The two exceptions to this rule are that: (*a*) uterine brothers and sisters are excluded by the daughter or the agnatic granddaughter, and (*b*) agnatic brothers and sisters are not excluded by the grandfather in the majority view. (Competition between the grandfather and the collaterals is the particular subject of Chapter 6.)

When the group of secondary heirs is admitted to succession through the absence of any male agnatic descendant or ascendant, priorities within it are basically determined by al-Jabarī's rule. However, the quartet of Qur'anic heirs within the group – the three types of sister and the uterine brother – stand outside this internal system of priorities. None of them, as a Qur'anic heir, excludes or is excluded by any other member of the group, the solitary exception being the exclusion of the consanguine sister by the germane brother on the ground of the superior strength of the agnatic blood-tie.

Such being the basic system of *de jure* priorities among the relatives of the inner family, the principles governing the distribution of the inheritance within the three groups will be the subject of the three chapters that follow.

3. PRIMARY HEIRS

Apportionment of an estate does not involve any distinction between moveables and immoveables or between real and personal property. The estate available for the legal heirs consists of all the assets of the deceased that remain after the satisfaction of funeral expenses, debts and valid bequests. Female heirs suffer from no disability, at least in Sunnī law, to succeed to land or real estate. Each heir's entitlement is simply expressed in terms of a fractional share and attaches *in specie* to the various properties which make up the inheritance.

Distribution of an estate on a residual basis among male agnate heirs is a comparatively straightforward process: the inheritance is divided between the entitled claimants in equal shares. It is the position of the Qur'anic heirs which occasions the complexities of the Islamic system. Distribution is not always simply a matter of allotting a fixed portion of the estate to those relatives nominated by the Qur'ān and giving the residue thereof to the male agnates. In the first place Qur'anic heirs may in certain circumstances inherit a residual share instead of a Qur'anic portion. In the second place the Qur'anic portion they inherit is not "fixed" in the sense that it is constant in all cases. The mother of the praepositus, for example, inherits a share of the estate amounting to (*a*) one-quarter, in competition with a wife and a father; (*b*) one-sixth, in competition with a son and a daughter; (*c*) one-third, in competition with a husband and a uterine brother; (*d*) two-thirteenths, in competition with a husband and two daughters; (*e*) $\frac{7}{32}$, in competition with a wife and a daughter. This is perhaps sufficient to indicate that the share of inheritance which a Qur'anic heir receives depends entirely upon the presence or absence of other relatives. By way of a brief analysis, the mother in case (*a*) above takes as a residuary heir; in case (*b*) she takes her basic Qur'anic portion; in case (*c*) this basic portion is increased through the absence of certain relatives, while in cases (*d*) and (*e*) the basic portion has to be adjusted because of the number and nature of the other heirs with whom she is in competition. A Qur'anic portion, therefore, is "fixed" only to the extent that it establishes the proportionate entitlement of a Qur'anic heir in any given circumstances; and for this reason it is hardly logical to speak of a "normal" Qur'anic entitlement, since this postulates the survival of certain other heirs as normal. The presence of a Qur'anic heir among the entitled claimants in fact poses three distinct questions: Does the relative concerned inherit a Qur'anic portion?

If so, what is the basic portion? Does the presence or absence of other relatives necessitate adjustment of this basic portion? It will therefore be apparent that the various factors which affect the position of the Qur'anic heirs lie at the root of questions of apportionment. These factors will now be considered in relation to the individual relatives who constitute the group of primary heirs.

1. The spouse relict

A spouse relict inherits only as a Qur'anic heir, and the one factor which determines the basic Qur'anic portion is the survival or otherwise of a descendant of the praepositus. "Descendant" here means descendant of the inner family – i.e. a child or agnatic grandchild how low soever – and it is immaterial whether the child belongs to the surviving spouse or is the issue of another marriage of the deceased spouse.

In the presence of a descendant the basic Qur'anic portion of the husband is one-quarter of the estate, and in the absence thereof one-half. A surviving wife's portion is precisely half these respective amounts. In the presence of a descendant her portion is one-eighth, and in the absence of a descendant one-quarter. But the wife's portion is a collective one in the case of polygamous unions. Two or more surviving wives will share equally in the portion of one-eighth or one-quarter as the case may be.

2. Children

"Allah ordains concerning your children that the male shall have a share equivalent to that of two females. If the children are females numbering two or more, their portion is two-thirds of the inheritance. If there is a single female child her portion is one-half". This Qur'anic provision (Sūra 4, verse 11), which is the only one relating to the rights of inheritance of children, makes it clear that the position of daughters depends upon whether or not the praepositus is survived by a son.

2.1. The principle of *ta'ṣīb*: sons and daughters as residuaries

When a son is present the children inherit as residuary heirs, sharing the estate, or the residue thereof, in the proportion of two parts to a son and one part to a daughter. This is known as the principle of *ta'ṣīb*. A son converts his sister, the daughter of the praepositus, into an *'aṣaba* or residuary heir, and the daughter is said to inherit in these circumstances as *'aṣaba bi ghayrihā*, or "residuary by another", as opposed to the son who is *'aṣaba bi nafsihi*, or "residuary in his own right". *Ta'ṣīb* is not confined to the children of the praepositus. It may be stated as a strict rule of succession that agnatic female relatives who are Qur'anic heirs are always converted into residuaries by a male relative of the same class, degree and strength of blood-tie. Of the group of female Qur'anic heirs only the wife, grandmother and uterine sister are unaffected by *ta'ṣīb*. With its essential corollary of double share to the male, the principle clearly establishes the superiority of the male agnates as legal heirs; and its application, as will be seen, is in fact extended by Sunnī jurisprudence to secure an advantage for the male agnate in two particular cases which are not competitions between male and female blood relatives of identical relationship.[1]

An example of the operation of *ta'ṣīb* among children would be the case of P who is survived by her:

Husband	(Qur'anic portion)	$\frac{1}{4}$
Father	(Qur'anic portion)	$\frac{1}{6}$
Mother	(Qur'anic portion)	$\frac{1}{6}$
Two sons	(Residuaries) ($\frac{5}{12}$)	$\frac{1}{6}$ each
Daughter		$\frac{1}{12}$

The residue of five-twelfths of the estate which is left for the sons and daughter in this case after the satisfaction of the Qur'anic portions is in fact the minimum share of inheritance that children of the praepositus, as a group, will ever take. They are reduced to this minimum by the presence of the husband, the father and the mother, and in any other circumstances their collective entitlement must exceed five-twelfths of the estate.

2.2. Daughters as Qur'anic heirs

In the absence of any son of the praepositus daughters always take as Qur'anic heirs. The basic Qur'anic portion of one daughter is one-half. Two or more daughters share equally in a portion of two-thirds. These basic portions, unlike those of the spouse relict or the mother, are not subject to variation through the presence or absence of any other relative.

[1] The cases of (*a*) the father in competition with the mother and the spouse relict (pp. 45–6 below), and (*b*) the grandfather in competition with agnatic sisters (pp. 84–9 below).

3. Parents

The Qur'ān (Sūra 4, verse 11) regulates the rights of succession of parents by providing that: "To each of the parents goes one-sixth of the inheritance if the deceased has left a child. If there is no surviving child and the parents are the legal heirs, the mother takes one-third, except where the deceased has left brothers, when the mother takes one-sixth". Juristic interpretation of these basic rules had the following results.

3.1. Father inherits as Qur'anic heir or as residuary or in dual capacity

The father of the praepositus inherits as a Qur'anic heir, with a basic portion of one-sixth, in the presence of any lineal descendant of the inner family. As in the case of the spouse relict, the term "child" used in the Qur'ān is regarded as including agnatic grandchildren how low soever. In the absence of any child or agnatic grandchild, the father is the male agnate heir with highest priority under al-Jabarī's rule and thus inherits as a residuary. This, in fact, is his basic character as a legal heir; and while he will be excluded as a residuary by a male agnate descendant, he will not be so excluded by a female descendant. Accordingly, in competition with a daughter or agnatic granddaughter, the father may inherit in a dual capacity, taking first his Qur'anic portion and then any residue there may be as the nearest male agnate.

Where, for example, the other heirs competing with the father are the mother (one-sixth) and two daughters (two-thirds), the father is restricted to his Qur'anic portion of one-sixth, since the sum of the portions exhausts the estate. But if the other surviving heirs are the wife (one-eighth) and one daughter (one-half), the satisfaction of the Qur'anic portions (including the father's one-sixth) leaves a residue of $\frac{5}{24}$. This goes to the father, giving him a total share of three-eighths of the inheritance. In these two cases the apportionment of the estate would, in fact, be precisely the same if the father inherited solely as a residuary heir. But the purpose of giving him a Qur'anic entitlement in the presence of a female descendant is to ensure that he receives a respectable share of the inheritance in any event. If he were to rank solely as a residuary, his share would be $\frac{1}{24}$ in the presence of a wife, mother and two daughters, and nothing in the presence of a husband, mother and two daughters.

3.2. Mother's portion of one-third restricted to one-sixth by a lineal descendant or collaterals

The mother of the praepositus takes as a Qur'anic heir a basic portion of either one-third or one-sixth, being restricted to the latter portion in the presence of either a child or agnatic grandchild or "brothers" of the praepositus. It is settled law according to all the Sunnī schools that the Qur'anic term "brothers" means either brothers or sisters, germane, consanguine or uterine, and that any two or more such collaterals will restrict the mother to one-sixth – although Ibn 'Abbās, an authority of the Prophet's generation, is on record as maintaining that three or more collaterals were needed to restrict the portion of the mother, on the ground that the Qur'ān uses the plural and not the dual form of the word "brothers".[1] It is also settled law that collaterals will restrict the mother's portion whether they themselves inherit or not.

Where the collaterals are in fact legal heirs the purpose of the rule is clearly to increase their share in the inheritance at the expense of that of the mother, just as the restriction of the Qur'anic portions of the spouse relict and the mother by a lineal descendant is designed for the latter's benefit.

However, where there is no surviving descendant whose presence would in any case restrict the mother to one-sixth, collaterals will be excluded from inheritance only by the father (and, in certain cases, the grandfather). Accordingly, the restriction of the mother by the collaterals benefits only the father (or the grandfather), giving him in effect, as residuary heir, an extra share of one-sixth of the estate. Systematically, therefore, the collaterals restrict, or partially exclude, the mother and then are themselves in turn excluded by the father to his sole advantage. Expressed in another way, the principle is that the mother's portion is always reduced by collaterals and she is not allowed to profit from the fact that the collaterals happen to be themselves excluded by another heir.[2]

Looking beyond the immediate distribution of the estate in these cases, the rule of restriction will, in fact, ultimately benefit the agnatic collaterals in the normal course of events. For when the father dies, the bulk of the extra portion which he obtains through their presence will devolve upon them as his children and primary heirs. Consanguine collaterals particularly stand to benefit, since, unlike germanes, they will not be the legal heirs of the mother of the praepositus when she dies, so that whatever she

[1] The dual form of a word in the Arabic language denotes precisely the number of two. It is generally accepted, however, that the plural form of a word can be used to indicate a number of two or more.

[2] This same principle appears in (*a*) a variant view relating to a competition between the father and grandmothers (p. 64 below), and (*b*) the so-called *Mu'ādda* cases, where, in a competition between the grandfather, a germane brother and a consanguine brother as residuary heirs, the consanguine brother counts against the grandfather so as to reduce his share but is then himself excluded by the germane brother to the latter's sole advantage (pp. 85–6 below).

takes from the estate of her child, their consanguine brother or sister, will be lost to them forever. On the other hand uterine collaterals manifestly suffer from the rule. Their presence in effect causes one-sixth of the estate of their deceased brother or sister to be taken from the mother, whose primary heirs they will eventually be, and given to the father from whom they will never inherit. In both the short and the long term, therefore, the rule operates exclusively to the benefit of the agnatic relatives of the deceased.

3.3. Parents in competition with a spouse relict: the *'Umariyyatān*

Considerable controversy was provoked in the early days by the particular problem of the relative rights of the father and mother when the only other surviving heir is the spouse relict. Ibn 'Abbās maintained that in this case the mother was entitled to a Qur'anic portion of one-third of the estate, since the Qur'ān clearly stated that the mother's share was to be one-third in the absence of any lineal descendant or collaterals. According to him, therefore, in competition with a husband, who takes a portion of one-half, the mother takes one-third and the father, as residuary, one-sixth; while in competition with a wife, who takes one-quarter, the mother takes one-third and the father five-twelfths as residuary.

This view was firmly rejected by Sunnī jurisprudence as a whole. According to all schools, the mother in these circumstances does not take a Qur'anic portion but shares in the residue with the father, taking half as much as he does, after the deduction of the spouse relict's portion. Thus, in competition with the husband, the mother takes one-sixth and the father one-third of the estate; and in competition with the wife, the mother takes one-quarter and the father one-half of the inheritance. Sunnī law claims for these solutions the authority of the general consensus of the Prophet's contemporaries following the view of 'Umar, the second Caliph of Islam from 639 to 644, who allegedly first resolved the case of parents competing with the husband and then, by analogy, the case of parents competing with the wife. Accordingly, the cases are generally known as the *'Umariyyatān* or the "Two Decisions of 'Umar".

Formally, these cases are reconciled with the Qur'ān, which states that where "the parents are the legal heirs, the mother takes one third", by interpreting the text to mean either "where the parents are the only legal heirs", or "the mother takes one third of the residue". Neither of these interpretations however, is intrinsically as sound as the obvious interpretation adopted by Ibn 'Abbās. And as the classical jurist Ibn Qudāma admits (*al-Mughnī*, VI, 180): "the argument of Ibn 'Abbās would prevail were it not for the consensus of the Prophet's companions to the contrary". The real reason behind the decisions, and behind the forced interpretations of the Qur'ān, was simply the refusal to accept the possibility of the mother of the deceased taking a greater share in the inheritance than the father. As the Mālikī authority al-'Adawī states (*Ḥāshiyat*, II, 346):

The majority felt that to give the mother one-third in these two cases would lead to a contradiction of basic principles. For if, in competition with the husband, she takes one-third of the whole estate, she takes twice the share of the father; and there is no parallel case of a female, in competition with a male of the same class and degree of relationship, taking double the share of the male.

Accordingly, the remedy was deemed to lie in extending the principle of *ta'ṣīb* to cover these cases. Converted into a residuary by the father, the mother is entitled to one-third of the residue. For this reason the cases are also known as "*al-Gharrawāni*", or the "Two Deceivers", the mother being deceived in the sense that "she takes one-third in name but not in substance".

Once it had been decided that the principle of *ta'ṣīb* must apply where the parents were in competition with the husband, the same principle was systematically applied, by analogy, where the parents were in competition with the wife – although in this latter case the father's entitlement as a residuary would exceed that of the mother's full Qur'anic portion of one-third. Certain early jurists, in fact, distinguished between the two cases on this ground, applying *ta'ṣīb* in the case of a competition with the husband but giving the mother her Qur'anic portion of one-third in the case of a competition with the wife. In this latter case, they argued, there was no reason to depart from the obvious meaning of the text of the Qur'ān. Sunnī jurisprudence, however, rejected this distinction in the interests of consistency. And while the initial controversy surrounding the issue illustrates the difficulties attendant upon the amalgamation of the two categories of heirs, the old heirs of the customary law and the new heirs of the Qur'ān, the ultimate solution clearly endorses the principle of the superiority of the male agnate heirs. In order to preserve the customary pre-eminence of the father as an agnatic heir the Qur'anic legislation was restrictively interpreted.

4. Adjustment of Qur'anic portions

The estate of a deceased Muslim may be over-subscribed, in the sense that the sum of the fractional portions therein to which surviving Qur'anic heirs are entitled may exceed unity. Equally, an estate may be under-subscribed when the sum of the fractional portions of Qur'anic heirs falls short of unity and there is no residuary heir to take the surplus. Provision is made for such circumstances by the principles of *'awl* and *radd*; and while these principles are examined here in the context of succession by primary heirs, they apply equally to cases of succession by substitute and secondary heirs.

4.1. The doctrine of *'awl* or proportionate reduction

The doctrine of *'awl* applies when the estate is over-subscribed. To obtain the necessary unity all the basic Qur'anic portions are reduced *pro rata*. As will be appreciated from the illustration that follows, the simple arithmetical method by which this result is achieved is to increase the common denominator of the basic Qur'anic portions to a number which represents the sum of the original numerators. And this explains why the process of decreasing the Qur'anic portions is in fact called "increase", or *'awl*. It is a significant feature of Islamic legal method that the emphasis is commonly placed upon the means by which a result is obtained rather than upon the end result itself.

Where, for example, the deceased is survived by her husband, father and two or more daughters, *'awl* operates as follows:

Husband	$\frac{1}{4} = \frac{3}{12}$	by *'awl*	$= \frac{3}{13}$
Father	$\frac{1}{6} = \frac{2}{12}$		$= \frac{2}{13}$
Daughters	$\frac{2}{3} = \frac{8}{12}$		$= \frac{8}{13}$

Some Arab authorities state that this case was in fact the first historical instance of the application of *'awl*. 'Abbās b. Abī Ṭālib is alleged to have proposed this solution when summoned as one of a group of scholars by the Caliph 'Umar to advise upon the case. Other writers, however, assert that the doctrine originated in rather more picturesque circumstances, in the "Pulpit" case – *al-Minbāriyya*. 'Alī, the cousin and son-in-law of the Prophet, was delivering a sermon in the mosque when he was interrupted by a questioner from the congregation who asked what a wife's right of inheritance was when her deceased husband was also survived by both his parents and his two daughters. Without a moment's hesitation, the anecdote goes, 'Alī replied: "The wife's one-eighth becomes one-ninth". 'Alī's mental arithmetic in the pulpit, or *minbār*, which gives the case the name of *al-Minbāriyya*, is explained as shown on p. 48.

Father	$\frac{1}{6} = \frac{4}{24}$	by *ʿawl*	$= \frac{4}{27}$
Mother	$\frac{1}{6} = \frac{4}{24}$		$= \frac{4}{27}$
Daughters	$\frac{2}{3} = \frac{16}{24}$		$= \frac{16}{27}$
Wife	$\frac{1}{8} = \frac{3}{24}$		$= \frac{3}{27}$ $(\frac{1}{9})$

4.2. The variant view of Ibn ʿAbbās

Natural and equitable though the principle of proportionate abatement may appear, it is not the only possible solution where the Qur'anic portions exceed unity. In the early days opposition to the principle was voiced by Ibn ʿAbbās on the ground that it reduced the share of certain heirs below the portion expressly and specifically prescribed by the Qur'ān as their minimum entitlement. Ibn ʿAbbās maintained that in this context a distinction should be drawn between two types of Qur'anic heir. On the one hand, there were those relatives who were allotted a Qur'anic portion solely in order to assure them of a minimum share of inheritance in any circumstances. This group comprised the spouse relict, mother, grandmother, uterine sister, uterine brother, father and grandfather (assuming, of course, in the case of the last two relatives, the presence of a lineal descendant of the praepositus). To hold that their minimum prescribed portions could be further reduced, argued Ibn ʿAbbās, was to contradict the very purpose and the express terms of the Qur'ān itself. On the other hand, the allotted portions of the remaining four Qur'anic relatives – the daughter, granddaughter, germane sister and consanguine sister (who are all entitled, subject to the rules of exclusion, to a basic portion of one-half) – did not in the same way represent their minimum entitlement. For, according to the terms of the Qur'ān itself, these females were to inherit as residuaries in the presence of their respective brothers, in which case their share in the estate would be considerably less than the Qur'anic portion. Since, therefore, the fixed portions of this latter group were not guaranteed to the same extent as those of the first group, they could properly be reduced where necessary. Ibn ʿAbbās accordingly maintained that where an estate was over-subscribed the burden of the necessary reduction should fall exclusively upon the daughters, granddaughters or agnatic sisters. In the circumstances of the "Pulpit" case, for example, his distribution of the estate would be: father one-sixth, mother one-sixth, wife one-eighth, daughters 13/24. It will be evident, of course, that there can be no case of an over-subscribed estate unless a daughter, granddaughter or agnatic sister is an entitled heir.

Although the arguments of Ibn 'Abbās were endorsed by Shī'ī law, under which, as will be seen, only the portions of daughters or sisters are subject to reduction, Sunnī jurisprudence rejected them and has consistently maintained that the burden of reduction is to be borne rateably by all entitled Qur'anic heirs. '*Awl* rests on the view that a Qur'anic portion does not represent an entitlement which is "fixed" in an absolute sense, but one which is "fixed" only in its ratio to other allotted portions. Thus, whether an estate is over-subscribed or not, a daughter's share will be twice that of a husband, three times that of a mother and four times that of a wife. "Equity is equality" seems to be the guiding principle here, just as it is in the doctrine of the proportionate abatement of creditors' claims in cases of bankruptcy.

4.3. The doctrine of *radd*, or proportionate "return"

A more general controversy arose during the formative period of Sunnī jurisprudence in regard to cases in which the only surviving relatives of the inner family were Qur'anic heirs whose prescribed portions did not exhaust the estate. Early Mālikī and Shāfi'ī law adopted the view that the residue of the estate in these circumstances should go to the Public Treasury and be used for the general benefit of the Muslim community as a whole, since it was not permissible to allow any relative a share of the inheritance greater than that specified by the Qur'ān. Mālikī law remained faithful to this principle.

4.3.1. No *radd* in Mālikī law

All the traditional authorities of this school hold that the Public Treasury is a residuary heir and entitled to succeed as such in the absence of any male agnate relative of the praepositus. Consequently, the possibility of an estate without a residuary heir is not contemplated by Mālikī law, since it assumes that a Public Treasury, in one form or another, will always exist. This doctrine of the Public Treasury is perhaps the supremely distinctive feature of the Mālikī law of succession. Not only does it prevent any Qur'anic heir from taking more than his or her prescribed portion; it also excludes all relatives of the outer family from any rights of succession and imposes an additional restriction on the power of testamentary disposition (pp. 91 and 243 below).

Shāfi'ī law, however, from the classical period onwards, qualified the position of the Public Treasury as an heir by the condition that it should be "properly administered" – that is to say its existence and organisation as a function of state should be strictly in accordance with the constitutional precepts of Sharī'a doctrine which, *inter alia*, precisely defined the mode of expenditure of its revenues. Most Shāfi'ī authorities admit that the political circumstances of Islam, in all but its first few decades, prevented the Treasury from being so "properly administered" and accordingly from being a legal heir. In effect, therefore, the Shāfi'īs align themselves with the other schools, the Ḥanafīs and the Ḥanbalīs, who had from the outset denied to the Treasury the role of legal heir.[1]

These schools based their view on the Qur'anic text (Sura 33, verse 6) which states: "Blood relatives are nearer, the one to the other, than other believers." In the first place, they argued, this text implied that any blood relative must have a right of inheritance superior to that of strangers, or the community as a whole represented by the Public Treasury. No text of the Qur'ān spoke of the Treasury as a legal heir, and therefore it could claim an estate only by escheat, that is to say in default of any surviving blood relative of the deceased. In the second place, the nomination by the Qur'ān of certain blood relatives as entitled to prescribed portions of the estate was a clear indication that those relatives were to be given priority over any others in regard to any residue which remained after the satisfaction of their basic portions and which was not claimed by any male agnate.

4.3.2. The spouse relict is barred from *radd*

Accordingly, the Ḥanafī, Ḥanbalī and Shāfi'ī schools apply in these circumstances the doctrine of *radd*, under which the surplus of the inheritance is returned to all the entitled Qur'anic heirs, except the spouse relict, *pro rata* their basic portions. Thus, as far as blood relatives are concerned, the ratio of their respective rights, as established by the Qur'ān, is preserved. The spouse relict does not participate in *radd* simply because he or she is not a blood relative, and it is only to blood relatives that the Qur'anic text on which the doctrine is based gives priority. A spouse relict is liable to suffer a reduction in his or her Qur'anic portion under the doctrine of *'awl* but not to enjoy a corresponding increase by *radd*; and therefore the portion of one-half or one-quarter, as the case may be, is strictly a maximum entitlement. Where no other relative of the inner family survives, the residue of the estate will pass to relatives of the outer family or, in the absence of the latter, by escheat to the Public Treasury.

[1] In Zanzibar today, however, the original Shāfi'ī doctrine is still applied on the ground that the Public Treasury exists and is properly administered. See J. N. D. Anderson, *Islamic Law in Africa* (London, 1954), p. 75.

4.3.3. Method of calculation of *radd*

Where there is no spouse relict among the entitled claimants, the arithmetical method involved in *radd* is precisely the same as that involved in *'awl*: the common denominator of the basic portions is changed to a number which represents the sum of the original numerators. Thus:

Mother	$\frac{1}{6}$	by	$= \frac{1}{4}$
Daughter	$\frac{3}{6}$	*radd*	$= \frac{3}{4}$

When a spouse relict is among the entitled heirs, calculation of the proportionate increase is slightly more complicated. According to the texts, the amount of the surplus has first to be ascertained; this surplus has then to be divided among the Qur'anic heirs, less the spouse relict, in accordance with the ratio of their basic portions, and their final entitlement will be obtained by adding these shares in the surplus to their original portions. The same result, however, is more simply achieved by dividing the residue of the estate left after the deduction of the spouse relict's portion among the other heirs in accordance with the ratio of their basic portions.

In a competition, for example, between a wife, two daughters and a mother, the ratio of the collective share of the daughters to that of the mother is 4:1. The residue of the estate after the deduction of the wife's share is therefore divided into five parts, four of which go to the daughters and one to the mother:

Wife	$\frac{1}{8}$		$\frac{1}{8}$
Daughters	$(\frac{2}{3})$	$\frac{4}{5} \times \frac{7}{8}$	$= \frac{28}{40}$
Mother	$(\frac{1}{6})$	$\frac{1}{5} \times \frac{7}{8}$	$= \frac{7}{40}$

4. SUBSTITUTE HEIRS

1. Substitution is not representation

Grandchildren and grandparents, at the second or a more distant degree of removal from the praepositus, may properly be called substitute heirs for the children and parents of the praepositus inasmuch as they inherit, when entitled to do so, on broadly the same principles as the latter. But the principle of substitution must be carefully distinguished from that of representation. Representation, in its strictly technical sense as a principle of succession, means that a more distant relative steps into the shoes of a nearer relative of the deceased and is treated for purposes of inheritance exactly as if he were in fact that nearer relative. This is not the case with the substitute heirs. They succeed in their own right as the relatives nearest in degree along a certain line of connection with the praepositus. And because they stand at the second or further degree of removal from the deceased, their position as legal heirs, both as regards their own entitlement and the effect their presence has on the entitlement of other relatives, is not always precisely the same as the position of the respective primary heirs would be in similar circumstances.

2. Grandsons

An agnatic grandson (the son of a son how low soever) is *de jure* excluded from succession by any son of the praepositus, whether this latter be his own father or his paternal uncle, but not by any other relative. In the absence of any son, the grandson is the residuary heir with highest priority, and in relation to all relatives except daughters and granddaughters his position is precisely the same as that of the son would be. Thus, he reduces the spouse relict and the mother to their minimal portions; in his presence the father of the praepositus takes as a Qur'anic heir, and he totally excludes from succession all lineal descendants of a lower degree than himself and all secondary heirs.

In the presence of daughters and granddaughters, however, the position of the grandson differs from that of the son because of his degree of removal from the praepositus. The normal doctrine of *ta'ṣīb* applies so that he converts an agnatic granddaughter of equal degree into a residuary heir. But the grandson does not so convert a daughter into a residuary heir. She takes in his presence her Qur'anic portion, and for this reason the grandson may find himself *de facto* excluded from succession.

Where, for example, the relatives competing with the grandson are two daughters (two-thirds), the father (one-sixth) and the mother (one-sixth), the Qur'anic portions exhaust the estate and nothing remains for the grandson as the residuary heir.

As an exception to the normal operation of *ta'ṣīb*, a great grandson at the third or lower degree of removal from the praepositus converts into a residuary heir a higher agnatic granddaughter who is not entitled to take as a Qur'anic heir (p. 57 below).

3. Grandfathers

In the absence of the father of the praepositus, agnatic grandfathers (the single line of the father's father how high soever) are admitted to succession, the normal principle applying that the nearer in degree excludes the more remote. Like the father, the grandfather inherits as a residuary heir in the absence of any lineal descendant of the inner family; as a Qur'anic heir entitled to a portion of one-sixth in the presence of a son or agnatic grandson, and potentially in a dual capacity in the presence of a daughter or agnatic granddaughter – taking first his Qur'anic portion and then any residue that there may be.

The fact that the grandfather is entitled as a Qur'anic heir saves him from any possibility of *de facto* exclusion, and thus he appears at first sight to enjoy a relatively stronger position, as a substitute heir, than the grandson.

In a competition, for example, with the husband, mother and two daughters of the praepositus, a grandson would be de facto excluded, whereas a grandfather would take a Qur'anic portion (reduced by *'awl*) of two-fifteenths of the estate.

Moreover, although it is highly improbable in practice that a praepositus will be survived by both a grandfather and a grandson who are entitled legal heirs, in such a hypothetical case a *de facto* exclusion of a grandson could in effect result from the presence of the grandfather.

For example, nothing will remain for a grandson as residuary heir in the presence of two daughters (two-thirds), a mother (one-sixth) and a grandfather (one-sixth) of the praepositus.

Both these cases, however, merely underline the fact that while the position of a grandfather depends solely upon the presence or absence of one relative – the father, that of a grandson depends upon the presence or absence not only of any son but also of any daughters of the praepositus. For this reason the grandson cannot be a substitute heir for the son in the same systematic way as the grandfather is a substitute heir for the father. But the real point at issue is the relative entitlement of the class of descendants as a whole as against that of the class of ascendants as a whole; and this remains basically the same whether it is the primary or the substitute heirs of either class that in fact inherit. Certainly the entitlement of the class of descendants as a whole is never less in the presence of a grandfather than it is in the presence of a father.

There are two situations in which the grandfather does not inherit on precisely the same principles as the father would do.

3.1. In competition with the mother and spouse relict

First, in competition with the mother and the spouse relict only, the grandfather takes as a residuary heir after the deduction of the mother's and the spouse relict's portions. Since he is at the second or further degree of removal from the praepositus, he does not convert the mother into a residuary heir as the father does in the same situation (the two cases known as the *'Umaryyatān*).

3.2. In competition with agnatic brothers and sisters

Secondly, the Sunnī majority hold that the grandfather does not, as the father does, exclude the agnatic brothers and sisters of the deceased from succession. This particular problem is the subject of Chapter 6 below, but it may be briefly observed here that the principle ground for the distinction is the difference between the father and the grandfather in the degree of their relationship with the praepositus.

4. Granddaughters

Abū Mūsā was asked about succession by a daughter, a son's daughter and a sister. He answered: "The daughter takes one-half and the sister one-half. Go and ask Ibn Mas'ūd, who will certainly agree with me." But when Ibn Mas'ūd was approached and informed of Abū Mūsā's opinion, he replied: "Then you have been misled. I myself do not claim any infallible authority, but I would decide this case precisely as the Prophet himself decided it. The daughter takes one-half, the son's daughter one-sixth – to complete the two-thirds – and the sister takes the residue." When Abū Mūsā was informed of Ibn Mas'ūd's statement, he observed: "Ask me no further questions as long as you have such a learned scholar among you."[1]

[1] Quoted by the Mālikī authority al-'Adawī in *Ḥāshiyat*, II, 349 ff.

4.1. The nature of the Qur'anic entitlement

From this alleged decision of the Prophet emerges the basic principle that granddaughters (the term being used here to describe any daughter of the praepositus' son how low soever) are deemed to be included in the group of "female children" to which the Qur'ān allots a collective portion of two-thirds of the estate. Entitlement of the members of the group to this portion, or *farḍ*, depends upon their relative degree of removal from the deceased. Where there are two or more daughters of the praepositus surviving, the *farḍ* is exhausted by them and nothing remains for a granddaughter, who thus suffers a *de facto* rather than a *de jure* exclusion. But where only one daughter survives and takes her specified share of one-half of the estate, there is left from the collective *farḍ* a surplus amounting to one-sixth of the estate ($\frac{2}{3} - \frac{1}{2} = \frac{1}{6}$), which will go to the nearest granddaughter or granddaughters, a plurality sharing equally therein. In the absence of a daughter of the praepositus, the whole portion of two-thirds is available for granddaughters, and by strict analogy with the above principle great granddaughters become entitled to the surplus of one-sixth when only one granddaughter survives. A granddaughter who takes one-sixth of the estate in these circumstances is not therefore taking a separate and individual portion, but a part of the collective *farḍ* of two-thirds; and one result of this is that, as a joint owner, she will have a pre-emptive right in the event of her co-heir selling the half of the estate which she has inherited.[1]

As distinct, then, from the three other substitute heirs, who are always totally excluded from succession by the relative for whom they are a substitute, the granddaughter is never *de jure* excluded by the daughter. Under the rule of degree she will be excluded by a son or nearer grandson of the praepositus, but apart from this she generally takes the position of the daughter in the latter's absence. Like the daughter she excludes the uterine collaterals from succession, and when entitled she inherits on the same principles, taking either as a Qur'anic heir or as a residuary through the rule of *ta'ṣīb* when in company with a grandson of equal degree.

4.2. The effect of *ta'ṣīb*: the cases of the "Lucky and Unlucky Kinsman"

The variable effect of the rule that the granddaughter loses her Qur'anic entitlement in the presence of a grandson and must always be converted

[1] Pre-emption arises when the owner of an undivided share in real property sells that share. The co-owner then has the right to substitute himself for the purchaser and take the property sold on the agreed terms.

into a residuary heir by him is aptly illustrated in the cases known as the "Lucky and Unlucky Kinsman".

The case of the "Lucky Kinsman" arises when the principle of *ta'ṣīb* operates to the advantage of the granddaughter. Here, as in any other case where there are two or more daughters of the praepositus surviving, the granddaughter would inherit nothing in the absence of the grandson; for the residue would be returned to the Qur'anic heirs under the doctrine of *radd*, or be inherited by the Public Treasury in Mālikī law. As far as the granddaughter is concerned, therefore, the grandson is a "lucky kinsman", in the sense that his presence is fortunate for her, admitting her to a share of the inheritance which she would otherwise not have taken.

Mother	(Qur'anic portion)	$\frac{1}{6}$
Daughters	(Qur'anic portion)	$\frac{2}{3}$
Grandson	(Residuaries)	$\frac{2}{18}$
Granddaughter	(Residuaries)	$\frac{1}{18}$

Conversely, in the case of the "Unlucky Kinsman" the principle of *ta'ṣīb* operates to the disadvantage of the granddaughter. Since the Qur'anic portions have exhausted the estate, the residuary heirs are *de facto* excluded. Had the granddaughter not been converted into a residuary by the grandson, she would have been entitled to share in the "daughters' *farḍ*", her basic portion of one-sixth then being reduced by *'awl* in these circumstances to two-fifteenths. Since she is in fact denied this share by the presence of the grandson, he is here, as far as the granddaughter is concerned, an unlucky kinsman.

Husband	(Qur'anic portion)	$\frac{3}{12}$	Reduced	$\frac{3}{13}$
Father	(Qur'anic portion)	$\frac{2}{12}$	by	$\frac{2}{13}$
Mother	(Qur'anic portion)	$\frac{2}{12}$	*'awl*	$\frac{2}{13}$
Daughter	(Qur'anic portion)	$\frac{6}{12}$	to:	$\frac{6}{13}$
Grandson Granddaughter	(Residuaries)	—		—

In the broadest sense, of course, the presence of a grandson will always be fortunate or unfortunate for the granddaughter, inasmuch as the *quantum* of her entitlement must necessarily be affected thereby. Normally *ta'ṣīb* will operate to her disadvantage, but in exceptional cases it will secure her a larger share of the inheritance. Six granddaughters in competition with a single daughter, for example, will share one-quarter of the estate (the Qur'anic portion of one-sixth increased by *radd*); but where there is also a grandson present their collective share as residuaries will be three-eighths of the inheritance. This, however, is to say no more than that the entitlement of any one relative always depends upon the number and nature of other relatives who survive, and that the presence of any other heir is always to a degree "unfortunate" for him or her. The cases technically known as the "Lucky and Unlucky Kinsman" are strictly confined to circumstances in which a Qur'anic heir, by virtue of being converted into a residuary, is either totally excluded from inheritance or admitted to a share in the inheritance when she is excluded from a Qur'anic entitlement. Apart from the granddaughter, the only other female relative who can be affected by *ta'ṣīb* in the same way is a consanguine sister (pp. 69–71 below).

4.3. Corollary to the strict principle of *ta'ṣīb*

While a granddaughter must always be converted into a residuary heir by a grandson of the same degree as herself, whether this operates to her benefit or detriment, she will also be converted into a residuary heir by a grandson of lower degree than herself when a plurality of daughters prevents her from taking as a Qur'anic heir. This is one of the exceptions to the strict principle that *ta'ṣīb* occurs only between male and female relatives of equal degree, and is based on the ground that if a great grandson must share his residual entitlement with a granddaughter of equal degree, he must *a fortiori* share it with a granddaughter who is nearer in degree to the praepositus than himself and who would otherwise not inherit.

In the presence of one daughter of the praepositus, granddaughters (without grandsons of equal degree to convert them into residuaries) must always take as Qur'anic heirs and will not be converted into residuaries by the great grandson, whether this would or would not be advantageous to them in terms of the *quantum* of their entitlement. When the only Qur'anic heirs present are a daughter and a great number of granddaughters, the latter are at a relative disadvantage with the great grandson, since he takes the whole residue of one-third of the estate while they must share one-sixth among themselves. On the other hand, a great grandson may in effect be *de facto* excluded by a granddaughter, when her Qur'anic portion, added to those of other Qur'anic heirs, exhausts the estate. In sum, therefore, a great grandson may play the role of a "lucky kinsman" for a granddaughter but not that of an "unlucky kinsman".

4.4. The variant doctrine of Ibn Mas'ūd

To Ibn Mas'ūd, the famous companion of the Prophet, are ascribed two rules relating to succession by the granddaughter which differ from the law described above.[1] First, he held that a granddaughter was not to be converted into a residuary heir by a grandson when the Qur'anic *farḍ* of two-thirds was exhausted by a plurality of daughters or nearer granddaughters. In other words, he did not accept the principle of the "Lucky Kinsman".

Secondly, he held that granddaughters, when in competition with one daughter and a grandson or grandsons, should take either the Qur'anic portion of one sixth, or their share as residuary heirs, whichever was less. This rule can apply only in the case of a plurality of granddaughters. One granddaughter will always take as a residuary, as she does under the normal doctrine, because her residual share can never be greater than one-sixth. It will, in fact, always be less than this amount where there is either another Qur'anic heir or a plurality of grandsons. In many cases, however, the collective residual share of two or more granddaughters will exceed one-sixth of the estate; and here they will, under Ibn Mas'ūd's rule, be restricted to a portion of one-sixth as Qur'anic heirs. The following case is solved under the normal doctrine. According to Ibn Mas'ūd, the granddaughters would be restricted to a collective Qur'anic portion of one-sixth (i.e. 1/24 each) and the grandson would take the residue of 5/24.

Wife	(Qur'anic portion)	$\frac{1}{8}$
Daughter	(Qur'anic portion)	$\frac{1}{2}$
Grandson	(Residuaries)	$\frac{1}{8}$
Four granddaughters	(Residuaries)	$\frac{1}{16}$ each

This doctrine of Ibn Mas'ūd is now of historical interest only, inasmuch as it did not become part of the classical law of any school. But it serves as an apt reminder of the initial controversies that were engendered in the early days by the attempt to harmonise the twin principles of Qur'anic and agnatic succession.

Classical jurisprudence rejected both the rules of Ibn Mas'ūd on the ground that they rest upon a false premise – namely, that the female descendants of the praepositus, as a group, are restricted to a maximum share of two-thirds of the inheritance. For while two-thirds may be their

[1] Ibn Mas'ūd has something of a reputation for an individual approach to problems of inheritance. He is on record as disagreeing with the rest of the companions of the Prophet on several issues. See, for example, p. 71 and p. 80 below.

maximum entitlement as a Qur'anic portion (subject to its augmentation by *radd*), the residual entitlement of a number of female descendants may well exceed this. Where the heirs, for example, are six daughters and one son, or six granddaughters and one grandson, the collective share of the females as residuaries will be three-quarters of the estate.

It might, however, be argued that the principle behind Ibn Mas'ūd's rules is somewhat more subtle than the absolute restriction of female descendants to a maximum share of two-thirds. Assuming that Ibn Mas'ūd would admit that the collective residual entitlement of either daughters or granddaughters might exceed two-thirds, his doctrine is that the principles of Qur'anic and residual entitlement ought not to be combined within the class of female descendants as a whole to the disadvantage of a grandson who is a residuary heir. If daughters and granddaughters together are to be regarded as a composite group with whom the grandson is in competition, then it seems reasonable to argue that because, say, five daughters will not restrict the grandson to less than one-third as residue, *a fortiori* one daughter and four granddaughters should not do so.

In the majority view, however, daughters and granddaughters only form a composite group as Qur'anic heirs. When a grandson is present, the female descendants fall into two distinct categories. The daughters take as Qur'anic heirs and the granddaughters as residuaries, whatever the number of the latter and whatever the effect, in terms of their entitlement, may be. This, of course, is the result of the strict and systematic application of the principle of *ta'ṣīb*, under which agnatic females who are Qur'anic heirs must always be converted into residuaries by their brothers. At root, therefore, it is the classical principle of *ta'ṣīb* with which Ibn Mas'ūd's doctrine is in conflict. Under his doctrine, granddaughters, when a daughter is present, are only converted into residuaries by the grandson when it is to the latter's advantage. If the rule is confined to grandsons it is certainly anomalous, whatever particular arguments may be adduced in its support from consideration of daughters and granddaughters as a composite group. But it may well be that Ibn Mas'ūd's rules represent a partial survival of an original principle of *ta'ṣīb* which was equally as consistent as its classical counterpart: namely, that daughters, granddaughters, germane and consanguine sisters share as residuaries in the presence of their respective brothers *within the limit of their collective Qur'anic entitlement*. Such a view of *ta'ṣīb*, as a principle operating in every case to the advantage of male relatives, would at least be in accordance with its basic purpose, which was indubitably to reduce, and not to increase, the Qur'anic entitlement of females.

5. Grandmothers

5.1. The Qur'anic portion of a grandmother

A grandmother how high soever, being a substitute heir for the mother, inherits only in the latter's absence. Like the mother, she does not exclude any other heir of the inner family and, by virtue of an alleged ruling of the Prophet, she is entitled to one-sixth of the estate as a Qur'anic heir, two or more entitled grandmothers sharing equally therein.

Once again, however, the entitlement of the substitute heir is not always the same as the entitlement of the primary heir would be in similar circumstances. Grandmothers inherit only as Qur'anic heirs and their fixed portion, subject to *radd* or *'awl*, is always one-sixth of the estate. A grandmother's portion is never increased to one-third, as is the mother's, in the absence of children or collateral relatives of the praepositus. Nor is she ever converted into a residuary heir by any male agnate, as the mother is so converted by the father in the two cases of the *'Umariyyatān* (pp. 45–6 above).

But while the *quantum* of the grandmother's share is common ground to all the Sunnī schools of law, there is considerable divergence between them on the basic problem of the circumstances in which a grandmother of the praepositus will be entitled to take this share. Three principal issues are involved.

5.2. The grandmothers who are potentially Qur'anic heirs

There appears to have been some initial hesitation as to whether a paternal grandmother should be admitted to succession as a substitute heir for the deceased's mother. Abū Bakr, the first Caliph of Islam, is said to have been the judge in a case where the praepositus, whose parents were predeceased, was survived by both his paternal and maternal grandmothers. He decided that the *farḍ* of one-sixth should go wholly to the maternal grandmother, on the ground that she was the more proper representative of the deceased's mother than the deceased's father's mother. But this decision was apparently criticised on the ground that it ignored the principle of reciprocity; for it excluded the grandmother from whom the present praepositus, as the son's son, would have inherited, in favour of the grandmother from whom the present praepositus, as a daughter's son, would not have inherited. Abū Bakr then is said to have revised his decision and given both grandmothers equal shares in the *farḍ*. This precedent was subsequently adopted by all the Sunnī schools of law.

Beyond this the fundamental principle common to all the Sunnī schools is that a grandmother how high soever is not an ordinary legal heir if she is connected with the praepositus through a male ascendant who is not himself a member of the inner family – i.e. a non-agnatic grandfather. This eliminates, on the maternal side, all grandmothers except the single line of the mother's mother how high soever, and leaves on the paternal side the several unbroken female lines of the mother and the mother's mother how high soever of the father and the agnatic grandfathers how high soever. It is with regard to the paternal grandmothers who are to be accounted legal heirs of the inner family that the schools differ.

Mālikī law admits to succession only the single line of the mother or mother's mother how high soever of the praepositus' father.

Ḥanbalī law admits the two lines of mothers how high soever of the praepositus' father and father's father.

Ḥanafī and Shāfi'ī law admit all the lines of mothers how high soever of the praepositus' father and father's father how high soever.

These rules are, of course, primarily of academic interest only, since the possibility of succession by great grandmothers or grandmothers of an even higher degree is in practice remote. From a theoretical standpoint, however, it may be observed that at the third or any higher degree of removal from the praepositus, the number of grandmothers, maternal and paternal together who may inherit as heirs of the inner family never exceeds two in Mālikī law and three in Ḥanbalī law. Under Ḥanafī and Shāfi'ī law, the number of grandmothers so entitled is three at the third degree of removal from the praepositus and increases by one in each successive higher generation.

5.3. The rules of exclusion between grandmothers

As with other classes of heirs, the basic principle applies that the nearer in degree excludes the more remote. But the effect of this principle depends upon whether all grandmothers are regarded as constituting a single group, or whether a distinction is drawn between the paternal and the maternal sides.

The Ḥanafīs and Ḥanbalīs treat all grandmothers as a single group and apply the rule of degree regardless of side, so that a nearer paternal or maternal grandmother excludes more remote grandmothers on both her own and the other side.

In the contemplation of Mālikī and Shāfi'ī law, on the other hand, the class of grandmothers contains the two distinct maternal and paternal groups. Within each group the nearer excludes the more remote. And because the mother excludes any paternal grandmother, so also a nearer maternal grandmother excludes a more remote paternal grandmother. But a nearer paternal grandmother does not exclude a more remote maternal grandmother. Since the father himself does not exclude any maternal grandmother, *a fortiori* a female ascendant connected with the praepositus through him does not do so.

5.4. Exclusion of the paternal grandmother by the father

Only the Ḥanbalīs maintain that the father does not exclude a paternal grandmother from succession. The other three Sunnī schools hold that the father does exclude a paternal grandmother – a rule which constitutes the solitary exception to the principle that a grandmother, as a substitute heir for the mother, is not excluded by any other member of the inner family.

Here, as in the previous question, the Ḥanbalīs regard all grandmothers as a single class. Paternal, no less than maternal, grandmothers are representatives of the deceased's mother, and as such are no more subject to exclusion by the father than she would be.

Shāfi'ī and Mālikī law are equally consistent in deciding this question on the basis that the maternal and the paternal grandmothers form two distinct groups. Just as a mother excludes a mother's mother, and a father excludes a father's father, a paternal grandmother is excluded by the father simply because he is the nearer in degree along a particular line of connection with the deceased. Expressed more precisely, the rule is that a paternal grandmother how high soever is excluded by the father or the father's father how high soever through whom she is connected with the praepositus – the rule naturally having a more restricted application in Mālikī law, which recognises only the one line of mothers how high soever of the father as grandmothers of the inner family. Thus, a father's mother's mother is excluded by the father but not by the father's father. It goes without saying that a paternal grandmother will not be excluded by her own son, who is not the father or grandfather, but the paternal uncle or great uncle of the praepositus.

Ḥanafī law, perhaps, betrays some inconsistency in subscribing to the view that the father excludes a paternal grandmother. In regard to the issue of priorities among grandmothers, the Ḥanafīs maintain that a nearer paternal grandmother excludes a more remote maternal grandmother because they regard all grandmothers as forming a single group. In other words they ignore in that context the particular connection of the paternal grandmother through the father. On the present issue, however, this same connection is recognised by the Ḥanafīs as the effective cause of the exclusion of the paternal grandmother by the father.

5.5. Illustration of different doctrines

The following hypothetical case may serve to summarise the principal divergencies of doctrine between the different schools.

P's four sole surviving relatives are his father, F, and three grandmothers – X, his father's mother, Y, his father's father's mother, and Z, his mother's mother's mother.

	Ḥanafīs	Mālikīs	Shāfi'īs	Ḥanbalīs
F	All	$\frac{5}{6}$	$\frac{5}{6}$	$\frac{5}{6}$
X	—	—	—	$\frac{1}{6}$
Y	—	—	—	—
Z	—	$\frac{1}{6}$	$\frac{1}{6}$	—

5.5.1. Ḥanafī law

Y and Z are both excluded by the nearer grandmother X, who is in turn excluded by F. Although Y is in fact also excluded by F, Z is not. This, therefore, is one of only two instances in the Islamic law of inheritance of a relative (Z) being totally excluded from a share in the estate by, and only by, another relative (X) who in turn suffers *de jure* exclusion.[1]

5.5.2. Mālikī law

Y is not a legal heir of the inner family. X is excluded by F, who takes the residue of the estate after the deduction of Z's Qur'anic portion.

5.5.3. Shāfi'ī law

Y is recognised as ordinary legal heir, but is excluded by the nearer paternal grandmother X (or by F). The solution is then the same as under Mālikī law.

5.5.4. Ḥanbalī law

X, as the nearer grandmother, excludes both Y and Z. But she herself is not excluded by F and therefore takes the Qur'anic *farḍ*.

[1] The only other instance occurs under the Ḥanbalī law of succession by the outer family (illustration on p. 96 below). Perhaps the nearest parallel to these two anomalous cases is the restriction of the mother to a portion of one-sixth, which may be regarded as a case of partial exclusion, by brothers or sisters of the praepositus, who are themselves *de jure* excluded by the father.

5.6. A variant view on the effect of the father's exclusion of the paternal grandmother

One refinement of the Mālikī, Shāfi'ī and Ḥanafī doctrine of the exclusion of the paternal grandmother by the father remains to be noted. Certain jurists argued that a maternal grandmother, when in competition with the father and a paternal grandmother whom she herself does not exclude, should not be allowed to profit from the exclusion of the paternal grandmother by the father, but should be restricted to the share that she would have received had such exclusion not taken place.

As applied to the hypothetical case above, this variant view would not affect the Ḥanafī solution, since the great maternal grandmother is excluded. But if it were applied by the Mālikīs and Shāfi'īs, X would initially be counted against Z and then excluded by F to his sole advantage. Z would therefore take a Qur'anic portion of one twelfth, and F the residue of eleven twelfths. The variant view would have the same effect in Ḥanafī law if X and Z were grandmothers of the same degree.

However, although the authoritative legal manuals give some prominence to this view, it did not succeed in becoming the dominant doctrine of any school.[1]

[1] This same principle is in fact recognised and applied by the Mālikī, Shāfi'ī and Ḥanbalī schools in the case of a competition between a grandfather and germane and consanguine brothers or sisters. It is known in that context as the *Mu'ādda* doctrine (pp. 85–6 below).

5. SECONDARY HEIRS

1. Qur'anic provisions relating to succession by brothers and sisters

Although the group of secondary heirs includes all male agnates, however remote, other than lineal descendants or ascendants, it is the brothers and sisters of the praepositus who occupy pride of place within the group. Qur'anic legislation relating to inheritance by brothers and sisters is confined to two brief statements.

(*a*) If the heirs of a deceased man or woman are collateral relatives and a brother or sister survives, then he or she takes one-sixth. But if there is more than one brother or sister, they share one-third (Sūra 4, verse 12).

(*b*) Allāh ordains concerning collateral relatives that if a man dies without a child and leaves a sister, she takes half of the inheritance; and he will be her heir if she dies without a child. If there are two sisters, they take two-thirds of the inheritance. If the collaterals include both males and females, then the male takes a share equivalent to that of two females (Sūra 4, verse 176).

While the Arabic words rendered here as "collateral relatives", "brother" and "sister" are precisely the same in both passages, the consensus of juristic opinion maintains that text (*a*) refers solely to uterine brothers and sisters, and text (*b*) solely to agnatic collaterals, the germane and consanguine brothers and sisters of the deceased.[1] On this basis the fundamental principles of succession by collaterals as laid down in the Qur'ān are clear enough. Uterine brothers and sisters take a fixed portion as Qur'anic heirs. Agnatic sisters are allotted fixed portions but are converted into residuary heirs by agnatic brothers of the praepositus. But in this as in other aspects of the law the Qur'anic provisions are only the bare rudiments of the completed system. It was left to the explanatory decisions of the Prophet and the juristic reasoning of the early authorities to supply the details of the relative priorities among the different types of collaterals and, in particular, to define the precise circumstances in which brothers

[1] The Qur'anic term translated here as "collateral relatives" is *kalāla*, the precise meaning of which is a matter of some doubt. It is clearly a derivative of the root Arabic term with the three consonants k.l.l., one meaning of which is "to surround". *Iklīl*, another derivative of the same root, is the term for a crown or a type of headwear which sits around the head rather than on top of it. *Kalāla*, therefore, refers to those relatives who form the lateral branches of the praepositus' family tree, standing on either his paternal or maternal side, as opposed to those relatives who stand directly above or below him in the perpendicular branches of ascendants and descendants. However, some scholars maintain that the term describes the relatives themselves and means all relatives other than ascendants or descendants, while others think that it describes the praepositus, meaning a person who has no surviving ascendants or descendants.

and sisters would be entitled legal heirs. And in this respect Sunnī jurisprudence provides an illuminating example of the dominant role played by alleged precedents of the Prophet in the formation of legal doctrine.

2. The explanatory role of *sunna*

Without any apparent ambiguity the Qur'ān declares, in passage (*b*) translated above, that agnatic brothers and sisters are entitled to inherit only in the absence of any child (*walad*) of the praepositus. But in the case of the estate of Sa'd (p. 29 above), the Prophet allowed the brother to inherit when two daughters of the deceased survived, and in a case reported by Ibn Mas'ūd (p. 54 above), he allowed the sister to inherit when the deceased was survived by a daughter and a granddaughter. Both these alleged precedents were accepted by Sunnī jurisprudence as authentic and therefore binding. The problem was simply to explain the apparent conflict between the Prophet's decisions and the text of the Qur'ān.

Sunnī legal theory admits in principle that a precedent or *sunna* of the Prophet may repeal or abrogate a text of the Qur'ān, but in practice endeavours to reconcile any apparent conflict between the two sources of law by interpretation. Such reconciliation was achieved in this case by interpreting the word *walad* in the Qur'ān to mean "a male child". In its natural and obvious sense, of course, *walad* means a male or female child. And this is the meaning given to the term when it appears in other passages of the Qur'ān – where, for example, it is enacted that the portion of the inheritance to which a mother or a spouse relict is entitled is limited by the survival of a *walad* of the deceased. But the restrictive interpretation of the term in the context of succession by brothers and sisters was necessitated by the accepted precedents of the Prophet on the subject. In the contemplation of Sunnī jurisprudence, therefore, the Qur'ān declares that brothers and sisters do not inherit in the presence of a male child but leaves open the question of their rights of succession in the presence of a female child – a lacuna which was subsequently filled by the explanatory decisions of the Prophet. In short, it was the settled law of all Sunnī schools from the beginning that agnatic brothers and sisters were totally excluded from inheritance by a son or agnatic grandson of the deceased, but not by a daughter or agnatic granddaughter.

3. Uterine collaterals

A uterine brother or sister is totally excluded from succession by any child or agnatic grandchild, or by the father or agnatic grandfather how high soever of the praepositus. Of those blood relatives, therefore, who are primary or substitute heirs only the mother and the grandmother do not exclude the uterines. But the uterines are not excluded by any agnatic brother or sister or by any other secondary heir.

When entitled to succeed, the uterines inherit always as Qur'anic heirs, one brother or sister taking a basic portion of one-sixth and two or more sharing equally, regardless of sex, in a basic collective portion of one-third. The rule that a male relative takes twice the share of a corresponding female relative is a principle of agnatic succession which does not apply to uterines. As is the case with other Qur'anic heirs, the basic portions of the uterines are subject to increase by *radd* or decrease by *'awl.*

4. Agnatic brothers

Agnatic brothers and sisters are *de jure* excluded from succession by the son, agnatic grandson, or father of the praepositus, but not by the daughter, granddaughter, mother or grandmother, nor by the grandfather in the majority view.

As between the agnatic collaterals themselves, a germane brother totally excludes a consanguine brother or a consanguine sister because of the superior strength of his blood-tie, but a consanguine brother is not excluded by a germane sister.

When they are entitled to inherit, agnatic brothers take as residuary heirs, and under the principle of *ta'ṣīb* convert into residuary heirs sisters of the praepositus whose blood-tie is precisely the same as their own. Germane sisters are therefore converted into residuaries only by germane

Husband	(Qur'anic portion)	restricted by child	$\frac{1}{4}$ =	$\frac{3}{13}$
Mother	(Qur'anic portion)	restricted by child	$\frac{1}{6}$ =	$\frac{2}{13}$ by
Daughter	(Qur'anic portion)		$\frac{1}{2}$ =	$\frac{6}{13}$ *'awl*
Granddaughter	(Qur'anic portion)		$\frac{1}{6}$ =	$\frac{2}{13}$
Germane brother, Germane sister	(Residuaries)		—	—
Consanguine sister	Excluded by germane brother		—	—

3-2

brothers and consanguine sisters only by consanguine brothers, whether, in this last case, the relationship between the brother and sister themselves is a germane or a consanguine one.

Although agnatic brothers are not *de jure* excluded by any female descendant or ascendant, they may be *de facto* excluded as residuary heirs when the Qur'anic portions allotted to the females exhaust the estate, as in the hypothetical case shown on p. 67.

5. Agnatic sisters

Germane and consanguine sisters, when entitled to inherit, may either (*a*) take as Qur'anic heirs, or (*b*) be converted into residuary heirs by brothers, or (*c*) inherit under the special title of "accompanying residuaries".

5.1. Agnatic sisters as Qur'anic heirs: the case of the "Hen and her Chicks"

Where no daughter, agnatic granddaughter or agnatic brother of the praepositus survives, germane and consanguine sisters take as Qur'anic heirs. The Qur'anic entitlement of agnatic sisters is strictly analogous to that of female descendants. A portion of one-half is prescribed for one sister and a collective portion, or *farḍ*, or two-thirds for a plurality of sisters. In the distribution of this collective *farḍ* among sisters, germanes are given precisely the same precedence over consanguines (by virtue of their superior blood-tie) as daughters are given over granddaughters (by virtue of their superior degree) in the distribution of their collective *farḍ* of two-thirds. Thus, two or more germane sisters will exhaust the *farḍ* and any consanguine sisters will be *de facto* excluded. Where only one germane sister survives and takes her allotted portion of one-half (or three-quarters of the collective *farḍ*), a portion amounting to one-sixth of the inheritance (or one-quarter of the collective *farḍ*) remains for a consanguine sister or sisters, who will share equally therein. Where no germane sister survives, a consanguine sister takes the full portion of one-half and two or more consanguine sisters share two-thirds, just as granddaughters take the place of daughters in the latters' absence.

Agnatic sisters who inherit as Qur'anic heirs do not *de jure* exclude any other relative of the inner family. In the following case a nephew, uncle or cousin would take the residue in the absence of the consanguine brother. However, like the consanguine brother, they would suffer *de facto* exclusion if the deceased had also been survived by a mother or a grandmother.

Wife	(Qur'anic portion)	$\frac{1}{4}$
Two germane sisters	(Qur'anic portion)	$\frac{2}{3}$
Consanguine brother	(Residuary)	$\frac{1}{12}$

The comparatively large portions allotted to agnatic sisters, coupled with the fact that they do not exclude uterines from succession or reduce the spouse relict's entitlement, produces the situation in which an estate is over-subscribed by the Qur'anic portions to the maximum possible extent, and the individual heirs accordingly must suffer the greatest possible reduction in their basic portions. To this particular case Muslim jurists give the rather curious title, the "Hen and her Chicks" (*Umm al-furūkh*). In some mysterious way the initial common denominator of the fractional shares appeared to resemble a mother hen, and the greatly increased denominator resulting from *'awl* her brood of chickens.

Husband	$\frac{3}{6}$	by *'awl*	$= \frac{3}{10}$
Mother	$\frac{1}{6}$		$= \frac{1}{10}$
Germane sister	$\frac{3}{6}$		$= \frac{3}{10}$
Consanguine sister	$\frac{1}{6}$		$= \frac{1}{10}$
Uterine sisters	$\frac{2}{6}$		$= \frac{2}{10}$

It may be recalled that the early scholar Ibn 'Abbās denied the validity of *'awl* and maintained that the burden of any necessary reduction in basic Qur'anic portions should fall exclusively upon daughters, granddaughters or agnatic sisters. According to his view, therefore, the germane and consanguine sisters in this case would have no share at all in the inheritance.

5.2. Sisters converted into residuaries by brothers: the cases of the "Lucky and Unlucky Kinsman"

A germane sister is converted into a residuary heir by a germane brother, and a consanguine sister by a consanguine brother. In this respect there is a striking parallel between the position of agnatic sisters and that of female descendants of the praepositus. In precisely the same way as it affects a granddaughter, the principle of *ta'ṣīb* may operate either to the benefit or the detriment of a consanguine sister and produce two further cases of a "Lucky and an Unlucky Kinsman".

A consanguine brother will be a lucky kinsman as far as the consanguine sister is concerned when his presence enables her to take a residual share in the estate, although the survival of two or more germane sisters excludes her from a Qur'anic entitlement.

Germane sisters	(Qur'anic portion)	$\frac{2}{3}$
Grandmother	(Qur'anic portion)	$\frac{1}{6}$
Consanguine sister	(Residuaries)	$\frac{1}{18}$
Consanguine brother	(Residuaries)	$\frac{2}{18}$

In the absence of the consanguine brother the consanguine sister would receive nothing. The residue of one-sixth remaining after the satisfaction of the basic Qur'anic portions of the germane sisters and the grandmother would revert to the germane sisters and the grandmother by *radd* according to the majority, or be claimed by the Public Treasury under Mālikī law.

Conversely, the presence of a consanguine brother will be unfortunate for a consanguine sister when the principle of *ta'ṣīb* deprives her of her basic Qur'anic portion of one-sixth in the presence of one germane sister, and no residue remains after the satisfaction of the portions of the entitled Qur'anic heirs.

Husband	(Qur'anic portion)	$\frac{3}{6}$	by *'awl*	$\frac{3}{7}$
Mother	(Qur'anic portion)	$\frac{1}{6}$	by *'awl*	$\frac{1}{7}$
Germane sister	(Qur'anic portion	$\frac{3}{6}$	by *'awl*	$\frac{3}{7}$
Consanguine sister	(Residuaries)	—		—
Consanguine brother	(Residuaries)	—		—

Here the consanguine sister would have taken a portion of one-eighth of the estate in the absence of the consanguine brother. But of course the loss of one heir is always the gain of another; and the presence of the consanguine brother does benefit the husband, mother and germane sister, who in effect share proportionately the one-eighth portion the consanguine sister would otherwise have taken.

According to all the Sunnī schools, therefore, the position of a consanguine sister as a legal heir is strictly analogous to that of a granddaughter. The only difference between them is that a granddaughter will be converted into a residuary heir by a grandson of lower degree than herself when she would otherwise not inherit, but a consanguine sister will never be converted into a residuary by a male collateral of lower degree, i.e. a consanguine brother's son. In the case of the granddaughter the argument for the modification of the strict principle of *ta'ṣīb* is that a great grandson must share his residual entitlement with a great granddaughter and therefore, *a fortiori*, must share it with a granddaughter who is nearer in degree to the praepositus. This same argument does not apply to the case of the consanguine sister, for the simple reason that a female collateral of lower degree than herself – i.e. the consanguine brother's daughter – is not a legal heir of the inner family and would not share in any residue to which her brother, as an agnatic nephew of the praepositus, might be entitled.

5.2.1. The variant view of Ibn Mas'ūd

As has been observed above (pp. 58–9), the early authority Ibn Mas'ūd diverged from the majority view on the question of a granddaughter's rights of inheritance. He maintained that where a daughter or daughters of the praepositus survived, the principle of *ta'ṣīb* could not operate to the benefit of granddaughters so as to give the female descendants as a whole a collective entitlement exceeding two-thirds of the inheritance. Consistently with that approach he held in regard to agnatic sisters that the maximum entitlement of germanes and consanguines collectively was two-thirds of the estate. Accordingly, in his view, (*a*) a consanguine sister is totally excluded from inheritance in the presence of two germane sisters, whether a consanguine brother is present or not, and (*b*) in competition with one germane sister and a consanguine brother or brothers, consanguine sisters take either a *farḍ* portion of one-sixth, or their share as residuaries, whichever is less.

For example, where the surviving heirs are a germane sister, three consanguine sisters and a consanguine brother, the three consanguine sisters will take one-tenth each, and the consanguine brother one-fifth, under Sunnī law. According to Ibn Mas'ūd, each consanguine sister would take one-eighteenth, and the consanguine brother one-third.

5.3. Agnatic sisters as "accompanying residuaries"

In the presence of a daughter or agnatic granddaughter, and in the absence of brothers who would convert them into residuaries, germane or consanguine sisters inherit as "accompanying residuaries". Sunnī jurisprudence formally rests this doctrine upon the authority of a precedent of the Prophet who, according to the report of Ibn Mas'ūd (referred to on p. 54 above), resolved a competition between a daughter, a granddaughter and a sister by giving the daughter one-half, the granddaughter one-sixth, and the sister the residue of one-third. The Qur'ān itself provides no support for the doctrine. On the contrary, the relevant passage of the Qur'ān declares in effect that a sister is entitled to one-half of the inheritance in the absence of a child. The result of this doctrine, in the case where the sole heirs are a daughter and a sister, is to give the sister one-half of the inheritance in the presence of a child. However, as has been observed, Sunnī law here acknowledges the overriding authority of the Prophet's decision and regards the Qur'ān as referring only to cases in which there is no surviving male child of the deceased.

The rationale of the doctrine appears to be that female descendants, while not excluding agnatic sisters from succession, should nevertheless have precedence over them as regards the *quantum* of the inheritance they take. To allow a sister to inherit as a Qur'anic heir along with a daughter would give both relatives a parity of entitlement. The obvious and indeed the only alternative was that the sister should take as a residuary. Accordingly, she is said to inherit in these circumstances as "an accompanying residuary", or *'aṣaba ma'a ghayrihā* ("residuary along with another" – i.e. the daughter or granddaughter). *'Aṣaba*, which is the only word known to Islamic legal terminology to describe a residuary heir, literally means "male agnate" and therefore requires some qualification when it is applied to females inheriting in a residual capacity. Females who are converted into residuary heirs by males are known as *'aṣaba bi ghayrihā*, or "residuaries by another". "Accompanying residuary" is merely a term of convenience invented for these particular cases of a germane or consanguine sister inheriting along with a daughter or granddaughter, and does not apply to any other heir.

5.3.1. A sister as residuary excludes any inferior residuary

In effect, therefore, an agnatic sister inherits in the presence of a female descendant precisely as a brother of her own blood tie would do. In her capacity as a residuary, she may herself be *de facto* excluded from succession – in competition, for example, with the husband, mother and two daughters of the praepositus; but she also assumes the power to exclude

Wife	(Qur'anic portion)		$\frac{1}{8}$
Granddaughter	(Qur'anic portion)		$\frac{1}{2}$
Germane sister	(Residuary)		$\frac{3}{8}$
Consanguine sister } Consanguine brother }	(Residuaries)	Excluded by germane sister	—
Uterine brothers	(Qur'anic portion)	Excluded by granddaughter	—

others in accordance with al-Jabarī's rule. Accordingly, a germane sister inheriting under this special title *de jure* excludes a consanguine sister or consanguine brother, and either a germane or a consanguine sister excludes any inferior *'aṣaba*, such as agnatic nephews, uncles and cousins.

6. Germanes and uterines in competition: the "Case of the Donkey" or *al-Ḥimāriyya*

For the peoples of the Arabian peninsula Islam marked a transition in social values and standards which is represented, in the laws of inheritance, by the attempt to harmonise the claims of the *'aṣaba*, the traditional heirs of the customary law, with those of the new heirs nominated by the Qur'ān. Inevitably, during the early period, there existed a basic tension between these two classes of heirs. As far as collateral relatives are concerned, that tension lay between the agnatic brothers and the uterine brothers of the praepositus; and for two agnatic brothers at least the tension reached breaking point in the case known as *al-Ḥimāriyya*.

A deceased woman was survived by her husband, her mother, two germane brothers and two uterine brothers. At the first hearing of the case, 'Umar, following the golden rule of distribution, allotted the prescribed Qur'anic portions of one-half to the husband, one-sixth to the mother and one-third to the uterine brothers, with the result that the germane brothers, as residuary heirs, were *de facto* excluded from succession. Since the rights of the husband and mother, as an heir by marriage and an ascendant respectively, were undisputed, the case resolved itself into a straightforward competition for the remaining one-third of the estate between the germane and the uterine collaterals. In a sense, therefore, this competition between the *'aṣaba* and the Qur'anic heirs epitomised the conflict between the old and the new order of society; and the germane brothers, despite their traditional pre-eminence as agnatic heirs, had in effect been totally ousted from succession by the new uterine heirs. However, on appeal by the germane brothers, 'Umar revised his decision and ordered that the one-third of the estate remaining after the deduction of the husband's and mother's portions should be distributed in equal shares among the germane and the uterine brothers.

6.1. *Ratio decidendi*

On appeal the germane brothers abandoned their original contention that their agnatic tie gave them absolute priority over the uterines and produced a more temperate and logical argument. As germane relatives, they asserted, they had the same mother as the deceased, and thus possessed the very same quality of relationship which was the exclusive basis of the uterine brothers' right of inheritance. At least, therefore, they should stand on a parity with the uterines. The fact that they also had the same father as the deceased was beside the point. If they gained no advantage from this agnatic tie, then by the same token they should not be penalised because of it. Accepting the validity of this argument, 'Umar conceded the necessity for an equitable modification of the golden rule of distribution in these particular circumstances and allowed the germane brothers to inherit *qua* uterines. The case takes its name from the way in which the germane brothers explained that they wished to waive their character of agnates, in the sense that their connection with the praepositus through their father should not be taken into account. "O Commander of the Faithful", the common version of the case has them say, "suppose our father were a donkey (*ḥimār*), do we not still have the same mother as the deceased?" The case is also given the somewhat more prosaic title of the *Mushtaraka*, or "the case of the Divided Inheritance", since the portion of one-third was equally divided among the germane and uterine brothers.

6.2. The *Ḥimāriyya* rule – accepted by Mālikī and Shāfi'ī law

As adopted by the Mālikī and Shāfi'ī schools, the *Ḥimāriyya* rule applies only where germanes as residuary heirs would be totally excluded from succession owing to the presence of uterines. The only combination of surviving relatives which can produce this result is that of a husband, a mother or a grandmother, and two or more uterine brothers or sisters. If the surviving spouse were a wife, or if no mother or grandmother survived, or if only one uterine brother or sister were present, the rule would not apply since the Qur'anic portions would not completely exhaust the estate, however inferior, in this event, the residual share of each of a number of germanes might be to the Qur'anic portion of an individual uterine. Germane sisters who are converted into residuaries by germane brothers are covered by the *Ḥimāriyya* rule, and since in this case they inherit *qua* uterines, male and female take equal shares. In the absence of any germane brother, germane sisters would take as Qur'anic heirs, and for this reason they might well have cause to lament, on material grounds, the presence of a germane brother.

For example, a germane sister in competition with a husband, mother, germane brother and four uterine brothers will receive one-eighteenth of the estate under the *Ḥimāriyya* rule. But if no germane brother had survived, she would take one-third as her Qur'anic portion after *'awl*. The share of each uterine brother would be one-eighteenth, whether the germane brother were present or absent.

Consanguine brothers and sisters cannot claim the benefit of the *Ḥimāriyya* rule, for the obvious reason that they do not have a maternal connection with the praepositus.

6.3. The *Ḥimāriyya* rule – rejected by Ḥanafī and Ḥanbalī law

'Umar's equitable compromise between the traditional heirs of the tribal law and the new heirs introduced by the Qur'ān did not win the support of the Ḥanafī and Ḥanbalī schools. They maintained that 'Umar's decision at first instance was systematically sound and correct in principle, and that he had been ill-advised to reverse it on appeal. Precedents of the Prophet had drawn a clear-cut distinction between the two categories of the *ahl al-farā'iḍ* and the *'aṣaba* as legal heirs, and laid down the golden rule that the *ahl al-farā'iḍ* had absolute priority in the distribution of the estate, in the sense that their allotted portions were the first charge upon it, even if this resulted, as it admittedly did on many occasions, in the *de facto* exclusion of the *'aṣaba* as residuary heirs. Therefore, once an *'aṣaba*, always an *'aṣaba*. The character of a male agnate as a residuary heir was a permanent one which could not be conveniently discarded in particular circumstances. Whatever logic might support the *Ḥimāriyya* rule, the fact remained that it contradicted the express terms of the Qur'ān itself. In the first place, the uterines were deprived of their prescribed collective portion of one-third of the estate; and in the second place, germane brothers and sisters took equal shares under the rule when the Qur'ān had ordained that the male should take twice the share of the female.

For the Ḥanbalī jurist Ibn Qudāma, the *Ḥimāriyya* rule had little logical appeal.[1] It was settled law, he argued, that in competition with a husband and a mother, one uterine brother would take a portion of one-sixth and germane collaterals, even if there were a hundred of them, would share the one-sixth residue. If, therefore, there was no objection to one uterine brother taking one hundred times as much of an inheritance as a germane brother, why should not two uterines exclude the germanes altogether? Furthermore, the principle of ignoring a particular type of relationship was a dangerous one, inasmuch as it could apply to other cases of succession, and so play havoc with the delicately balanced system of the two categories of heirs. For example, it was agreed in the case of the "Unlucky Kinsman"

[1] Ibn Qudāma refutes the *Ḥimāriyya* rule at length in *al-Mughnī*, VI, 180 ff.

that a consanguine sister was converted into a residuary heir by a consanguine brother and so *de facto* excluded from succession in the presence, say, of a husband and one germane sister whose Qur'anic portions exhausted the estate. But it could be argued, on the *Ḥimāriyya* principle, that the relationship of the consanguine sister with the praepositus remains the same whether the consanguine brother is there or not. If he had not survived, the consanguine sister would be entitled to a basic Qur'anic portion of one-sixth. Why, therefore, should she not be able to claim that the presence of the consanguine brother is immaterial and no account should be taken of him, so that she can shed her character as a residuary heir and revert to her Qur'anic status? As Ibn Qudāma tartly enquires: "Why not assume here that the consanguine brother is a donkey?"

6.4. The fundamental jurisprudential issues involved

From the standpoint of Islamic legal theory, the case of the *Ḥimāriyya* raises the fundamental issue of the role that may be played by human reason in the elaboration of Sharī'a law. Classical Sunnī jurisprudence stands foursquare upon the principle that law-making is for Allāh alone. His comprehensive law had been revealed in the Qur'ān and the divinely inspired activities of the Prophet Muḥammad. The task of jurisprudence was simply to ascertain the precise terms of that law as it applied to any given case. Human reason, therefore, could not make law by freely speculating, in terms of social desirability, upon the ends or purposes that law should serve, and formulating appropriate rules therefor. It could only discover Allāh's law through the interpretation of the divine revelation and the proper application of the principles established therein to cases not specifically regulated by the divine texts themselves. Within these accepted limits the jurisprudential debate turned upon the precise modes of reasoning which could legitimately be employed. Analogical deduction, or *qiyās*, was accepted by the general consensus of opinion as a valid method of extending the principle embodied in a specific ruling of the Qur'ān or *sunna* to cover closely parallel cases. For many jurists, indeed, this was the only acceptable method of reasoning. But others maintained that in particular cases strict analogy could occasion injustice, and it was then permissible to resolve a problem on broad equitable considerations. To this admittedly vague and ill-defined process was given the label *istiḥsān*, which means "seeking the best solution" or "juristic preference". And in the contemplation of classical jurisprudence the *Ḥimāriyya* rule can rest only upon the principle of *istiḥsān*. In the particular circumstances of that case it was deemed preferable or more equitable that the germane brothers should inherit as uterines rather than retain their normal character of male agnate residuaries as strict analogy would require.

Seen in these terms the *Ḥimāriyya* controversy reveals two basically distinct attitudes towards the problem of the juristic interpretation of the principles established by divine revelations. All jurists had the same ultimate purpose of ascertaining what was justice for the germane brothers in the circumstances of this case. And justice could obviously be measured only in terms of the religious law. But for one side justice meant the strict application, by way of analogy, of the letter of the golden rule of distribution formulated by the Prophet, under which the germane brothers of necessity ranked as residuary heirs. For the other side, the spirit of the golden rule was of greater significance than its letter, and justice required a relaxation of its strict terms in this particular case. The principle of *istiḥsān* is akin to Equity, and the division between the jurists of Islam on the *Ḥimāriyya* issue is as fundamental as that which arose in the English legal system when the champions of the strict letter of the common law rules were challenged by the advocates of Equity.[1]

Sharī'a law is often described as a law which did not grow out of society but was imposed upon society by the divine command from above. In principle this is true enough. It is also true in principle that Sharī'a law is a doctrinal system, the authority of which stems from the views of qualified scholars and not from the decisions of courts in actual cases. But this does not mean that the Sharī'a is a system of religious ideology which developed in complete isolation from the currents of human experience. Juristic debate and development, at least in the early years, often derived their impetus from actual social problems, even if not always in such picturesque circumstances as those of the "Case of the Donkey".

7. Nephews, uncles, cousins and other male agnates

As members of the inner family, these male agnates are entitled to succeed as residuary heirs in the absence of any male agnate descendant or ascendant or any agnatic brother of the praepositus. Priorities among them are

[1] The division of the four Sunnī schools on the *Ḥimāriyya* issue is rather curious in view of their respective doctrines on jurisprudential theory. The two schools who accept the *Ḥimāriyya* rule – the Mālikīs and Shāfi'īs – do not in theory approve of *istiḥsān*. Shāfi'ī himself, in fact, unequivocally condemned it as tantamount to man-made legislation. On the other hand, the Ḥanafīs, who are reputedly the particular champions of *istiḥsān*, reject the *Ḥimāriyya* rule. Only the Ḥanbalīs appear to be systematically consistent in this respect, rejecting the principle of *istiḥsān*, and with it the *Ḥimāriyya* rule.

determined strictly by al-Jabarī's rule. A nephew or more remote male agnate is not *de jure* excluded by any female, except by an agnatic sister when she inherits as an accompanying residuary, although he is, of course, liable to *de facto* exclusion. The incidence of this will naturally be higher than in the case of an agnatic brother, since neither the nephew nor any more distant male agnate converts a sister of the praepositus into a residuary heir.

6. GRANDFATHER AND COLLATERALS IN COMPETITION

1. The scope of the problem: "The Tatters" case

"If anyone is attracted by the prospect of rushing headlong into the depths of hell-fire, let him attempt to adjudicate a competition between the grandfather and the collaterals." These are the alleged words of the Caliph 'Umar,[1] referring to one of the most complex problems of the law of intestacy in terms which, as this chapter proceeds, may appear as not unduly pessimistic. It is the problem of the comparative strength of the claims of two classes of agnatic relatives – on the one hand the deceased's father's father how high soever, and on the other hand his germane or consanguine brothers and sisters. For the sake of convenience we shall refer to the two parties throughout this chapter as the grandfather and the collaterals of the deceased. Non-agnatic grandfathers, however, such as a maternal grandfather or a father's mother's father, are not involved in the problem; nor are uterine brothers and sisters, for it is settled law that they are excluded from succession by the father's father. It is also obvious that a direct competition between the grandfather and the collaterals can only arise in the absence of those relatives who would exclude either party – i.e. the deceased's father, who would exclude both the grandfather and the collaterals, and the son or son's son how low soever, who would exclude the collaterals.

In the absence of any explicit text of the Qur'ān or the *sunna* regulating such a competition, controversy was inevitable. A convenient starting point to the problem, and one which will serve to indicate the great diversity of prevailing views, is provided by the case of *al-Khuraqā'*, or "The Tatters" – so-called simply because of the extent to which the early authorities were torn and divided on the issues involved. Here, no less than seven variant solutions were put forward as to how an estate should be apportioned in the relatively simple case where the praepositus was survived by three relatives only – his mother, germane sister and grandfather.

Of these solutions Muslim jurisprudence soon discarded the last four; and for the purposes of both the traditional and the modern law it is the first three only which are of importance. As it emerges from "The Tatters" case, the distinction between these three views may be summarised as

[1] Quoted by the Shāfi'ī authority al-Ramlī, *Nihāyat al-Muḥtāj*, v, 20.

follows. According to Abū Bakr, the grandfather totally excludes the sister. Zaid and 'Alī, on the other hand, are agreed that the sister is not excluded by the grandfather and inherits along with him, but differ as to the principles upon which the estate should be apportioned between them. Zaid maintains that both take as residuary heirs, the male taking double the share of the female, while 'Alī holds that the sister takes her Qur'anic portion of one-half, and the grandfather the residue of one-sixth.

	Mother	Germane sister	Grandfather
1. Abū Bakr	$\frac{1}{3}$	—	$\frac{2}{3}$
2. Zaid b. Thābit	$\frac{1}{3}$	$\frac{2}{9}$	$\frac{4}{9}$
3. 'Alī	$\frac{1}{3}$	$\frac{1}{2}$	$\frac{1}{6}$
4. 'Umar	$\frac{1}{6}$	$\frac{1}{2}$	$\frac{1}{3}$
5. Ibn Mas'ūd (i)	$\frac{1}{6}$	—	$\frac{5}{6}$
6. Ibn Mas'ūd (ii)	$\frac{1}{4}$	$\frac{1}{2}$	$\frac{1}{4}$
7. 'Uthmān	$\frac{1}{3}$	$\frac{1}{3}$	$\frac{1}{3}$

With this brief indication of the fundamental lines of divergence we may now proceed to examine the three separate doctrines in detail.

2. Abū Bakr's doctrine

2.1. The rule of total exclusion of collaterals – accepted by Ḥanafī law

Abū Bakr's view that the grandfather completely excludes all brothers and sisters of the deceased was endorsed by Abū Ḥanīfa and subsequently became the authoritative doctrine of the Ḥanafī school.

In deciding this basic question of whether the grandfather should or should not exclude the collaterals, the scholars undoubtedly took into account the practical effect that their conclusion would have in terms of the distribution of wealth among the family group. According to the legal texts, however, the issue was resolved upon purely juristic arguments.

2.2. The juristic arguments in support of exclusion

Abū Bakr and his supporters see the grandfather in these circumstances as the nearest member of the class of male agnate ascendants which, as a whole, is superior to the class of collateral relatives. As regards the class of male agnate descendants, it is an established rule that, in the absence of the son, the nearest member of the class – the son's son how low soever – takes precisely the same position in the scheme of priorities that the son would have occupied. Similarly, in the absence of the father, the grandfather, as the nearest male agnate ascendant, should occupy the same position as the father and exclude the collaterals just as he would have done.

To support this general principle that the grandfather ranks as a father and as such has priority over the collaterals, three major arguments are adduced.

(i) In linguistic usage the term "father" (*abū*) is commonly applied to male agnate ascendants. The Qur'ān, for example, speaks of Abraham as the "father" of the Muslim community.

(ii) The legal relationship between grandfather and grandchild is in many particulars parallel to that between father and child. Thus the penalties of death for deliberate homicide, of flogging for defamation[1] and of amputation of the hand for theft do not apply where the offender is the father or grandfather of the victim, but do apply in the case of a brother or a sister. Again, a grandfather is bound to provide maintenance and support for his grandchild who is in need thereof, but no such duty, in the majority view, falls upon a brother or sister.

(iii) Under settled principles of succession the grandfather inherits upon the same basis as the father in the latter's absence – as a residuary heir in the absence of any child or son's child of the deceased, as a Qur'anic heir in the presence of a son or son's son how low soever, and potentially in a dual capacity in the presence of a daughter or son's daughter. Finally, the superior position of the grandfather is underlined by the fact that he is excluded from succession only by the deceased's father, whereas collaterals are excluded not only by the father but also by a son or son's son how low soever, or, in fact, by the presence of Qur'anic heirs whose shares exhaust the estate.

2.2.1. Reasons for dissent by the majority

The doctrine of the exclusion of collaterals by the grandfather did not, however, find favour with the majority of early jurists, for whom the arguments cited above were not sufficiently decisive to deprive the collaterals of their rights of inheritance which had been clearly defined in the Qur'ān. In the first place, they contended, this is a competition between relatives who are precisely equal in their degree of removal from the deceased, both parties being connected with him through the same intermediate link of his father; and in fact, since the claims of descendants are superior to those of ascendants, it is the collaterals who have the stronger agnatic tie with

[1] The criminal offence of an unproved allegation of illicit sexual intercourse (*qadhf*).

this common intermediate link.[1] Secondly, they argued, it is by no means axiomatic that the grandfather should stand in the same position *vis à vis* the collaterals as the father, for it is already established that the respective positions of the father and the grandfather differ in one other case – namely, in a competition with the deceased's mother and spouse relict.[2]

2.2.2. The problem for the majority: apportionment

On these grounds the majority held that the collaterals should be admitted to succession along with the grandfather. For them, therefore, the problem was to achieve an acceptable mode of distribution between the two parties in accordance with the established principles of succession. As has been emphasised before, the central feature of the whole law of intestacy is the attempt to harmonise the claims of two distinct categories of heir – the Qur'anic heir and the agnatic residuary. And nowhere, perhaps, are the complexities of this process more in evidence than in the two major schemes for apportionment between the grandfather and the collaterals that may be referred to as the doctrines of 'Alī and Zaid respectively.

3. 'Alī's doctrine

Under this doctrine the position of the collaterals on the one hand and the grandfather on the other is separately determined by reference to the other heirs competing, and both parties then inherit on normal principles.

3.1. 'Alī's doctrine: normal principles apply subject to the "advantage rule"

Thus, germane brothers, always taking as residuaries, will totally exclude consanguine brothers or sisters. Consanguine brothers take as residuaries in the absence of germane brothers but will not exclude a germane sister from her Qur'anic portion, while both germane and consanguine brothers convert their respective sisters into residuary heirs. Sisters unaccompanied

[1] This argument that considerations of *degree* may cut across and override the recognised priorities of *class* was denounced as arbitrary by the supporters of Abū Bakr's doctrine. They pointed out that if the principle were systematically applied a father's father's father, for example, would stand on an equal footing with a brother's son; but in fact no jurist would deny the total exclusion of the latter by the former.

[2] Pp. 45–6 and p. 54 above. The principle of *ta'ṣīb* applies between the father and the mother, so that the father takes two-thirds and the mother one-third of the residue left after the deduction of the spouse's share, while the grandfather takes the residue after the deduction of both the spouse's and the mother's Qur'anic portions.

by brothers take as Qur'anic heirs, except in the presence of a daughter or son's daughter where they inherit as "accompanying residuaries".

Similarly the grandfather, in accordance with normal principles, will usually inherit as a residuary heir of equal standing with brothers who are so entitled, but will take as a Qur'anic heir in the presence of a daughter or son's daughter of the deceased. To this general principle, however, there are two exceptions.

(i) The grandfather takes advantage of his status as a Qur'anic heir to claim a basic portion of one-sixth, where his entitlement as a residuary would be less than this owing to either the plurality of competing collaterals or the presence of other Qur'anic heirs or both.

(ii) Notwithstanding the presence of a daughter or son's daughter, the grandfather in competition with a brother takes as a residuary where this is more advantageous to him than his Qur'anic portion of one-sixth.

3.2. 'Alī's doctrine illustrated

(*a*)	Wife	Qur'anic portion	$\frac{1}{4}$
	Two germane brothers	Residuaries	$\frac{1}{4}$ each
	Consanguine brother	Excluded by germane brother	—
	Grandfather	Residuary	$\frac{1}{4}$
(*b*)	Mother	Qur'anic portion, reduced by collaterals	$\frac{1}{6}$
	Germane sister	Qur'anic portion	$\frac{1}{2}$
	Consanguine brother }	Residuaries	$\frac{1}{6}$
	Grandfather }		$\frac{1}{6}$
(*c*)	Son's daughter	Qur'anic portion	$\frac{1}{2}$
	Consanguine sister	"Accompanying residuary"	$\frac{1}{3}$
	Grandfather	Qur'anic portion	$\frac{1}{6}$
(*d*)	Husband	Qur'anic portion	$\frac{1}{2}$
	Mother	Qur'anic portion, reduced by collaterals	$\frac{1}{6}$
	Germane brother }	Residuaries	$\frac{1}{12}$
	Two germane sisters }		$\frac{1}{24}$ each
	Grandfather	Qur'anic portion, under advantage rule (i)	$\frac{1}{6}$
(*e*)	Daughter	Qur'anic portion	$\frac{1}{2}$
	Germane brother }	Residuaries	$\frac{1}{5}$
	Germane sister }		$\frac{1}{10}$
	Consanguine sister	Excluded by germane brother	—
	Grandfather	Residuary under advantage rule (ii)	$\frac{1}{5}$

4. Zaid's doctrine

4.1. Zaid's doctrine is more favourable to the grandfather: the advantage rules

Zaid b. Thābit, the secretary of the Prophet, is alleged to have been the originator of principles for resolving the competition between a grandfather and collaterals, which, with certain refinements subsequently introduced, became the authoritative doctrine of the Mālikī, Shāfi'ī and Ḥanbalī schools.

Under this doctrine the grandfather is always, basically, a residuary heir (whether a daughter or son's daughter of the deceased is present or not), and the sum result is that his position is more favourable than it is under the doctrine of 'Alī: for, in addition to the rule that the grandfather always takes his Qur'anic portion of one-sixth where this is to his benefit, Zaid introduced two further advantage rules which seriously qualify the normal principles of entitlement applicable to the grandfather and collaterals respectively.

(i) Sisters never take as Qur'anic heirs, but by the principle of *ta'ṣīb* are converted into residuaries by the grandfather who will accordingly take double their share.

(ii) The grandfather is entitled to a minimum portion of one-third of the collective entitlement of himself and the collaterals, whether this be the whole estate or the residue after the deduction of other Qur'anic portions.

Under this last advantage rule the grandfather is, in effect, regarded as a *quasi*-Qur'anic heir, his portion being fixed at one-third on the grounds that: (*a*) in competition with the deceased's mother alone he is entitled to twice as much as she is, and (*b*) since collaterals in competition with the mother alone do not reduce her to a portion of less than one-sixth, they cannot reduce the grandfather to a portion of less than twice that amount.

4.2. Zaid's doctrine illustrated

(*a*)	Daughter	Qur'anic portion	$\frac{1}{2}$
	Germane sister	Residuaries	$\frac{1}{6}$
	Grandfather		$\frac{1}{3}$
(*b*)	Wife	Qur'anic portion	$\frac{1}{4}$
	Four germane brothers	Residuaries	$\frac{1}{8}$ each
	Grandfather	Under "one-third" advantage rule	$\frac{1}{4}$

Under 'Alī's doctrine, the grandfather would, in both the above cases, be reduced to one-sixth as a Qur'anic heir (see illustrations (*c*) and (*d*), p. 83 above).

4.3. The *Mu'ādda* rule

One detail of Zaid's doctrine, however, affects the position of the grandfather adversely. Since the grandfather does not himself exclude consanguine brothers and sisters, his entitlement as a residuary heir is calculated by taking account of *all* the collaterals present (brothers or sisters, germane or consanguine), and then consanguines are excluded by germanes, upon normal principles, to the sole advantage of the latter. The cases in which this rule applies are known as the *Mu'ādda*, or "Computation", cases, because the consanguines are *counted* initially in the distribution against the grandfather.

		Initially	Finally
(*c*)	Grandfather	($\frac{1}{3}$)	$\frac{1}{3}$
	Germane brother	($\frac{1}{3}$)	$\frac{2}{3}$
	Consanguine brother	($\frac{1}{3}$)	—

Under 'Alī's doctrine the grandfather and the germane brother would each take one-half of the estate.

		Initially		Finally
(*d*)	Grandfather	($\frac{1}{6}$)		$\frac{1}{6}$
	Daughter	($\frac{1}{2}$)		$\frac{1}{2}$
	Germane brother	($\frac{1}{6}$)	Portion of consanguine sister then	$\frac{2}{9}$
	Germane sister	($\frac{1}{12}$)	goes to germanes on normal principles	$\frac{1}{9}$
	Consanguine sister	($\frac{1}{12}$)		—

Under 'Alī's doctrine the grandfather would take one-fifth of the estate (see illustration (*e*), p. 83 above).

It will be obvious, however, that the disadvantage which the grandfather suffers through the *Mu'ādda* doctrine is to a large degree offset by the rule that he takes a minimum of one-third of the collective entitlement of himself and the collaterals. In effect, when consanguines are present, he can be in a worse position than he would be under 'Alī's doctrine only where he is in competition with one germane brother, or one germane brother and one germane sister. For example, in the circumstances of illustration (*a*) (p. 83 above) the grandfather would still take one-quarter of the estate under Zaid's advantage rule.

4.3.1. The restricted exclusion of consanguines by a germane sister

It remains to note with regard to the *Mu'ādda* doctrine that, whereas a germane brother totally excludes all consanguines, a germane sister does not exclude them beyond the extent that is necessary to make up her own portion to one-half of the inheritance – this being, of course, her normal entitlement as a Qur'anic heir in the presence of consanguine brothers or sisters. Since the germane sister has thus only a restricted capacity to exclude the consanguines, the cases where this occurs are known as the cases of *al-Mukhtaṣara*, or "The Restricted Female". In the following case the residue of five-sixths is first apportioned between the grandfather and all the collaterals. Then the germane sister takes from the collective share of the consanguines sufficient to make up her own portion to one-half of the inheritance. The remainder of the consanguines' share is then divided between brother and sister, double share to the brother.

(*e*)	Initially		Finally
Mother	($\frac{1}{6}$)		$\frac{1}{6}$
Germane sister	($\frac{5}{36}$)	$+\frac{13}{36}$	$\frac{1}{2}$
Consanguine brother	($\frac{10}{36}$) }	$-\frac{13}{36} = \frac{2}{36}$	{ $\frac{2}{54}$
Consanguine sister	($\frac{5}{36}$) }		{ $\frac{1}{54}$
Grandfather	($\frac{10}{36}$)		$\frac{10}{36}$

As a matter of principle the texts state that two or more germane sisters will exclude consanguines only to the extent of taking their maximum collective portion of two-thirds of the inheritance. In practice, however, this means that consanguines will in every case be totally excluded by two or more germane sisters, since the grandfather will take the remaining one-third under the advantage rule.

4.4. Later refinements of Zaid's doctrine: three anomalous cases

Three particular refinements of Zaid's doctrine were adopted by later jurisprudence with the common objective of improving upon the position which the grandfather would occupy under normal principles when the husband and mother of a deceased woman have taken the bulk of the estate as Qur'anic heirs. The first two refinements, however, (the *Mālikiyya* and *Shibh al-Mālikiyya*) are peculiar features of Mālikī law and rest upon arguments of a certain plausibility concerning the effect that the presence of uterines has upon the position of germane and consanguine brothers; while the third case of the *Akdariyya*, representing Shāfiʿī and Ḥanbalī as well as Mālikī law, is little more than a feat of juridical juggling for the sole purpose of securing a greater share of the inheritance for the grandfather.

4.4.1. *al-Mālikiyya* (Mālik's Rule)

Husband	$\frac{1}{2}$
Mother (reduced by collaterals)	$\frac{1}{6}$
Uterine brothers (or sisters)	—
Consanguine brother(s)	—
Grandfather	$\frac{1}{3}$

Here the uterines are excluded by the grandfather, and distribution upon normal principles would result in the grandfather taking one-sixth (either as a residuary or a Qur'anic heir under the advantage rule) and the consanguine brother(s) taking the remaining one-sixth. Mālik, however, argued that if the grandfather were not present in this case the consanguine brother(s) would receive nothing as residuary heir(s) because the estate would be exhausted by the Qur'anic heirs, the uterines taking one-third in this capacity. Since, therefore, it is the grandfather alone who excludes the uterines, the consanguine brother(s) cannot properly claim in this case to stand on an equal footing with him as residuary heir(s), and the exclusion of the uterines must operate to the sole advantage of the grandfather.

4.4.2. *Shibh al-Mālikiyya* (Analogy with Mālik's rule)

Husband	$\frac{1}{2}$
Mother	$\frac{1}{6}$
Uterine brothers (or sisters)	—
Germane brother(s)	—
Grandfather	$\frac{1}{3}$

In this, as in the previous case, Mālikī law determines the position of the germane brother(s) by reference to the heirs other than the grandfather. In the absence of the grandfather, the germane brother(s) would not, like the consanguine brother(s), be totally excluded, but would share with the uterines in one-third of the estate under the *Ḥimāriyya* principle (p. 73 above). However, since they would then inherit solely *qua* uterines, they retain this character in the presence of the grandfather and are excluded by him just as are the uterine brothers proper.

4.4.3. *al-Akdariyya* (the "Confounding Rule")

This case of a competition between the deceased's husband, mother, grandfather and germane *or* consanguine sister involves a dual anomaly.[1] In the first place, Zaid's basic rule of *ta'ṣīb*, that a sister is converted into a residuary heir by the grandfather, is here contradicted. Since, argue the texts, only one-sixth of the estate remains after the Qur'anic portions of the husband and mother have been satisfied, the sister cannot share in this residue because one-sixth is the recognised minimum entitlement of the grandfather. On the other hand, none of the heirs present excludes the sister: she must, therefore, as a matter of principle, take in the only alternative capacity of a Qur'anic heir.

It is, however, the second stage in the solution of the *Akdariyya* which constitutes a much more serious anomaly and which "confounds" not only the principles of Zaid but also the fundamental principles of succession as a whole. For the Qur'anic portions of the grandfather and the sister, as finally determined by the necessary *pro rata* reduction (*'awl*), are then consolidated and re-apportioned between them, the grandfather taking twice as much as the sister on the ground that in competition with her he ranks as a brother. Accordingly the solution is as follows:

Husband	$\frac{1}{2}$		$= \frac{3}{9}$			$\frac{3}{9}$
Mother	$\frac{1}{3}$	All Qur'anic portions by *'awl*	$= \frac{2}{9}$			$\frac{2}{9}$
Grandfather	$\frac{1}{6}$		$= \frac{1}{9}$	$\frac{4}{9}$	$\times \frac{2}{3}$	$= \frac{8}{27}$
Sister (germane or consanguine)	$\frac{1}{2}$		$= \frac{3}{9}$		$\times \frac{1}{3}$	$= \frac{4}{27}$

The solution of the *Akdariyya* depends, as has been seen, upon the preliminary argument that the sister must take as a Qur'anic heir because she would otherwise be excluded from inheritance despite the fact that none

[1] While the popular view is that this case takes its name from the Arabic verb *akdara* ("to throw into confusion"), others maintain that it was so-called because the rule was first enunciated by the jurist al-Akdar. Mālik himself refers to the case as *al-Gharrā'*, which means, say the commentators, either "The Unique case" (from *ghurra*, the distinctive blaze on a horse's forehead) or "The Deceit", because the sister is deceived (*gharra*) by being initially allotted a share of one-half which is later reduced to 4/27.

of the heirs present in principle excludes her. This, of course, can apply only where there is one sister competing with the husband, mother and grandfather: for two or more sisters would reduce the mother to a portion of one-sixth, and thus a residue of one-sixth would be available for distribution among the sisters after the satisfaction of the grandfather's minimum entitlement.

The argument, however, appears on closer examination to be somewhat superficial. In the first place, once the basic principle is accepted that a sister in competition with the grandfather is converted into a residuary heir by him, she does not, or ought not to, lose this character simply because the grandfather, in the particular circumstances, takes as a Qur'anic heir under the advantage rule. If, for example, a plurality of sisters were in competition with the husband (one-half), mother (one-sixth) and grandfather (one-sixth), the latter taking as a Qur'anic heir, they would share the remaining one-sixth as residuaries. In the second place, there is, throughout the law of intestacy, a clear-cut distinction between a residuary heir who is *de jure* excluded by the presence of an heir of superior class, degree or strength of blood-tie, and one who is *de facto* excluded simply because the Qur'anic portions exhaust the estate. What objection, then, can there be in principle to regarding the sister in the circumstances of the *Akdariyya* as a residuary heir who is *de facto* excluded? This would indeed be the unfortunate lot of a germane or consanguine brother in competition with the same relatives.[1]

Thus lacking any real foundation in principle, the argument that the sister must be treated as a Qur'anic heir may well appear as nothing more than a convenient peg upon which to hang the subsequent and unparalleled stratagem of so combining the rules of Qur'anic and residual succession as to increase the grandfather's share to almost one-third of the estate. Viewed in this light the *Akdariyya* perhaps provides the key to the attitude underlying the traditional doctrine on the whole question of a competition between the grandfather and the collaterals.

'Alī's doctrine, recognising a parity of entitlement between grandfather and collaterals, represents a systematic application of the normal principles of succession to both parties. By contrast, the view of Zaid, as adopted by the Sunnī majority, has a distinctly arbitrary and opportunist flavour.

[1] Ibn Qudāma in *al-Mughnī* (VI, 225) indicates the effect of the sex and number of collaterals present in these circumstances by quoting the case of a lady who died survived by her husband, her grandfather and her mother who was pregnant. The latter reflected thus: "If I give birth to a boy my share in my daughter's estate will be one-third. If my child is a daughter it will be two-ninths. Twins will reduce me to one-sixth."

From the elaborate "advantage rules" and the anomalous cases it is clear that this doctrine, while admitting as a matter of juristic principle that the grandfather does not exclude the collaterals, nevertheless attempts to give him that position of relative superiority over them which his social standing in the patriarchal family group seemed to require. The manipulation of basic principles which this attitude engendered is epitomised by the *Akdariyya* – aptly named, indeed, as a case of confusion worse confounded.

7. SUCCESSION BY THE OUTER FAMILY

Relatives are relegated to the outer family for the purposes of succession not because of their distance or the degree of their removal from the praepositus but because of the nature of their relationship or their sex. Among the vast complex of female and non-agnatic relatives which constitutes the outer family are persons who are as "near" to the praepositus as members of the inner family. For example, a father's father, a son's child or a brother's son are "ordinary heirs" of the inner family; but a mother's father, a daughter's child or a brother's daughter are members of the outer family. It is also apparent that, outside the circle of the praepositus' closest relatives, in any given class of relatives – such as that of nephews and nieces – the number of members of the outer family is potentially far larger than that of members of the inner family, so that the likelihood of this class being represented solely by members of the outer family is correspondingly greater.

1. The conflicting doctrines of the Sunnī schools

Cases of succession by members of the outer family are, however, exceptional. Under Mālikī law the outer family is never admitted to inheritance because, failing the survival of any male agnate relative of the praepositus, the Public Treasury succeeds as a residuary heir. In Ḥanafī, Shāfi'ī and Ḥanbalī law, rights of inheritance do pass to relatives of the outer family, but only in the absence of any blood relative of the inner family; and since they are thus, in this majority view, totally excluded by any Qur'anic heir save the spouse relict, or by any male agnate however distant, the prospect of their being in fact called to succession is somewhat remote.

This sphere of the law is not, of course, by any means devoid of practical importance: indeed, it is precisely in the exceptional circumstances for which it caters that the jurisdiction of the courts is most likely to be invoked. But perhaps the law here has a greater and a more particular significance from the standpoint of doctrinal theory and legal methodology: for the variety of juristic principles which are applied to the subject provides one of the most striking illustrations of the fact that Islamic law is by nature a self contained comparative system.

Two major doctrines exist to regulate cases of succession by relatives of the outer family. The Shāfi'ī and Ḥanbalī schools adopt the doctrine of *tanzīl*, under which the rights of these relatives are basically determined by reference to the link of the ordinary heir – i.e. relative of the inner family – through whom they are connected with the praepositus. This is, therefore the sole instance of a system of complete representation in the traditional Islamic law of inheritance. The Ḥanafī school, on the other hand, adopts the principle of *qarāba*, or "relationship", under which the rights of the relatives are determined by the nature of their own relationship with the praepositus. But once priorities have been settled by the rules of *qarāba*, there is a divergence of view as to the method of apportioning the inheritance among the entitled heirs. The one view, sponsored by Abū Yūsuf, favours the simple method of apportionment *per capita*; the other view, that of Shaybānī, supports the principle of apportionment *per stirpes*. This chapter, therefore, will examine these various principles in some detail, albeit that some of the cases illustrating their application can hardly be of common occurrence in practice.

2. The doctrine of *tanzīl*: Shāfi'ī and Ḥanbalī law

Tanzīl, or representation, is the principle that a relative of the outer family steps into the shoes of that relative of the inner family, or ordinary legal heir, through whom he or she is connected with the praepositus and inherits what that relative would have inherited had he or she survived the praepositus.

In all cases the relative of the outer family represents the first ordinary legal heir, whether Qur'anic heir or agnatic residuary, who appears when the line of connection is traced back to the praepositus. Thus, a son's daughter's child represents the son's daughter of the praepositus, not the praepositus' son; and a cousin who is the daughter of the praepositus' father's germane brother represents the germane paternal uncle of the praepositus, not his father or grandfather. Grandchildren will therefore step into the shoes of their own ascendants, as will nephews and nieces, while grandparents will represent their own descendants. Uncles and aunts, however, and through them their issue, step into the shoes not of their parents but of their brother or sister, and so represent not the grandparent of the deceased but his father or mother.

Where only one relative of the outer family survives, he or she naturally inherits the whole estate, or the residue thereof after the deduction of the spouse relict's portion. Competition between several relatives is regulated by the five major rules which follow.

2.1. Rule 1: priority by degree of removal from common link

Among relatives who are connected with the praepositus through the same ordinary heir, the nearer in degree to this heir excludes the more remote. Thus, the daughter's daughter, the immediate child of the ordinary heir she represents (the deceased's daughter), will exclude the daughter's daughter's son, whether this great grandson is her own child or the child of her sister. Similarly the paternal aunt, being at the first degree of removal from the ordinary heir she represents (the deceased's father), will exclude those cousins of the praepositus who are either her own children or the children of other paternal aunts. In the case below, where P is survived by an aunt, a great grandmother and a second cousin, all connected with P through the same link of his mother, the aunt (at the first degree of removal from this link) excludes the grandmother (at the second degree of removal), who in turn and in the absence of the aunt would exclude the cousin (at the third degree of removal).[1]

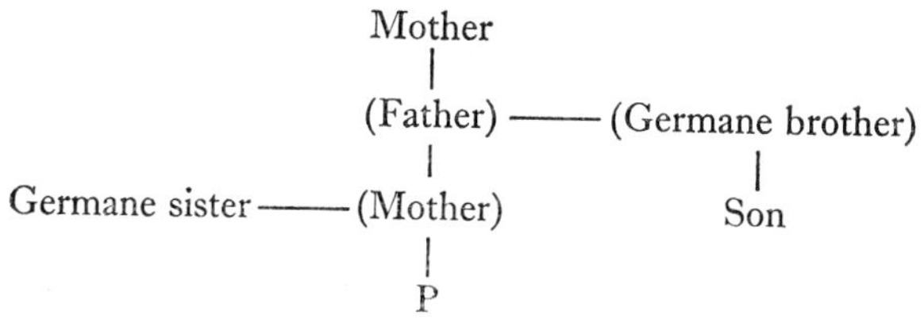

2.2. Rule 2: common link as the notional praepositus

Relatives connected with the praepositus through the same ordinary heir and at the same degree of removal from this link inherit on the basis of their relationship with this link. The application of this rule has three principal effects.

(i) Where the relatives succeeding are the lineal descendants of the ordinary heir they represent, there is a distinction between Shāfi'ī and Ḥanbalī law.

[1] A variant doctrine ignores this rule of priority by degree where the common link of several relatives is the mother of the praepositus, and maintains that the entitlement of the relatives should be determined solely by their relationship with the mother, i.e as though the mother herself were the praepositus. Applied to the illustration in the text, this principle would mean that none of the three relatives would be excluded. As a germane sister, grandmother and agnatic cousin of the mother, the supposed praepositus, they would be entitled, respectively, to one-half, one-sixth and one-third of the estate of the actual praepositus.

According to Shāfiʿī law these relatives inherit, as the sons or daughters of the ordinary heir, in accordance with the basic rule of double share to the male. This does not, however, apply to the issue of a uterine brother or sister of the praepositus, where male and female share equally following the normal principle of distribution among the uterine heirs.

According to Ḥanbalī law the male and female descendants of *any* ordinary heir share equally, on the ground that in these cases the connection with the praepositus is always through a female.

(ii) Where the relatives concerned are uncles and aunts of the praepositus, and thus represent either his mother or his father, the rule not only affects the *quantum* of share but may also result in the total exclusion of some of the relatives, because the rules of exclusion and distribution relating to brothers and sisters will apply.

(Father)	Uterine brother	Germane sister	Germane sister	Consanguine sister
P	$\frac{1}{5}$	$\frac{2}{5}$	$\frac{2}{5}$	—

Here, the paternal aunt who is the consanguine sister of the praepositus' father is *de facto* excluded by the presence of two germane sisters of the father. The basic Qur'anic portions of the germane sisters and the uterine brother are then increased by *radd*.

(Mother)	Germane sister	Consanguine brother	Consanguine sister
P	$\frac{1}{2}$	$\frac{1}{4}$	$\frac{1}{4}$

Here, after the mother's germane sister has taken her Qur'anic portion, the consanguine maternal uncle and aunt take the residue in equal shares. As between maternal uncles and aunts who have the same blood-tie (whether germane, consanguine or uterine) with the mother of the praepositus, the rule of double share to the male does not apply.

A germane maternal uncle would totally exclude the consanguine maternal uncle and aunt, while all maternal uncles and aunts would be excluded by the maternal grandfather: for although the latter is no nearer in degree to the praepositus' mother than the uncles and aunts, he will, as the father of the heir represented, exclude the brothers and sisters of the same link.

Precisely the same rules regulate succession by great uncles and aunts who represent the mother's mother or the father's father of the praepositus.

(iii) Where the succeeding relatives are cousins of the praepositus and have different parents, they inherit the share which their parent would have received, had he or she survived, under the rules of section (ii) above. Under this system of representation within representation, the male and female children of any uncle or aunt take equal shares in Ḥanbalī law. In Shāfiʿī law the children of a maternal aunt or uncle, and the children of the praepositus' uterine paternal uncle or aunt, share equally in their parent's portion. But among the children of the praepositus' germane or consanguine paternal aunt the rule of double share to the male applies.

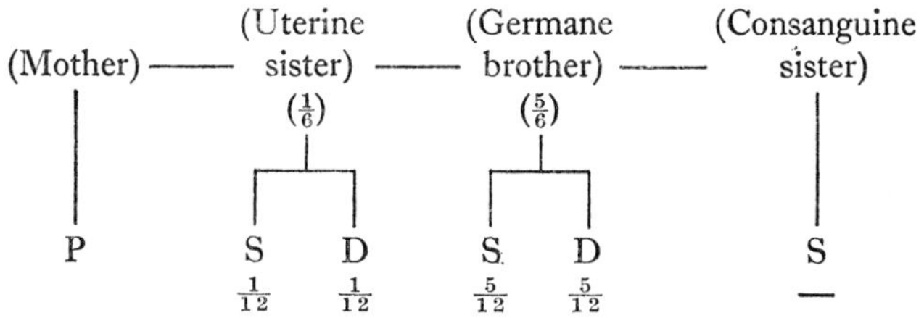

P = Praepositus, S = Son, D = Daughter.

The same principles govern succession by the issue of cousins, the share that each parent would have received if he or she had survived descending to his or her children.

2.3. Rule 3: notional distribution among different links

Relatives who are connected with the praepositus through different ordinary heirs, and who are equal in the degree of removal from their respective links, inherit what the ordinary heir they represent would have inherited in competition with the other ordinary heirs represented.

In the following example all the relatives are one degree removed from the ordinary heirs they severally represent. The praepositus' cousin, nephew and niece are excluded, because the heirs they represent – the paternal uncle, brother and sister – would be excluded by the father who is represented by the paternal aunt. (In the latter's absence the cousin would, similarly, be excluded by the niece but not by the nephew.) In the presence of a germane brother and sister, even though they are themselves excluded, the mother is restricted to a portion of one-sixth. This is then divided among the maternal aunts as though the mother herself were the praepositus (Rule 2). The father's representative, the uterine paternal aunt, then succeeds to the residue.

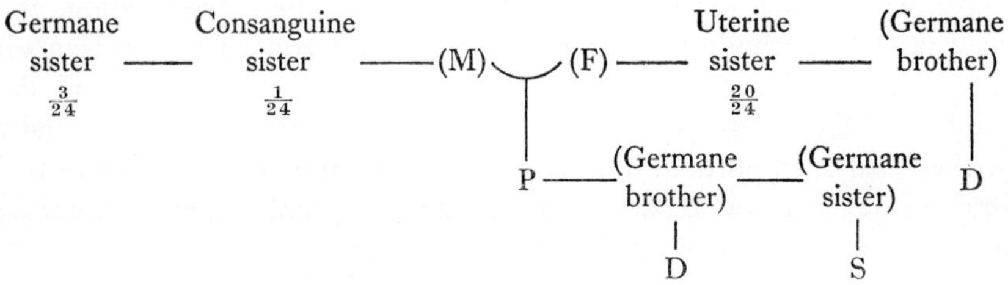

M = Mother, F = Father.

2.4. Rule 4: priority by degree of removal from different links

Where relatives connected with the praepositus through different ordinary heirs vary in their degree of removal from the heirs they severally represent, the relative nearer in degree to the heir represented (i) under Shāfiʿī law excludes all other relatives; (ii) under Ḥanbalī law excludes all other relatives of the same general class. For the purposes of this rule Ḥanbalī law recognises three classes of relatives – descendants, paternal relatives and maternal relatives. In the class of descendants, for example, there are two ordinary heirs, the daughter and the son's daughter. A son's daughter's daughter will therefore exclude a daughter's daughter's son, but *under this*

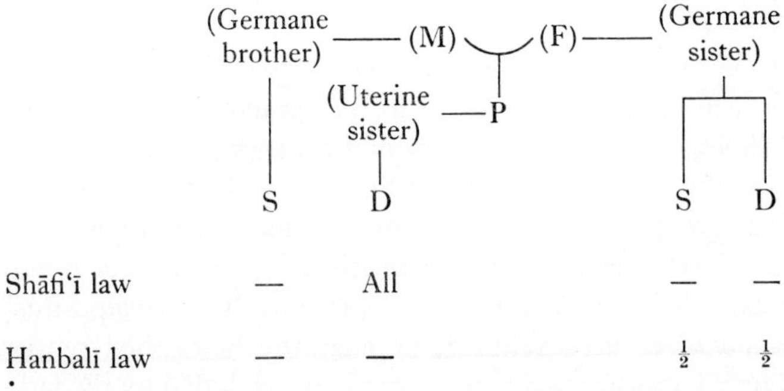

rule she will not exclude any paternal or maternal relative, however far removed from the ordinary heir represented, while under Shāfi'ī law she will exclude any such relative who is more than one degree removed from the heir represented. Hence, the case on p. 96 is solved as follows.

(i) Under Shāfi'ī law the niece, as the only relative at the first degree of removal from the ordinary heir she represents, excludes all other relatives.

(ii) Under Ḥanbalī law the niece excludes the maternal cousin, but is in turn excluded by the paternal cousins, since the ordinary heir the latter represent (the father) excludes the heir whom the niece represents (the uterine sister). The paternal cousins then take equal shares in accordance with the normal Ḥanbalī doctrine. Here, the presence of the niece obviously benefits the paternal cousins, since without her the maternal cousin would have been entitled to one-third of the estate.[1]

2.5. Rule 5: maximum portion for spouse relict

A spouse relict succeeding along with relatives of the outer family is in no way affected by the representational principles of *tanzīl*. The spouse relict, as the only surviving member of the inner family, stands outside this system of representational succession. His or her portion is not subject to reduction by the presence of relatives who represent the deceased's daughter or son's daughter, nor by the process of *'awl*. The spouse relict always takes the maximum Qur'anic portion, and the rights of the relatives of the outer family then attach only to the residue of the estate.[2]

[1] See p. 63 above for the only other parallel case of an excluding heir being in turn excluded. The Ḥanbalī texts reflect some controversy on the question of how many different classes of relatives (within each of which the relative nearer to an ordinary heir will exclude others) are to be recognised for the purposes of this rule. The jurist Abū'l-Khaṭṭāb suggested that five classes should be recognised – descendants, brothers' and sisters' issue, mother's relatives, father's relatives and germane or consanguine paternal uncles' descendants. But this principle, taken in conjunction with Rule 3, produces unacceptable results. For example, a paternal uncle's daughter would be excluded by the granddaughter of a paternal aunt. There would be no exclusion under Rule 4 since the two heirs belong to different classes, but under Rule 3 the relative representing the paternal uncle would be excluded by the relative representing the father. Similarly, any nephew or niece of the praepositus, representing the praepositus' brother or sister, would be excluded by the issue, how low soever, of a paternal aunt. Ibn Qudāma remarks: "Had Abu'l-Khaṭṭāb appreciated these results of his opinion, I suspect he would never have voiced it." The correct basis for the application of the Ḥanbalī rule, therefore, appears to be the recognition of three classes of relatives only.

[2] There exists a variant doctrine on this point, under which the rights of the relatives of the outer family may be affected by the presence of a spouse relict. This doctrine is that the estate should first be notionally distributed as though the ordinary heirs represented were in fact competing with the spouse relict. The spouse relict is then given the maxi-

Husband	$\frac{1}{2}$	
Daughter's daughter	$\frac{3}{12}$	($\frac{1}{2}$ of the residue)
Son's daughter's daughter	$\frac{1}{12}$	($\frac{1}{6}$ of the residue)
Germane sister's son	$\frac{2}{12}$	(residue of the residue)

3. The doctrine of *qarāba*

The Ḥanafī principle of *qarāba*, or "relationship", is best considered under two separate heads: first, the rules of exclusion, upon which there is general agreement, and second, the rules of apportionment, in regard to which there is an important divergence of doctrine.

3.1. Rules of exclusion

Under the doctrine of *qarāba*, relatives of the outer family are marshalled into an order of priority which is based broadly upon the same three major criteria that determine the order of priority among agnatic residuary heirs of the inner family.

3.1.1. The rule of class

Relatives are divided into four main classes, any member of a higher class totally excluding any member of a lower class. The four classes, in order of priority, are: I. descendants; II. ascendants; III. descendants of the praepositus' parents; IV. descendants of the praepositus' grandparents how high soever.

Class IV is further divided into subsidiary classes. The praepositus' own uncles and aunts (and their issue) precede, as a class, the uncles and aunts (and their issue) of his parents, who in turn precede the uncles and aunts (and their issue) of his grandparents. A great uncle or aunt is thus totally excluded by any child how low soever of a cousin of the praepositus.

mum Qur'anic portion and the residue is distributed among the ordinary heirs, and through them to their representatives, in accordance with the ratio of their several shares established by the first notional distribution. Applying this method to the illustration given in the text above, the first notional distribution will be: husband one-quarter, daughter's daughter one-half, son's daughter's daughter one-sixth, germane sister's son one-twelfth. The ratio of the shares of the last three relatives is therefore 6:2:1. When the husband is then given his full portion of one-half, and the residue of one-half is divided among the relatives in accordance with this ratio, the result is: daughter's daughter six-eighteenths, son's daughter's daughter two-eighteenths, germane sister's son one-eighteenth. It is evident, however, that a distribution different from that resulting from the normal doctrine can only occur where the ordinary heirs represented include both Qur'anic and residuary heirs.

3.1.2. The rule of degree

The rule that, among relatives of the same class, the nearer in degree to the praepositus excludes the more remote is absolute, and therefore applies, in Classes II, III and IV between all relatives, regardless of sex and whether they are on the paternal or maternal side. The daughter of a uterine sister will thus exclude the daughter of a germane brother's son, and any maternal aunt will exclude a paternal uncle's daughter.

3.1.3. The rule of strength of relationship

A final determinant of priority, among relatives of the same class and of equal degree, is provided by the comparative strength of their relationship with the deceased. A superior strength of relationship is deemed to result from either (*a*) immediate connection with the praepositus through a member of his inner family, or (*b*) connection through a stronger blood tie. These two factors affect priorities within the various classes of relatives as follows.

(i) In Class I the child of a Qur'anic or residuary heir (son's (how low soever) daughter or son) excludes other grandchildren of equal degree.

(ii) In Class II the father of a grandmother who is a Qur'anic heir excludes other grandparents of equal degree.[1]

(iii) In Class III both the factors establishing a superior strength of relationship may apply. First, among relatives of the same degree, the child of a member of the inner family excludes others. Then, among those that remain, the issue of germane brothers or sisters exclude the issue of consanguines, who in turn exclude the issue of uterines.

Thus, where the sole heirs of the praepositus are the son of his germane sister's son and the daughter of his consanguine brother's son, the latter will exclude the former.

As will be observed below (pp. 103–4), however, the rule of priority through strength of blood-tie does not apply, as it is here formulated, under the doctrine of Shaybānī. His principle of *per stirpes* apportionment merges into the rules of exclusion in this class of relatives.

(iv) In Class IV both the grounds of a superior relationship again apply, but in the reverse order to that observed in Class III. First, the germane

[1] The mother of a grandmother who is a Qur'anic heir is always, under Ḥanafī law, herself a Qur'anic heir, and the mother of any entitled agnatic grandfather (the father's father how high soever) is similarly always a Qur'anic heir. The above rule is observed in the Indian sub-continent and the Ḥanafī countries of the Middle East generally, although the dominant view of the classical jurists appears to be that no priority derives from such a connection in the case of grandparents.

relatives or issue thereof, exclude consanguines, who in turn exclude uterines. Then, among those that remain, the children of male aganate relatives exclude others. Both these rules, however, apply only among relatives on the same side, i.e. paternal or maternal. And clearly the second rule can apply only on the paternal side, where the child of a germane uncle will exclude the child of a germane aunt, or the child of a consanguine uncle will exclude the child of a consanguine aunt.

Thus, a germane paternal aunt's son or daughter will exclude a consanguine paternal uncle's daughter, though neither will exclude a uterine maternal aunt's child.

3.2. Rules of apportionment

As is the case under the doctrine of *tanzīl*, the spouse relict is in no way affected by the presence of relatives of the outer family, so that, where there is a spouse relict, the problem of apportionment applies only to the residue of the estate left after the deduction of the spouse relict's maximum Qur'anic portion.

3.2.1. The distinction between apportionment *per capita* and *per stirpes*

Towards this problem the two early Ḥanafī jurists, Abū Yūsuf and Shaybānī, adopted fundamentally different approaches, which may reflect the respective roles they played in early legal science. Although they are popularly known as "the two companions", Abū Yūsuf and Shaybānī had little in common apart from their pupillage under Abū Ḥanīfa. Abū Yūsuf was a practising lawyer, the chief justice of the central government at Baghdad, while Shaybānī was essentially an academic lawyer and a prolific author of works on legal doctrine. In keeping, perhaps, with this difference of personal character, Abū Yūsuf's solution of the present problem is simple and practical, while Shaybānī's is more complex because it seeks to express more fully the various theoretical implications of succession by members of the outer family.

According to Shaybānī, the share of the inheritance which relatives who are not excluded under the rules of priority will take is determined by the links through whom they are severally connected with the praepositus – a rule of distribution *per stirpes* which represents a partial adoption of the principle of representational succession.

Abū Yūsuf, however, does not look beyond the entitled heirs themselves but distributes the inheritance among them on a strictly *per capita* basis. The only concession he makes to the principle of representation is that, in Classes II and IV, entitled relatives on the paternal side take, collectively, two-thirds of the inheritance (the notional share of the praepositus' father), while relatives on the maternal side take one-third of the inheritance (the notional share of the praepositus' mother).

In principle, therefore, the distinction between the two doctrines is clear-cut. In practice, however, as may be appreciated from the illustrations which follow, it is only likely to result in different schemes of distribution among relatives of Class III – nephews, nieces and their issue. Competitions between relatives of other classes will, in all but the most improbable of cases, be resolved by the common rules of exclusion.

3.2.2. Descendants

Here Shaybānī's *per stirpes* principle comes into operation only where: (*a*) the entitled relatives are great grandchildren or a lower generation of the praepositus' descendants; (*b*) they are connected with the praepositus through different lines of descent; and (*c*) their respective intermediate links of the same generation differ in sex.

In these circumstances a notional distribution of the estate is made at the first generation of descent from the praepositus where the intermediate links differ in sex in accordance with the rule of double share to male relatives. The notional share of each intermediate link is then divided between the surviving relatives connected through this link, males taking double the share of females. This basic scheme, however, is subject to two refinements.

(i) At the notional distribution a male intermediate link counts as as many males as there are surviving relatives claiming through him, and a female link counts as as many females as there are surviving relatives claiming through her.

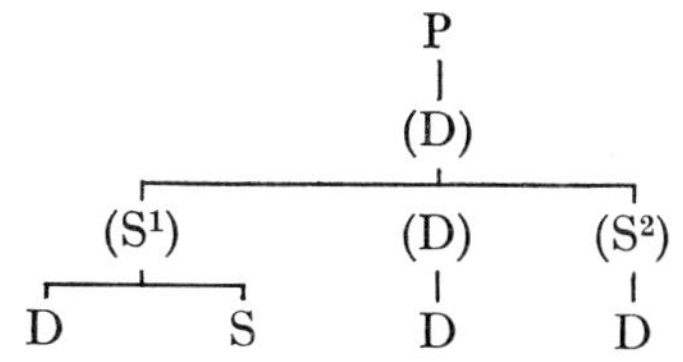

	D	S	D	D
Abū Yūsuf:	$\frac{1}{5}$	$\frac{2}{5}$	$\frac{1}{5}$	$\frac{1}{5}$
Shaybānī:	$\frac{3}{14}$	$\frac{6}{14}$	$\frac{2}{14}$	$\frac{3}{14}$

S = Son, D = Daughter.

(ii) Where there are three or more intermediate links taking part in the notional distribution, the collective share of the male links is apportioned between all relatives claiming through them, and the collective share of female links is apportioned between all their surviving descendants.

The case on p. 101 involves a notional distribution among three grandchildren. (S^1), counting as two males because there are two relatives claiming through him, takes four-sevenths, (S^2) two-sevenths and (D) one-seventh. The collective entitlement (six-sevenths) of (S^1) and (S^2) is then divided between the three relatives claiming through them, double share to the male.

Under both doctrines all the great grandchildren in this case would be excluded by the child of a son's daughter of the praepositus.

3.2.3. Ascendants

Both Abū Yūsuf and Shaybānī agree that in a competition between ascendants of the outer family, two-thirds of the inheritance goes to the paternal side and one-third to the maternal side. Since there is, among the four grandparents of the praepositus, only one member of the outer family – the mother's father – this rule of apportionment first comes into play among the deceased's great grandparents, and then only in a competition between the mother's mother's father and the father's mother's father, where the former would take one-third and the latter two-thirds of the inheritance. Either of these great grandfathers, being connected with the praepositus through a grandmother of the inner family, would totally exclude the only other two great grandparents who are members of the outer family – the parents of the mother's father. If the latter two great grandparents alone survived, the great grandfather would take two-thirds and the great grandmother one-third of the inheritance. Further investigation of the particular effect of Shaybānī's *per stirpes* principle upon grandparents of a higher generation seems quite pointless.

3.2.4. Descendants of the praepositus' parents

It is perhaps in regard to this class of relatives that the law has a greater practical significance, for it is not difficult to imagine circumstances in which an unmarried or childless praepositus is survived by nephews and nieces, or their issue, who are entitled to succeed as relatives of the outer family. It is here also that the divergent results of the respective doctrines of Abū Yūsuf and Shaybānī are particularly apparent. According to both jurists, among the children of nephews and nieces, or at any lower degree of their issue, the child of a male agnate relative will exclude all others.

Beyond this, however, Abū Yūsuf consistently applies a simple strength of blood-tie rule: the descendants of germane collaterals exclude the descendants of consanguines, who in turn exclude the descendants of uterines. Shaybānī, on the other hand, maintains that there should be a notional distribution of the inheritance among the links, the brothers and sisters of the praepositus, whose respective shares should then descend to the relatives claiming through them. This notional distribution follows the normal principles of Qur'anic and residual succession, but also involves those particular rules of Shaybānī (concerning the number of claimants through one link and the number of lines of connection) which apply to the class of descendants.

It is obvious, therefore, that Shaybānī's stirpital principle here affects not only the *quantum* of share but also the question of priorities. The children of uterine brothers or sisters are never excluded; the child of a consanguine brother is excluded by the child of a germane brother but not by the child of a germane sister, and the child of a consanguine sister is excluded by the child of a germane brother but only by two or more children of a germane sister. Among the entitled issue of germane or consanguine collaterals the male takes double the share of the female, but the issue of uterine collaterals share equally regardless of sex.

3.2.4.1. Nephews and nieces

	P — (Germane sister)	— (Consanguine sister)	— (Uterine brother)
	S	D	D
Abū Yūsuf:	All	—	—
Shaybānī:	$\frac{3}{5}$	$\frac{1}{5}$	$\frac{1}{5}$

According to Abū Yūsuf, the nephew, as the child of a germane relative of the praepositus, completely excludes the two nieces who are the children of consanguine and uterine relatives of the praepositus.

According to Shaybānī, there is a notional distribution between the brother and sisters of the praepositus (Qur'anic portions augmented by *radd*), whose respective shares then descend to their issue.

3.2.4.2. Issue of nephews and nieces

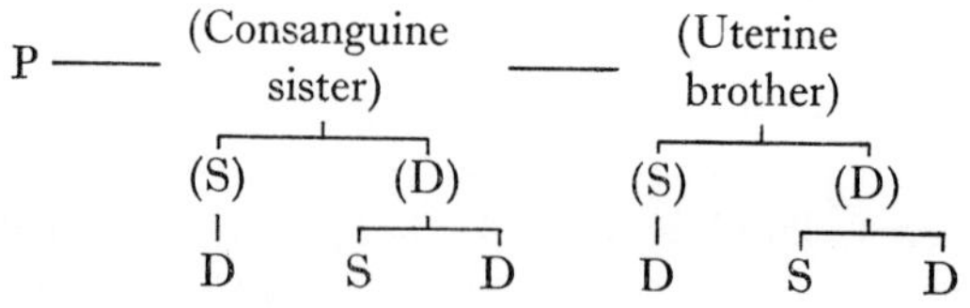

	D	S	D	D	S	D
Abū Yūsuf:	$\frac{1}{4}$	$\frac{1}{2}$	$\frac{1}{4}$	—	—	—
Shaybānī:	$\frac{3}{9}$	$\frac{2}{9}$	$\frac{1}{9}$	$\frac{1}{9}$	$\frac{1}{9}$	$\frac{1}{9}$

According to Shaybānī the notional distribution is between three consanguine sisters (two-thirds) and three uterine brothers (one-third). The consanguine sister's portion is then further notionally distributed among her children, the daughter counting as two daughters, and these shares then descend to their own children, the male taking double the share of the female. Among the issue of the uterine brother the difference of sex between the claimants and their intermediate links is disregarded.

According to Abū Yūsuf the rule of double share to the male in his *per capita* distribution applies to all relatives, including the issue of uterine brothers and sisters where they are entitled to inherit.

3.2.5. Descendants of the praepositus' grandparents

Following the rules of exclusion, under which, on the paternal and maternal sides independently, germane relatives (or the issue thereof) exclude consanguines who in turn exclude uterines, and then children of male agnates exclude others, Abū Yūsuf and Shaybānī recognise a common basic principle of apportionment. Paternal relatives take two-thirds, and maternal relatives one-third of the inheritance, the rule of double share to males applying in *all* cases.

Between the two jurists, therefore, different schemes of apportionment can only occur where the entitled relatives are the children of cousins or a lower generation. Then, Shaybānī's rules relating to the difference of sex in intermediate links, the number of lines of connection, and the number of claimants in each line will apply, and grandchildren of an aunt or uncle will be treated in exactly the same way as grandchildren of the daughter of the praepositus. In the following case a notional distribution is to be made to the praepositus' cousins, and the rules relating to difference of sex, number of claimants and lines of connection apply, both on the paternal and maternal sides and to uterines as well as to germanes and consanguines.

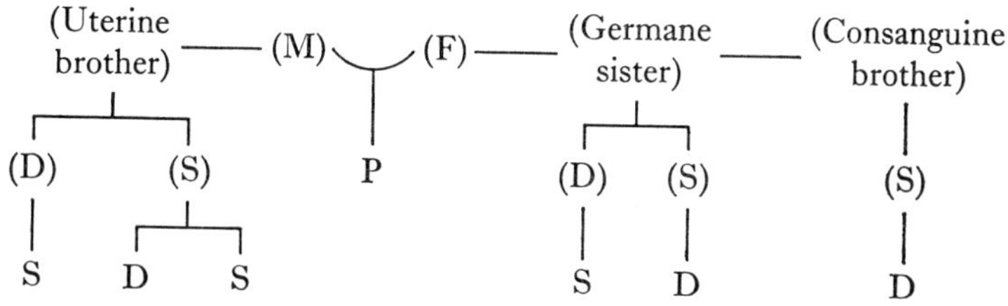

	S	D	S	S	D	D
Abū Yūsuf:	$\frac{6}{45}$	$\frac{3}{45}$	$\frac{6}{45}$	$\frac{20}{45}$	$\frac{10}{45}$	—
Shaybānī:	$\frac{3}{45}$	$\frac{4}{45}$	$\frac{8}{45}$	$\frac{10}{45}$	$\frac{20}{45}$	—

4. *Tanzīl* and *qarāba* compared

A few hypothetical cases may serve to show how the application of the doctrine of *qarāba* in the Ḥanafī school and of the doctrine of *tanzīl* in the Ḥanbalī and Shāfiʿī schools may produce widely divergent results.

(*a*)	Ḥanafīs	Shāfiʿīs	Ḥanbalīs
Mother's father	All	$\frac{1}{5}$	$\frac{1}{5}$
Germane sister's son	—	$\frac{2}{5}$	$\frac{2}{5}$
Germane sister's daughter	—	$\frac{2}{5}$	$\frac{2}{5}$

Under Ḥanafī law the rule of superior class applies, and under Shāfiʿī and Ḥanbalī law the rule of representational succession as by a mother and two germane sisters.

(*b*)	Ḥanafīs	Shāfiʿīs	Ḥanbalīs
Daughter's daughter	All	$\frac{3}{4}$	$\frac{3}{4}$
Son's daughter's daughter	—	$\frac{1}{4}$	$\frac{1}{4}$

This is the result in Ḥanafī law of the rule of degree among relatives of the same class, and in Shāfiʿī and Ḥanbalī law of the rule of representational succession as by a daughter and a son's daughter.

(c)	Ḥanafīs	Shāfiʻīs	Ḥanbalīs
Mother's father's mother	All	—	—
Uterine maternal aunt	—	All	All

This is the result in Ḥanafī law of the rule of superior class, and in Shāfiʻī and Ḥanbalī law of Rule 1 of the doctrine of *tanzīl*.

(d)	Ḥanafīs	Shāfiʻīs	Ḥanbalīs
Uterine paternal aunt	—	All	All
Germane brother's daughter	All	—	—

Under Ḥanafī law the rule of superior class applies. In Shāfiʻī and Ḥanbalī law the father, the heir represented by the aunt, excludes the germane brother, the heir represented by the niece.

(e)	Ḥanafīs	Shāfiʻīs	Ḥanbalīs
Daughter's daughter's daughter	All	—	$\frac{1}{2}$
Germane sister's daughter	—	$\frac{1}{2}$	$\frac{1}{2}$
Consanguine brother's daughter	—	$\frac{1}{2}$	—

In Ḥanafī law the rule of superior class applies. In Shāfiʻī law Rule 4 of the doctrine of *tanzīl* applies to exclude the great granddaughter. In Ḥanbalī law there is no exclusion under Rule 4, and distribution is as between a daughter, germane sister and consanguine brother, the germane sister in these circumstances inheriting as a residuary heir and thus excluding the consanguine brother under the strength of blood-tie rule.

(f)	Ḥanafīs	Shāfiʻīs	Ḥanbalīs
Uterine maternal aunt's daughter	$\frac{1}{3}$	—	$\frac{1}{3}$
Consanguine paternal uncle's daughter	—	All	$\frac{2}{3}$
Germane paternal aunt's son	$\frac{2}{3}$	—	—

In Ḥanafī law the paternal side takes two-thirds and the maternal side one-third of the estate, the strength of blood-tie rule excluding the consanguine uncle's child on the paternal side. In Shāfiʻī law Rule 4 of the doctrine of *tanzīl* applies to exclude both the aunts' children. In Ḥanbalī law exclusion under Rule 4 operates only among the paternal cousins, and there is then representational succession as between a mother and a consanguine paternal uncle.

(*g*)	Ḥanafīs	Shāfiʿīs	Ḥanbalīs
Uterine sister's daughter	All	$\frac{1}{6}$	$\frac{1}{6}$
Consanguine paternal uncle's son's daughter	—	$\frac{5}{6}$	$\frac{5}{6}$
Germane maternal aunt's son	—	—	—

In Ḥanafī law the rule of superior class applies. In Ḥanbalī and Shāfiʿī law the maternal cousin is excluded by the niece under Rule 4 of *tanzīl.*

(*h*)	Ḥanafīs	Shāfiʿīs	Ḥanbalīs
Germane paternal aunt's son	—	—	$\frac{2}{3}$
Uterine sister's daughter	All	$\frac{1}{3}$	—
Uterine maternal uncle	—	$\frac{2}{3}$	$\frac{1}{3}$

In Ḥanafī law the rule of superior class applies. In Shāfiʿī law the cousin is excluded under Rule 4 of the doctrine of *tanzīl,* and representational distribution between the niece and uncle is as between a uterine sister and a mother. In Ḥanbalī law the cousin, being a paternal relative, cannot be excluded by any maternal relative, and since representational succession is as between a father, uterine sister and mother, the uterine sister is excluded by the father.

8. INHERITANCE IN SHĪʿĪ LAW

1. The rejection of the criterion of agnatic relationship

Perhaps the most striking and significant divergence between the Sunnī and the Shīʿī legal systems as a whole lies in their respective laws of inheritance.[1] From a comparative standpoint the outstanding characteristic of the Shīʿī law of inheritance is its refusal to afford any special place or privileged position to agnate relatives as such – a fundamental distinction which is somewhat graphically expressed in the alleged dictum of the Shīʿī Imām, Jaʿfar al-Ṣadīq: "As for the *ʿaṣaba*, dust in their teeth." This basic approach of the Shīʿa to the subject of inheritance has two principal effects. In the first place, all blood relatives are embraced by a single and comprehensive system of priorities, and there is no major division, such as exists in Sunnī law because of the criterion of agnatic relationship, between an inner and an outer family. In the second place, female and non-agnatic relatives stand on an equal footing with male agnates in the Shīʿī scheme of succession in the sense that they exclude any relative who occupies an inferior position in the order of priorities. Exclusion of other relatives is not, as it is in the Sunnī system, the particular prerogative of male agnates. Most of the complexities of Sunnī law stem from the superior status which it grants to male agnates as legal heirs. By its firm repudiation of that principle of superiority the Shīʿī law of inheritance at least acquires the merit of comparative simplicity.

2. Priorities

2.1. Priority by *qarāba*, or "relationship"

As is the case in Sunnī law, the spouse relict stands outside the system of priorities, taking a fixed portion of the estate and neither excluding nor being excluded by any blood relative of the praepositus. Among blood relatives priority in succession depends upon the nature and quality of their relationship, or *qarāba*, with the deceased; and this is determined by the three usual criteria of class, degree and strength of blood tie.

[1] The term "Shīʿī law" is in many contexts as imprecise as "Sunnī" law, since the various branches of the Shīʿī movement diverge from one another on specific legal issues in much the same way as the schools of Sunnī Islam differ among themselves. The law here described is that of the numerically strongest group of the Shīʿa, the Ithnā ʿAsharīs. Ismāʿīlī succession law is basically the same, but the minority group of the Zaidīs has a law of inheritance which represents an amalgam of this "Shīʿī" and the Sunnī systems.

2.1.1. The rule of class

All blood relatives are divided into three classes as follows:

Class I: Parents and lineal descendants how low soever.

Class II: Grandparents how high soever, brothers and sisters and their issue how low soever.

Class III: Uncles and aunts, paternal and maternal, and their issue how low soever, followed by great uncles and aunts and their issue how low soever.

Any relative of Class I completely excludes from succession any relative of Class II, who in turn excludes any relative of Class III. Thus, an agnatic brother or nephew, and *a fortiori* an uncle or cousin, is excluded by the mother or daughter no less than by the father or son of the praepositus. In competition with a female or a non-agnatic relative of a higher class, a male agnate of a lower class takes nothing, or, following the expression of the Imām Ja'far, nothing more than a mouthful of dust.

2.1.2. The rule of degree

Within each class the rule that the relative nearer in degree to the praepositus excludes the more remote is of absolute application in so far as it covers both male and female and agnatic and non-agnatic relatives.

In Class I of the heirs, the parents and children of the praepositus must always inherit, and the rule of degree operates to exclude only lineal descendants. A daughter, just as a son, will *de jure* exclude any grandchild, male or female, agnatic or non-agnatic, and any grandchild will in turn exclude any lower grandchild.

Class II of the heirs contains the two distinct groups of ascendants and collaterals, and the rule of degree operates within each of the two groups but not between them. Thus, any great grandparent will be excluded by any grandparent, male or female, paternal or maternal. Any brother or sister will exclude any nephew or niece, so that, for example, a uterine sister will completely exclude a germane brother's son. But no grandparent, how high soever, will be excluded by any collateral, and no collateral or the issue thereof, how low soever, will be excluded by any grandparent.

Class III of the heirs in fact contains several sub-classes. Uncles and aunts of the praepositus, along with their issue how low soever, have priority as a rule of class over the uncles and aunts and the issue thereof of the praepositus' parents, who in turn have priority over the uncles and aunts and the issue thereof of the praepositus' grandparents. Within each of the sub-classes the rule of degree applies regardless of the sex, the "side" (paternal or maternal), or the strength of blood-tie of the relatives concerned. Thus a uterine maternal aunt *de jure* excludes from succession a germane paternal uncle's son.

2.1.3. The rule of strength of blood-tie

Among collateral relatives who are equal under the rules of class and degree, the final determinant of priority is the strength of the blood connection. Any germane, male or female, excludes any consanguine, but neither germanes nor consanguines exclude uterines. Similarly, where the surviving relatives are nephews and nieces or cousins of the praepositus, the issue of germanes exclude the issue of consanguines, but neither exclude the issue of uterines. Among relatives of Class III, however, this rule operates independently on the paternal and maternal sides. No paternal relative is excluded under this rule by any maternal relative and vice versa.

> P is survived by four cousins: A, the daughter of his germane paternal aunt; B, the son of his consanguine paternal uncle; C, the daughter of his consanguine maternal aunt, and D, the son of his uterine paternal aunt.

The only cousin who is not an entitled heir is B, who is excluded by A. (Under Sunnī law, B, as the only male agnate present, would take the whole estate.)

Through its basic doctrine of *qarāba* Shīʿī jurisprudence majestically sweeps aside all those troublesome distinctions and divisions, between Qur'anic and other heirs, and between agnatic and non-agnatic relatives, in which the generality of Muslim jurists were enmeshed because of their preoccupation with the traditional claims of the *ʿaṣaba*. Whatever appeal the doctrine of *qarāba* may or may not have to the Muslim religious conscience, the student of law may perhaps be forgiven if he looks upon it with the sense of deliverance of one who sees severed, at one clean stroke, the almost Gordian knot of Sunnī inheritance.

3. Apportionment of inheritance

Three basic principles govern the distribution of an estate among relatives who are entitled to succeed under the doctrine of *qarāba*.

3.1. Qur'anic portions and residual shares

The nine relatives specifically nominated by the Qur'an – the husband, wife, father, mother, daughter, germane sister, consanguine sister, uterine brother and uterine sister – take their prescribed portions in suitable circumstances, while other relatives such as the son and agnatic brothers take on a residual basis. In Shīʿī law, however, the term "residuary" is in no sense to be identified with "male agnate" as it is in Sunnī law. Shīʿī legal texts do not use the term *ʿaṣaba*, or its derivative *taʿṣīb*, to describe the basis of entitlement to inherit. A relative, male or female, agnatic or otherwise, is simply described as either *dhū qarāba* (lit. "the possessor of relationship") when entitlement is general or residual, or *dhū farḍ* ("the possessor of a prescribed portion") when entitlement is special or fixed.

Subject to the priorities of *qarāba*, the *quantum* of the Qur'anic portions and the circumstances in which they are taken are basically the same as in Sunnī law, since these questions were directly regulated by the Qur'ān. Thus, the spouse relict and the mother are restricted to their minimal portions by the survival of a child of the praepositus; the father takes as a Qur'anic heir when a child survives but otherwise as a residuary, and daughters and agnatic sisters take as residuaries in the presence of their respective brothers.

However, Shīʿī law has two distinctive features in this context. First, the grandfather, grandmother and agnatic granddaughter are not included in the list of Qur'anic heirs as they are in Sunnī law. Second, the system of priority by *qarāba* precludes any possibility of the *de facto* exclusion of residuary heirs such as may occur under Sunnī law when the portions of entitled Qur'anic heirs exhaust the estate. Exclusion of relatives from succession in Shīʿī law is always *de jure*.

3.2. Representational entitlement: the *per stirpes* principle

Where the entitled heirs are relatives more remote than the children, parents, brothers and sisters of the praepositus, the share of inheritance they take is basically determined by the principle of representation. Priorities apart, Shīʿī jurisprudence looks upon children, parents, brothers and sisters as the principal heirs, or "roots", of the system of inheritance. Other relatives are subsidiary heirs or "branches", and their derivative rights are determined by the standards applied to the root or principal heir through whom they trace their connection with the praepositus. In sum, therefore, where there are a number of subsidiary heirs competing who are connected with the praepositus through different principal heirs, each "root" transmits to its own "branches" the share of inheritance that it would notionally receive in competition with the other "roots" represented. This share, as a general rule, is then distributed among the "branches" as if the "root" itself were the praepositus.

Shī'ī law thus consistently applies to the whole range of the deceased's relatives the same principle of representational entitlement that Ḥanafī law, at least according to the doctrine of Shaybānī, applies to the relatives of the outer family. By comparison with Shaybānī's doctrine, however, the principle operates in a more straightforward and systematic fashion under Shī'ī law. Relatives claiming through one particular link take no more and no less than the notional entitlement of that individual link. There is no parallel in Shī'ī law to Shaybānī's two rules (*a*) that an intermediate link counts as as many links as there are relatives claiming through it, and (*b*) that the collective entitlement of all male intermediate links and that of all female intermediate links is shared by their respective issue pp. 101–2 above). At the same time Shī'ī doctrine in this regard does not represent such an outright adoption of the principle of representation as does the Shāfi'ī and Ḥanbalī doctrine of *tanzīl* in relation to succession by the outer family. *Tanzīl* is representation in the full sense of the term inasmuch as it determines both priority and *quantum* of share. But in Shī'ī law representation only comes into play to determine the *quantum* of share when priorities have been settled by the criteria of class, degree and strength of blood-tie under the doctrine of *qarāba*.

3.3. Relative entitlement of males and females

Subject to the principle of representational entitlement, the rule that a male takes twice the share of a corresponding female relative applies to lineal descendants and all relatives on the paternal side with the exception of uterines – i.e. those paternal uncles and aunts, or the issue thereof, who are the uterine brothers or sisters of the father or the paternal grandparents of the praepositus. Among these relatives, as among all relatives whose sole ultimate connection is through the mother of the praepositus, entitled males and females take equal shares. Shī'ī jurisprudence regards these rules as the logical extension of the principles embodied in the Qur'ān, which expressly provides that sons take twice as much as daughters and agnatic brothers twice as much as agnatic sisters but that uterine brothers and sisters share equally.

The operation of these three basic principles will be illustrated in the detailed consideration of the various classes of heirs which now follows.

3.4. The spouse relict

Shī'ī law concerning succession by the spouse relict is identical with Sunnī law in all but four particulars.

3.4.1. Variations from Sunnī law

(*a*) A surviving husband is restricted to a portion of one-quarter, and a surviving wife or wives to a portion of one-eighth, in the presence of *any* lineal descendant of the praepositus.

(*b*) The Qur'anic portion of the spouse relict is never subject to reduction by *'awl*. Where an estate is over-subscribed by Qur'anic heirs, Shī'ī law rejects the doctrine of *pro rata* abatement of all the Qur'anic portions and maintains, on the basis of arguments similar to those attributed to Ibn 'Abbās (p. 48 above), that the burden of necessary reduction is to be borne exclusively by daughters or agnatic sisters (or those relatives who succeed to their respective portions through the principle of representational entitlement).

(*c*) As in Sunnī law, the portion of a wife is never increased by *radd*. Where no relative of the praepositus survives, the residue of the estate goes to the Imām as the head of the Shī'ī community. But while a husband is also debarred from *radd* in the presence of any blood relative, in the absence thereof he succeeds to the residue of his deceased wife's estate by way of *radd* in preference to the Imām.

(*d*) A childless wife inherits no share in her deceased husband's lands.

3.4.2. The childless wife

"Childless" here means, according to the texts, that the surviving widow is without a child, alive or in embryo and subsequently born alive, at the time succession to the estate opens. A wife, therefore, suffers from this disability if she has had children by the praepositus who have died before the succession opens or if her only children are those of another marriage. The rule is clearly aimed at ensuring, to a large degree, that lands remain within the husband's family. A widow succeeds to a share in her husband's lands only when that share, or the greater part of it, will in the normal course of events be transmitted to the husband's issue upon her decease.

There does not appear to be any precise textual authority on the point whether a wife is caught by this rule if there survives any lineal descendant who is the issue of a predeceased child of herself and the praepositus. Although this lineal descendant is the primary heir of the wife at the time of her husband's decease, he or she would of course be excluded from succession by any further child born to the widow from a subsequent marriage. It would seem, however, that a wife in these circumstances should not suffer from the disqualification because it can only be the actual situation at the time of the husband's death which is relevant. Land actually inherited by a widow may eventually be lost to her former husband's family and go to her own collateral relatives if her children predecease her. The rule would therefore appear to be that a wife inherits a share in her husband's lands if there survives, at the time of his death, any lineal descendant of his who is at that time the primary heir of the wife. Such a lineal descendant would not, of course be the primary heir of the wife if she had living children from a previous marriage.

A childless wife's right of succession is subject to one further restriction. She does not inherit the immoveable property – buildings, trees etc. – of her husband *in specie*, but is entitled to receive the value of her share therein. In sum, her right of inheritance is a share of one-quarter or one-eighth, as the case may be, in the estate less the lands, but this right attaches *in specie* only to the moveable properties of the inheritance.[1]

3.5. Lineal descendants

3.5.1. The rights of the eldest son

A limited recognition of primogeniture exists in the rule that the eldest son is entitled to his father's clothing, sword, ring and copy of the Qur'ān. These personal effects of the deceased go to the eldest son over and above his normal right of inheritance, so that they do not form part of the estate to which the rights of other heirs attach. For this reason the specified articles may be validly bequeathed in accordance with the wishes of the owner and will not then be calculated as part of the one-third of his assets over which he has freedom of testamentary disposition. As regards all other properties, moveable and immoveable, which comprise the estate proper, all sons stand on an equal footing, as do all daughters.

3.5.2. Children

Where the praepositus is survived by a son, children inherit on a residual basis, a male taking twice the share of a female. If no son survives, one daughter takes a basic Qur'anic portion of one-half and two or more daughters share equally a collective portion of two-thirds of the estate. These portions may be increased by *radd*, or reduced where the estate is over-subscribed by other Qur'anic heirs. But since daughters exclude from succession any relatives other than the spouse relict and the parents, their minimum collective share in the estate of their deceased mother will be five-twelfths, and in the estate of their deceased father 13/24.

[1] Although there is considerable variance of view among the Shīʿī authorities on this question, the dominant doctrine appears to be that described here. At any rate this is the law as it is embodied in the current Civil Code of Iran (sections 946 and 947).

3.5.3. Grandchildren

Grandchildren inherit in the absence of any child of the praepositus and take strictly in accordance with the principle of representation. Thus, the children of a predeceased son of the praepositus will take their father's notional residual share, and in competition with them the children of a predeceased daughter will take the notional residual share of their mother. But where no child of a son survives the children of a daughter will share their mother's notional Qur'anic entitlement. In all cases the rule of double share to the male applies to grandchildren claiming through the same link.

> P is survived by her husband, her father and three grandchildren, A, B and C. A is the son of one predeceased daughter, while B is the son and C the daughter of a second predeceased daughter of P.

Here the notional Qur'anic entitlement of P's two predeceased daughters would be cut down from two-thirds to seven-twelfths (i.e. 7/24 each) in the presence of the husband and the father. A takes the whole of his mother's notional portion, while B and C share their mother's notional portion. Hence the final distribution will be: husband one-quarter, father one-sixth, A 7/24, B 14/72, C 7/72.

3.5.4. Great grandchildren

Great grandchildren become entitled legal heirs in the absence of any higher lineal descendant and take the notional share of their own parent. Hence, a notional distribution of the estate may have to be made at each of the two generations that intervene between themselves and the praepositus.

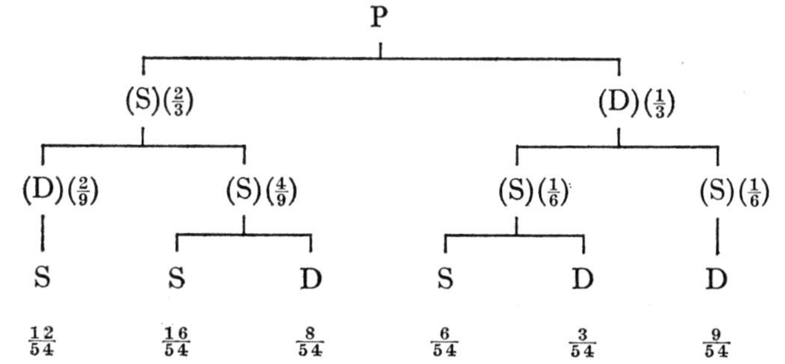

P = Praepositus, S = Son, D = Daughter.

3.6. Parents

3.6.1. The father

In competition with any lineal descendant of the praepositus the father takes exclusively as a Qur'anic heir. This basic portion of one-sixth represents his minimum share of the estate of his deceased child in any circumstances. It also represents his maximum share where the praepositus is succeeded by a son or a grandchild claiming through a son. But where the only entitled lineal descendants are daughters or grandchildren claiming through a daughter, the portion of one-sixth may be increased by *radd*. Where no lineal descendant survives the father always takes as a residuary.

3.6.2. The mother

The mother of the praepositus inherits exclusively as a Qur'anic heir. In the presence of any lineal descendant she takes a basic Qur'anic portion of one-sixth, which may be increased by *radd* in suitable circumstances. She is also restricted to a portion of one-sixth in the presence of the father and "collaterals" of the praepositus; and here the restriction is absolute, in the sense that she is debarred by the presence of the father and "collaterals" from participating in *radd*. Where neither of these restrictions applies, the mother is entitled to a basic Qur'anic portion of one-third.

All brothers and sisters are, of course, totally excluded from succession by the mother because of her priority in the scheme of *qarāba*, so that the restriction of her entitlement cannot operate to the direct benefit of the collaterals themselves. Shīʿī jurisprudence, however, maintains that the rule, as formulated in the Qur'ān, was designed to benefit the collaterals indirectly through the greater share of the inheritance that it gives to the father, upon whom the collaterals, as his issue, may be dependent for maintenance and from whom they will ultimately inherit. For this reason Shīʿī law, in a somewhat more systematic fashion than its Sunnī counterpart, excludes uterines from the ambit of the rule, on the ground that they have no right of maintenance or inheritance from the father of the praepositus and could only suffer from the restriction of their mother's entitlement. Accordingly, only germane or consanguine collaterals restrict the mother's portion. Further, two or more "brothers", according to the Qur'ān, must be present for the restriction to apply; and since the entitlement of a sister is generally half that of a brother, so here two sisters are ranked as equal to one brother. In Shīʿī law, therefore, the mother is restricted only by at least two brothers, or one brother and two sisters, or four sisters. But collaterals will never reduce the mother's portion unless the father of the praepositus is an entitled legal heir. The relevant Qur'anic passage (Sūra 4, verse 11) reads: "If there is no surviving child and the parents are the legal heirs, the mother takes one-third, except where the deceased has left brothers, when the mother takes one-sixth." Here Shī'ī juristic interpretation takes the exception clause closely with the whole of the preceding sentence – i.e. as applicable only when both parents are legal heirs – as opposed to the Sunnī interpretation which links the exception only to the phrase: "the mother takes one-third".

Collaterals will exclude the mother from *radd* only when a daughter, or a grandchild claiming through a daughter, succeeds to a Qur'anic portion along with the parents. When a son, or a grandchild claiming through a son, is an entitled heir, he or she will take as a residuary and there can be no *radd*. Similarly, in the absence of any lineal descendant, the father inherits as a residuary. Such exclusion of the mother from *radd*, therefore, must benefit both the daughter (or grandchild) and the father, the former to a greater extent than the latter.

3.7. Apportionment between spouse, parents and descendants illustrated

(*a*)	Husband	($\frac{1}{4}$)		= $\frac{1}{4}$
	Father	($\frac{1}{6}$)	by *radd*	= $\frac{3}{16}$
	Daughter	($\frac{1}{2}$)		= $\frac{9}{16}$
(*b*)	Husband			$\frac{1}{2}$
	Father (residuary)			$\frac{1}{6}$
	Mother			$\frac{1}{3}$
	Germane brother			—
	Germane sister			—
	Uterine brothers			—
(*c*)	Father	($\frac{1}{6}$)		= $\frac{1}{5}$
	Mother	($\frac{1}{6}$)	by *radd*	= $\frac{1}{5}$
	Daughter	($\frac{1}{2}$)		= $\frac{3}{5}$
	Three germane sisters	—		—
(*d*)	Wife			$\frac{1}{4}$
	Father			$\frac{7}{12}$
	Mother			$\frac{1}{6}$
	Two consanguine brothers			—
(*e*)	Father	($\frac{1}{6}$)	by *radd*	= $\frac{5}{24}$
	Mother	($\frac{1}{6}$)	—	$\frac{1}{6}$
	Daughter's son	($\frac{1}{2}$)	by *radd*	= $\frac{15}{24}$
	Germane brother	—		
	Two consanguine sisters	—		

By way of comparison with Sunnī law, it may be observed that *radd* applies in illustrations (*a*) and (*c*) when it would not so apply under Sunnī law because the father would rank both as a residuary and a Qur'anic heir. A much greater incidence of *radd* is a general characteristic of the Shīʿī system. It arises throughout the various classes of heirs because of the thorough integration of the Qur'anic heirs into the rules of priority and because of the principle of representational entitlement.

3.8. Grandparents

3.8.1. Paternal and maternal grandparents

Any grandparent is an entitled legal heir in the absence of any parent or lineal descendant of the praepositus and totally excludes from succession all relatives other than brothers and sisters or their issue. Apart, therefore, from a competition with collaterals (which is the subject of section 3.10. below), grandparents may inherit either alone or in competition with the spouse relict.

Under the principle of representational entitlement paternal grandparents take the notional share of the father and maternal grandparents that of the mother. Maternal grandparents, therefore, take a Qur'anic portion of one-third, which, in the absence of any paternal grandparent may be increased by *radd* to the extent of the whole estate or the estate less the spouse relict's portion. Paternal grandparents take the residual share of the father – i.e. the estate less either the portion of the mother or that of the spouse relict or both. The paternal grandfather takes twice as much as the paternal grandmother, but maternal grandparents share equally.

P dies, survived by his wife and his four grandparents.

Wife		$\frac{1}{4}$
Mother's father	$(\frac{1}{3})$	$\frac{1}{6}$
Mother's mother		$\frac{1}{6}$
Father's father	$(\frac{5}{12})$	$\frac{10}{36}$
Father's mother		$\frac{5}{36}$

3.8.2. Great grandparents

Great grandparents inherit in the absence of any grandparent and take the notional share that their own child, the grandparent of the praepositus, would have received had he or she survived. Here, and among higher grandparents should the case arise, male and female share equally if there is any female in their line of connection with the praepositus The rule of double share to the male, therefore, applies only to the parents of the paternal grandfather of the praepositus.

In the following hypothetical, if not wholly fanciful case, P is survived by five great grandparents.

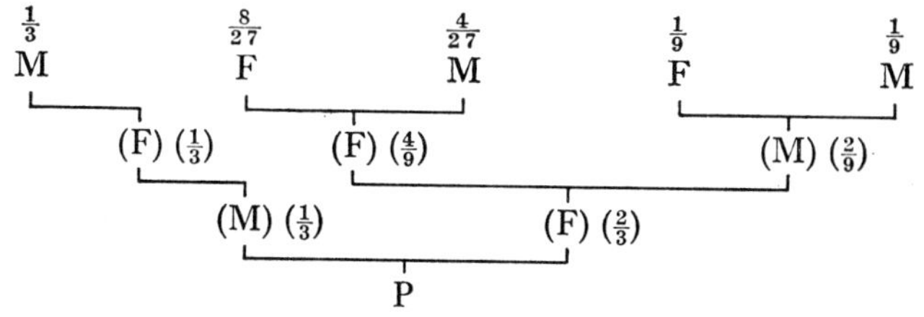

M = Mother, F = Father.

3.9. Collaterals and their issue

3.9.1. Brothers and sisters

Apart from any grandparent how high soever, the only other person who inherits along with brothers and sisters of the praepositus is the spouse relict. Uterines, excluded neither by germanes nor consanguines, take as Qur'anic heirs an individual portion of one-sixth or a collective portion of one-third. Subject to the rule that any germane totally excludes any consanguine, germane or consanguine brothers take as residuaries. Germane or consanguine sisters also take as residuaries in the presence of their respective brothers, but in the absence thereof take, in theory at least, as Qur'anic heirs an individual portion of one-half or a collective portion of two-thirds.

3.9.2. Sisters as Qur'anic heirs: adjustment of portions

In the event of the estate being over-subscribed the burden of necessary reduction falls exclusively upon the portions of germane or consanguine sisters.

Thus, to take the extreme example, in competition with the husband (one-half) and two or more uterines (one-third), a germane sister or sisters will take only one-sixth of the inheritance.

Where, on the other hand, an estate is under-subscribed, a germane, but not a consanguine, sister excludes any uterines from participating in *radd*.

Thus, in competition with the wife (one-quarter) and a uterine brother (one-sixth), a germane sister takes seven-twelfths of the estate. As between a wife, uterine brother and consanguine sister, only the spouse relict would be excluded from *radd*, and the distribution would be: wife, one-quarter; uterine brother, three-sixteenths, and consanguine sister, nine-sixteenths.

The result of these two particular rules of Shīʻī law is that a germane sister always inherits what is, in effect, a residual share. In the above two cases, and indeed in any other circumstances, a germane or consanguine brother succeeding instead of the germane sister would receive, as a residuary heir, precisely the same share of the inheritance. Given the system of priority by *qarāba* and the fact that the spouse relict is debarred from *radd*, the two rules mean that no case can arise where the prescribed Qur'anic portion of a germane sister or sisters has any special significance. A consanguine sister, when entitled to inherit, is largely in the same position; for it is only where the estate is under-subscribed and uterines are present that she takes strictly as a Qur'anic heir. One consanguine sister competing with uterines or with a wife and one uterine, and two or more consanguine sisters competing with one uterine will take a basic Qur'anic portion and share the surplus proportionately, by *radd*, with the uterines.

3.9.3. Nephews and nieces

In the absence of any brother or sister of the praepositus, nephews and nieces (or in their absence their issue) inherit on the representational principle. Children of germane or consanguine brothers and sisters take the notional entitlement of their parent on the basis of double share to the male, while the children of uterine brothers and sisters share equally. (In the case below the excluded nephew would take the whole estate under Sunnī law.)

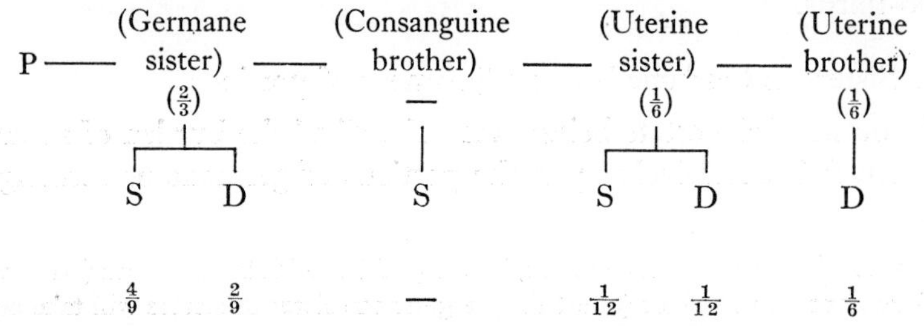

3.10. Grandparents and collaterals in competition

3.10.1. Grandparents counted as brothers or sisters

No grandparent, how high soever, excludes or is excluded by any brother or sister or their issue how low soever. Apportionment of the inheritance between grandparents and collaterals is simplicity itself when compared with the Sunnī law on this point. Grandparents are merged into the system of apportionment between collaterals by being counted, according to their sex, as either brothers or sisters. Maternal grandparents rank as uterine brothers or sisters, while paternal grandparents rank either as germanes or, where a consanguine brother or sister is an entitled heir, as consanguines. In these circumstances, therefore, grandparents no longer inherit as representative heirs of the father or mother of the praepositus.

3.10.2. Apportionment between grandparents and collaterals illustrated

(*a*)	Maternal grandfather	$\frac{1}{6}$
	Paternal grandmother	$\frac{5}{12}$
	Germane sister	$\frac{5}{12}$
	Consanguine brother	—

The consanguine brother is excluded by the germane sister. Ranking as a uterine brother, the maternal grandfather takes a Qur'anic portion of one-sixth, being excluded from *radd* by the germane sister. The germane sister and paternal grandmother take equal shares in the residue (in theory the collective Qur'anic *farḍ* of two-thirds augmented by *radd*).

(*b*)	Paternal grandfather	$\frac{4}{9}$
	Maternal grandfather	$\frac{1}{9}$
	Maternal grandmother	$\frac{1}{9}$
	Consanguine sister	$\frac{2}{9}$
	Uterine sister	$\frac{1}{9}$

The maternal grandparents and the uterine sister take equal shares in the collective Qur'anic portion of one-third. Ranking as a consanguine brother, the paternal grandfather shares the residue with the consanguine sister, double share to the male.

(*c*) Wife		$\frac{1}{4}$
Father's mother's	father	$\frac{7}{48}$
	mother	$\frac{7}{48}$
Germane sister's	son	$\frac{14}{72}$
	daughter	$\frac{7}{72}$
Uterine brother's	son	$\frac{1}{12}$
	daughter	$\frac{1}{12}$

Great grandparents in competition with collaterals or the issue of collaterals take under the representational principle, as do nephews and nieces in competition with grandparents or great grandparents. In the above case there is a notional distribution between the spouse relict (one-quarter), a uterine brother (one-sixth) and two germane sisters (taking equal shares in the residue of seven-twelfths, or, strictly, the Qur'anic *farḍ* less the necessary reduction). The notional entitlement of the germane sister then goes to her children according to the rule of double share to the male. But the children of the uterine brother share their father's entitlement equally, and the great grandparents also share equally in the entitlement of the paternal grandmother, since they are connected with the praepositus through a female.

3.11. Uncles, aunts and their issue

Apportionment of the estate among heirs of this final class represents a strictly systematic extension of the basic principles governing distribution among relatives of the preceding classes. Where the claimants are all on either the paternal or maternal side, they share the whole estate less the portion of the surviving spouse. Where there are entitled heirs on both sides, maternal relatives are representative sharers in the mother's notional Qur'anic portion of one-third, and paternal relatives in the father's notional residual entitlement of two-thirds or, where applicable, two-thirds less the portion of the spouse relict. On each side independently, claimants take according to the nature of their collateral relationship with the parent (or, in the case of great uncles and aunts, the grandparent) of the praepositus – i.e. precisely as if the parent or the grandparent were in fact the praepositus. Subject to this, however, maternal uncles and aunts who have the same blood-tie with the mother of the praepositus – whether germane, consanguine or uterine – share equally. On the paternal side, uterine uncles and aunts share equally, but the rule of double share to the male applies to germanes and consanguines. When cousins of the praepositus – the issue of uncles and aunts or of great uncles and aunts – are entitled heirs, they succeed by representation to the notional share of their parent, the rule of double share to the male then applying only to the issue of germanes and consanguines on the paternal side.

3.11.1. Apportionment between heirs of Class III illustrated

(*a*)	Husband	$\frac{1}{2}$	$\frac{1}{2}$
	Germane maternal aunt	($\frac{1}{3}$)	$\frac{1}{3}$
	Consanguine maternal uncle		—
	Consanguine paternal aunt	($\frac{1}{6}$)	$\frac{3}{24}$
	Uterine paternal uncle		$\frac{1}{24}$

On the maternal side the mother's germane sister excludes her consanguine brother. On the paternal side the father's consanguine sister and uterine brother share his notional entitlement in the ratio of three parts to the sister and one part to the brother (their respective Qur'anic portions increased by *radd*).

(*b*)	Consanguine maternal aunt's	son	$\frac{1}{6}$
		daughter	$\frac{1}{6}$
	German paternal aunt's	son	$\frac{20}{54}$
		daughter	$\frac{10}{54}$
	Consanguine paternal uncle's son		—
	Uterine paternal aunt's	son	$\frac{1}{18}$
		daughter	$\frac{1}{18}$

The maternal cousins share equally their mother's notional portion of one-third. On the paternal side, the notional distribution of the father's two-thirds is between his uterine sister ($1/6 \times 2/3 = 2/18$) and his germane sister, who excludes his consanguine brother completely and his uterine sister from *radd* and therefore takes the residue of the paternal side's share ($5/6 \times 2/3 = 10/18$). These notional shares of the two aunts then descend to their respective children. (In Sunnī law the agnatic cousin, here excluded, would be the sole legal heir.)

3.11.2. The anomalous case of a cousin excluding an uncle

Within this class of legal heirs composed of uncles, aunts and cousins occurs the one anomalous rule of the otherwise singularly systematic scheme of Shī'ī inheritance. In contradiction of the strict principle that the nearer in degree excludes the more remote, a consanguine paternal uncle is excluded from succession by a germane paternal uncle's son, when these two are the sole surviving relatives of the praepositus.

Political considerations explain the anomaly. Sunnī constitutional theory holds that a legitimate title to political sovereignty in Islam was vested in the 'Abbāsid dynasty, the succession of Caliphs who were the descendants of their progenitor 'Abbās. On the other hand, the Shī'a maintain that, following the death of the Prophet, leadership of the Muslim community properly passed to 'Alī and after him to his descendants. The anomalous rule of Shī'ī inheritance is clearly designed to reinforce their view as to who was the proper successor to the political authority of the Prophet, inasmuch as it resolves a hypothetical competition, as heirs of the Prophet, between 'Abbās and 'Alī in favour of the latter. For 'Alī was the cousin of the Prophet, the son of his germane paternal uncle Abū Ṭālib, while 'Abbās was the Prophet's consanguine paternal uncle.

4. Cases of Sunnī and Shī'ī inheritance compared

The crux of the distinction between the Sunnī and the Shī'ī systems of inheritance lies in the position of male agnates as legal heirs. A son of the praepositus, it is true, will always have precisely the same entitlement under both systems, whatever the number or character of other surviving relatives may be. But all other male agnates, particularly collaterals, are often much less favourably placed under the Shī'ī than under the Sunnī law, as the following cases will illustrate:

		Sunnī law	Shī'ī law
(*a*)	Son's son	$\frac{1}{2}$	—
	Daughter	$\frac{1}{2}$	All
(*b*)	Father	$\frac{2}{3}$	$\frac{1}{5}$
	Mother	$\frac{1}{3}$	$\frac{1}{5}$
	Daughter's son	—	$\frac{3}{5}$
(*c*)	Father's father	$\frac{3}{8}$	—
	Wife	$\frac{1}{8}$	$\frac{1}{8}$
	Daughter	$\frac{1}{2}$	$\frac{7}{8}$
(*d*)	Germane brother	$\frac{5}{24}$	—
	Wife	$\frac{1}{8}$	$\frac{1}{8}$
	Daughter	$\frac{1}{2}$	$\frac{7}{8}$
	Son's daughter	$\frac{1}{6}$	—
(*e*)	Germane brothers	$\frac{1}{3}$	—
	Husband	$\frac{1}{2}$	$\frac{1}{2}$
	Mother	$\frac{1}{6}$	$\frac{1}{2}$
(*f*)	Consanguine brother	$\frac{1}{2}$	—
	Son's daughter	$\frac{1}{2}$	$\frac{2}{3}$
	Daughter's son	—	$\frac{1}{3}$
(*g*)	Consanguine brother	$\frac{1}{2}$	—
	Germane sister	$\frac{1}{2}$	All
(*h*)	Germane brother's son	$\frac{5}{6}$	$\frac{20}{54}$
	Germane brother's daughter	—	$\frac{10}{54}$
	Father's mother	$\frac{1}{6}$	$\frac{5}{18}$
	Mother's father	—	$\frac{1}{6}$
(*i*)	Consanguine brother's son	$\frac{1}{3}$	—
	Husband	$\frac{1}{2}$	$\frac{1}{2}$
	Uterine brother	$\frac{1}{6}$	$\frac{1}{2}$

		Sunnī law	Shīʿī law
(*j*)	Germane paternal uncle	$\frac{5}{6}$	—
	Uterine brother	$\frac{1}{6}$	—
	Daughter's son	—	All
(*k*)	Consanguine paternal uncle's son	All	—
	Germane sister's son	—	All
(*l*)	Germane paternal uncle's son	All	—
	Uterine maternal uncle	—	$\frac{1}{3}$
	Germane paternal aunt	—	$\frac{2}{3}$

5. The jurisprudential basis of Shīʿī inheritance

It has been suggested that the "variants of Muhammadan law which are recognised by the... Shiites do not differ from the doctrines of the orthodox or Sunnī schools of law more widely than these last differ from one another"; that the differences which do exist are "features which in themselves were not necessarily either Shiite or Sunnī, but which became adventitiously distinctive for Shiite as against Sunnī law", and that the reason for this is that the Shīʿa adopted "Muhammadan law as it was being developed in the orthodox schools of law, introducing only such superficial modifications as were required by their own political and dogmatic tenets".[1]

There is little to commend this view as an assessment or an explanation of the Shīʿī system of inheritance. As opposed to the Sunnī law, which rests upon the concept of the extended family or tribal group, Shīʿī law rests upon the notion of the more limited or "nuclear" family group consisting of parents and lineal descendants. It is a gross underestimation to regard the latter system, which reflects a fundamentally different idea of family ties and responsibilities, as a "superficial modification" of the former. The fact is that such a view is dictated by the false premise that the Shīʿa in general followed Sunnī legal method; that the basic jurisprudential principles involved in the elaboration of Sharīʿa law were the same for both groups, and that it was merely a case of the Shīʿa adjusting some hypothetically common body of doctrine in order to support the personal authority of those whom the Shīʿa considered to be the legitimate political rulers of Islam. This is a false premise because it ignores the existence of certain distinctive features of Shīʿī jurisprudential and political theory, or at least seriously underestimates the role which these distinctive features played in the formation of the law. The view which will be put

[1] J. Schacht, *The Origins of Muhammadan Jurisprudence* (Oxford, 1950), pp. 260, 262.

forward here is that the divergent systems of Sunnī and Shīʿī succession were conditioned by different jurisprudential principles, which in turn derived from, or at least were inseparably allied with, fundamentally different political ideologies. In short, it is suggested that the individual scheme of Shīʿī inheritance, far from being "adventitiously distinctive", has a natural and integral place within the scheme of those particular beliefs, principles and values that make up the Shīʿī philosophy of Islam.

5.1. Sunnī and Shīʿī political theory

All systematic thinking about legal theory is linked at one end with philosophy and, at the other end, with political theory...Sometimes theory of knowledge and political ideology are welded into one coherent system, where the respective shares of the two are not easy to disentangle...But all legal theory must contain elements of philosophy...and gain its colour and specific content from political theory.[1]

These remarks have a particular relevance and truth for Islamic civilisation, where the theories of knowledge, of political power and allegiance and of legal authority all merge inextricably as interrelated aspects of a comprehensive scheme of life grounded upon religious belief. This totalitarian concept of Islam is common to both Sunnīs and Shīʿīs; but the two factions are at considerable variance in their views on the basic ingredients of the system and particularly in their respective doctrines concerning the nature and incidence of political authority.

According to the Sunnīs, the political head of State, or Caliph, should be a member of the Arab tribe of Quraysh who is elected to his office by the qualified members of the community. The Caliph has no legislative power as such, but is bound to rule according to the terms of Sharīʿa law as expounded in the authoritative manuals. This theory reflects the actual historical devolution of political power in Sunnī Islam, which passed, after the first four Caliphs, to the Umayyad and the ʿAbbāsid dynasties, both family branches of the tribe of Quraysh. The Shīʿa, on the other hand, maintained that the Prophet himself appointed his cousin and son-in-law ʿAlī as his successor, and that after the death of ʿAlī the title to the Imamate, or leadership, was hereditary, passing to the sons of ʿAlī from his marriage with the Prophet's daughter Fāṭima and thence to their lineal issue. To this line of Imāms was transmitted the same divine inspiration as had been given in the first place to their ascendant Muḥammad.

[1] W. G. Friedmann, *Legal Theory* (5th ed., London, 1967), p. 3.

5.2. Shīʿī law and particular political allegiances

There is clearly a close affinity between the Shīʿī rules of inheritance and their doctrine of the legitimate devolution of political authority in Islam. The principle of Shīʿī succession that any lineal descendant, and particularly the child of a daughter, has complete priority over all collaterals supports their view that the political title of the Prophet was properly inherited by his lineal descendants – the issue of his daughter Fāṭima – and not, as the Sunnīs claim, by the agnatic collaterals who were the issue of the Prophet's paternal uncle ʿAbbās. The question that arises is whether it was political considerations of this superficial kind which moulded the particular scheme of Shīʿī succession law. Are the distinctive features of the Shīʿī law attributable simply to their recognition of the authority of certain individuals as the legitimate political rulers of Islam?

It would appear that it was such considerations of personal political allegiance which were in the mind of the proponent of the view that the distinctive characteristics of Shīʿī law are "only such superficial modifications as were required by their own political...tenets". For the same author, speaking of the controversial institution of temporary marriage, or *mutʿa*, declares that "the Shiites recognised it, for no better reason than that its prohibition had been attributed to ʿUmar".[1] Certainly the Shīʿa had no cause to respect or accept the authority of the Caliph ʿUmar, whom they regarded as having usurped the leadership which rightly belonged to ʿAlī. But it is difficult to believe that such a negative approach as the out of hand rejection of the views of a political opponent was the dominating theme of Shīʿī jurisprudence. It surely does less than justice to Shīʿī jurists to suggest that their notions of what was good or bad law were based essentially on personal political animosities. The Shīʿīs themselves claim, with regard to *mutʿa*, that the practice was authorised by the Qur'ān itself. In other words, they claim to have a reason of juristic principle for rejecting the ruling of ʿUmar. And so it is with the Shīʿī laws of inheritance, which cannot be explained simply as reflecting Shīʿī aversion towards the decisions of Sunnī political authorities.

The Shīʿa, for example, rejected the decisions known as *al-ʿUmariyyatān* not simply because they were decisions of ʿUmar but because their own consistent method of interpretation of the Qur'ān, as will be seen shortly, produced a different solution for these cases. Similarly, it cannot be said that the Shīʿa rejected ʿUmar's decision, as such, in the celebrated case of *al-Ḥimāriyya*. The particular problems involved for the Sunnīs in the

[1] Schacht, *Origins*, p. 267.

circumstances of the *Ḥimāriyya* case were strictly irrelevant in the Shīʿī system, where the established rules of priority would result in the total exclusion of all collaterals from succession by the mother. There seems, in fact, to be only one rule of the Shīʿī law of inheritance which can properly be described as a "superficial modification" to conform to notions of personal political allegiance. This is the rule that the son of a germane paternal uncle excludes from succession a consanguine paternal uncle – a rule designed to establish the superiority of ʿAlī over ʿAbbās in a hypothetical competition between them as heirs of the Prophet. But this rule itself is an anomaly in a system which is otherwise fundamentally different from the Sunnī system, far more fundamentally different, in fact, than would be necessary if it were merely a matter of establishing the superiority of the Shīʿī Imāms over the Sunnī Caliphs as successors to the Prophet's political mantle. It is apparent, therefore, that the roots of the Shīʿī system of inheritance strike to much deeper issues than the bare question of political allegiance or hostility towards this ruler or that.

5.3. The distinction between Sunnī and Shīʿī political ideology

Politically, the rift between the Sunnīs and the Shīʿa was not merely a matter of support for different individuals as providing the best leadership. What was in issue was not so much the personal capabilities of the leaders but rather the legitimacy of their title. Behind the varying allegiances of the Sunnīs and the Shīʿa, and in fact producing them, lay a much deeper conflict of fundamental ideology concerning the basis and source of political authority in Islam.

In the Sunnī view political power in Islam continued to belong to the Arabian tribal aristocracy of pre-Islamic times because the basic Sunnī approach was to preserve the *status quo* unless it was clearly and unambiguously superceded by the dictates of the new religious faith. The political tradition of pre-Islamic Arabia was thus perpetuated and carried over into Islam, subject now, of course, to the new standards imposed by the divine law. Islam, in short, meant for the Sunnīs a reform, no doubt a profound reform, of past Arabian political tradition but not its complete obliteration.

Shīʿī political theory, on the other hand, rejects outright the notion of the continuing validity of pre-Islamic practice. In their view the ultimate and exclusive source of Islamic political authority on earth was the Prophet. After his death, therefore, leadership belonged naturally to the successor whom he had, in the Shīʿī belief, personally appointed – namely ʿAlī – and then to the issue of the latter by divine right. Far from being merely a reform of existing institutions, Islam meant for the Shīʿa the total abolition of those institutions. In the Shīʿī view the essence of Islam was that it constituted a new point of departure and a wholly novel system of State and society, which involved a clean break with past tradition and generated from within itself its own political standards and principles.

5.4. Sunnī and Shīʿī legal theory

These divergent political philosophies were the different soils in which the systems of Sunnī and Shīʿī jurisprudence were rooted and from which they derived their distinctive characteristics. Sunnī jurisprudence recognises two basic material sources of Sharīʿa law – the Qur'ān, the divine word itself, and the *sunna*, the divinely inspired precedents set by the Prophet Muḥammad. For the Sunnīs this constitutes the limit of divine revelation, since they believe that Muḥammad was the last person to have contact with the divine will. Accordingly, the further elaboration of the law was a process of juristic reasoning which involved, in particular, the extension of the principles embodied in the divine revelation by the method of analogical deduction, or *qiyās*. For the Shīʿa, however, divine revelation was not so limited in point of substance or time. In their belief the divine will continued to be transmitted, after the death of the Prophet, to the line of their own recognised leaders or Imāms. Accordingly, they maintained that, in addition to the Qur'ān and the *sunna*, the pronouncements of their Imāms constituted divine revelation and therefore binding law.

It might appear at first sight that the common ground of these respective legal theories outweighs their divergence. For they both recognise the primary source of law to lie in the Qur'anic revelations; they both accept the *sunna* of the Prophet as interpretative of and supplementary to the Qur'anic laws, and it is only beyond this point in regard to the further elaboration of the law that they differ. And even in this last respect it might be argued that the divergence was more a matter of ideal theory than of actual practice. For the last divinely inspired Imām, at least in the belief of the majority group of the Ithnā ʿAsharīs, "disappeared" in the year 874, and since that time, in the absence of the infallible word of the Imām, Shīʿī jurists have been just as active in interpreting and expounding the law as their Sunnī counterparts. In fact, however, the resemblance between Sunnī and Shīʿī legal theory is nominal and superficial – for two principal reasons.

5.5. The significance of the doctrine of Imamate

The first is a reason of material substance, namely, that the corpus of precedents of the Prophet which is recognised by the Shīʿa as constituting binding law differs considerably in content from that recognised by the Sunnīs. The reason for this is commonly said to be that the Shīʿa do not accept an alleged precedent of the Prophet as authentic unless the report of that precedent is transmitted by one of their Imāms. But it would perhaps be more accurate to say that the Shīʿa do not accept an alleged precedent of the Prophet as constituting binding law unless it is confirmed as such by one of their Imāms. For while it is often difficult to ascertain from the texts whether the Shīʿa regard an alleged precedent of the Prophet as authentic or not, what is certain is that they disregard that precedent if the authority of one of their Imāms supports a contradictory rule. The clearest instance of this, in the context of succession law, is provided by the alleged decision of the Prophet in Saʿd's case which, in establishing the residual succession rights of the *ʿaṣaba*, is the corner-stone of Sunnī inheritance. The Shīʿa completely ignore this precedent and rely instead upon the contradictory principle voiced by the Imām Jaʿfar: "Dust in the teeth of the *ʿaṣaba*." It is evident from this what a radically different balance is given to Shīʿī legal theory by the doctrine of the Imamate. In Sunnī jurisprudence the *sunna* of the Prophet constitutes a final and absolute authority, while in Shīʿī jurisprudence it is subject to the overriding authority of the infallible Imām. The pronouncements of the Imāms do not constitute merely a third source of Shīʿī law in addition to the Qur'ān and the *sunna*: they determine the very scope of the *sunna* of the Prophet as a source of law.

5.6. The Qur'ān as a source of law in Shīʿī legal theory

The second, and much more fundamental, reason for regarding the resemblance between Sunnī and Shīʿī legal theory as superficial is a matter of basic juristic approach. For both systems the primary material source of law was the common text of the Qur'ān. But the Qur'anic regulations on any topic, including that of succession which is perhaps covered in greater detail than any other, were by no means comprehensive. They provided only the skeleton outline of a *corpus juris* which was to derive its real substance from the supplementary decisions of the Prophet, from the pronouncements of the Shīʿī Imāms and from further juristic interpretation and elaboration. But the Sunnīs and the Shīʿa differed radically in the spirit of their approach to this whole process of giving substance to the bare bones of the Qur'anic laws because they started from totally different premises as to the nature and scope of the Qur'anic laws themselves. As a source of law the Qur'anic regulations have a very different significance for the Shīʿa and for the Sunnīs. And it is, at root, these different juristic attitudes towards the Qur'anic regulations, as they are reflected in those precedents of Muḥammad or statements of Imāms or juristic doctrines which each side holds as authoritative, which produce the major divergencies in their respective systems of inheritance.

5.7. The link between political doctrine and jurisprudence

Here it becomes apparent that jurisprudential and political thought share the same source of inspiration. In the contemplation of Sunnī jurisprudence the Qur'anic rules merely modified the traditional tribal law of inheritance in certain particulars. Consistently with their perpetuation of pre-Islamic standards in political doctrine, the Sunnīs regarded the norms of the pre-Islamic law as still operative insofar as they were not expressly superceded by the dictates of the Qur'ān. For Shīʿī jurisprudence, on the other hand, the Qur'anic rules were not simply particular reforms to be superimposed upon an existing legal institution but constituted the blueprint for a completely novel system of succession. Equally consistently with their own political ideology, the Shīʿa totally reject the notion of the continuing validity of pre-Islamic tribal law. For them the ultimate starting point of law in Islam was the Qur'ān. The standards of the pre-Islamic law were automatically repealed unless they were expressly endorsed by the Qur'ān, and it was the Qur'anic regulations themselves, not the traditional tribal practice, which provided the generative force for the further elaboration of the law. This basic view that the Qur'anic regulations provide a self-sufficient and comprehensive foundation for succession law, exclusive of any criteria derived from pre-Islamic custom, brings the Shīʿa into conflict with the Sunnīs, in the first place, on the issue of the precise meaning of the Qur'anic texts themselves.

5.8. Interpretation of Qur'anic texts

A consistent feature of Sunnī jurisprudence is the interpretation of the Qur'anic texts in the light of the customary criterion of the priority of male agnates in succession. This is, for example, the case in the decisions known as *al-ʿUmariyyatān*, which give the father twice as much of the inheritance as the mother when the parents succeed along with the spouse relict. The Qur'ān declares that where there is no surviving child or brothers and "the parents are the legal heirs, the mother takes one-third". In order, therefore, to justify the result of the '*Umariyyatān*, which is to reduce the mother's share to less than this amount, Sunnī jurisprudence had to read into this text the word "alone" after "parents", or the words "of the residue" after "one-third". Shīʿī jurisprudence, on the other hand, regards this as a wholly unwarranted process of forcing the text of the Qur'ān to conform to preconceived notions of succession, whether such notions were embodied in a decision of 'Umar or any other authority. They insisted that the words of the Qur'ān should be taken at their face value and that the mother should here take one-third of the whole estate as her Qur'anic portion, even if this meant that the father's residual share in the presence of a surviving husband was restricted to one-sixth of the inheritance.

What the Shīʿa consider to be an even more blatantly forced interpretation of the Qur'ān by the Sunnīs occurs in respect of the verse which states that a brother will be an heir only if the deceased "dies without a child (*walad*)". Here the Sunnīs took *walad* to mean "son or agnatic grandson", because, formally at any rate, the decision of the Prophet in Saʿd's case had allowed Saʿd's brother to inherit a residual share in his estate although Saʿd was survived by two daughters (pp. 29–30 above). But, of course, this decision clearly reflects the standards of agnatic succession, under which it would be difficult to accept the total exclusion of a brother by a female descendant of the deceased. Again, the Shīʿa here insist upon strict adherence to the obvious interpretation of the text of the Qur'ān. "*Walad*" means "any child or grandchild" and a brother is accordingly excluded from succession by the survival of any such descendant. Shīʿī jurisprudence can at least claim in this context the merit of consistency, since it takes the term *walad* to mean "lineal descendant" wherever it occurs in the Qur'ān. Sunnī jurisprudence, on the other hand, takes the term *walad* as it occurs elsewhere in the Qur'ān to mean "any child or agnatic grandchild" – as, for example, where the Qur'ān states that the spouse relict and the mother are restricted to their minimal shares by the survival of a *walad*. For Sunnī jurisprudence, of course, committed as it was to the notion of the agnatic family group, there could be no question of the term *walad* including, at least in the context of succession law, such non-agnates as daughters' children.

5.9. The Shīʿī extension of Qur'anic rules

Closely allied with this divergent approach towards the interpretation of the Qur'anic rules is a radical conflict between the Sunnīs and the Shīʿa as to the scope of those rules. For the Sunnīs the Qur'anic rules serve to qualify and mitigate the customary system of agnatic succession and do so, broadly speaking, only to the extent of their express terms. For the Shīʿa, on the other hand, the particular regulations of the Qur'ān embody, by implication, the general and fundamental principles of succession. It is this approach which constitutes the decisive determinant of Shīʿī law because it produces the two pre-eminently distinctive features of the system – the doctrines of priority by *qarāba* and of entitlement by representation.

The Qur'ān deals specifically only with the rights of inheritance of the spouse relict, parents, children and brothers and sisters. The essence of Shīʿī law is that these relatives are the principal heirs at the heart of the system, and the rules which govern their priorities and entitlement are extended to apply to more distant relatives as subordinate heirs.

As regards priorities, the inclusion of the daughter, mother and sister in the group of principal heirs nominated by the Qur'ān necessarily implied, for the Shīʿa, first, that females should be fully integrated into the system of priorities along with males and have the right to exclude inferior relatives, and second, that more distant female and non-agnate relatives should be included in the comprehensive scheme of priorities. Rights of inheritance should belong to those who were connected with the deceased through the principal female no less than the male heirs because the Qur'ān itself contained no indication that subordinate rights of succession depended upon an agnatic tie.

Similarly, for Shīʿī jurisprudence, the principle of representational entitlement is a logical extension of the Qur'anic provisions. The rights of inheritance of more distant relatives are derived through the principal heirs nominated by the Qur'ān, so that when they are entitled to succeed under the doctrine of *qarāba*, the nature of their entitlement (i.e. whether it be a fixed portion or a residual share) and its *quantum* depends upon that of the principal heir through whom they are connected with the praepositus.

All this, of course, is in sharp contrast with the Sunnī system where there is no such attempt to extend the underlying principles of the Qur'anic legislation. The Qur'anic heirs do not, as a general rule, exclude other relatives and therefore stand outside the system of priorities which is clearly derived from the customary tribal law. When they are not excluded, the Qur'anic heirs take their allotted portions, but beyond that point the system of succession is a purely agnatic one – at least as regards the inner family. The only way in which the Qur'anic provisions were extended by the Sunnīs was the recognition, by analogy, of the grandmother, paternal grandfather and son's daughter as substitute heirs for the mother, father and daughter respectively, and entitled, in appropriate circumstances to the fixed portion allotted by the Qur'ān to the latter. And clearly, in the last two cases at least, the analogical extension was conditioned by the agnatic criterion.

5.10. The law of succession and the Shīʿī philosophy of Islam

In the final analysis, then, the distinctive features of the Shīʿī system of succession are attributable to a particular jurisprudential view of the nature and scope of the Qur'anic legislation. This view was a natural and integral part of fundamental Shīʿī political ideology, which in turn was grounded upon the religious conviction that Islam meant a new way of life completely divorced from previous practice and not merely, as it did for the Sunnīs, a reform of that practice.

Inevitably, of course, the Shīʿa claimed that their law was closer to the Qur'ān and a more faithful reflection of its essential spirit than the Sunnī system. No doubt they saw themselves as the proponents of an objective interpretation of the divine revelation in opposition to those whose interpretation was persistently conditioned by traditional standards; in short as a purist movement opposing an Establishment which was concerned to preserve its vested interests from previous practice.

But to the external observer the Shīʿī premise as to the nature of Islam, on which their political and jurisprudential theory rests, is no more or no less valid than its Sunnī counterpart. For him, the external observer, Islam here simply provides a telling example of the universal truth that a system of law does not develop in isolation, but its threads are closely interwoven into the fabric of political ideals, social values and religious beliefs which gives a community its particular identity. For the two distinct systems of Sunnī and Shīʿī succession are natural manifestations of two basically different philosophies of Islam which give the two groups their distinct identities within the community of Muslims.

9. REFORMS IN THE TRADITIONAL SYSTEM OF PRIORITIES[1]

1. The social impetus for reform

'Aṣabiyya (from the root word *'aṣaba*) is the term used in Arabic literature to describe the solidarity of the extended agnatic family of traditional Islamic society – a notion of tribal ties and responsibilities which was the bedrock of the traditional Sunnī law of inheritance. In contemporary Islamic society, however, particularly in urban areas, the bonds of *'aṣabiyya* have become progressively weaker and in some places have altogether disappeared.

> The change from a pastoral or agricultural to an increasingly industrial economy, the growing concentrations of people within large impersonal cities and the movement of people from place to place, as their occupations demand, far from their ancestral homes – all these factors have tended to make the larger family of the past less meaningful as a social unit.[2]

Today, therefore, the focus of family ties has narrowed to centre upon what sociologists call the "nuclear family", the more limited group made up of parents and their lineal issue. And inevitably this has meant that within this immediate family circle the female – as wife, mother or daughter – occupies a much more prominent position and plays a much more effective and responsible role than hitherto. Over the past few decades the movement for the reform of the traditional family law has gathered increasing momentum throughout the Muslim world. It is a process of law reform which, because of the extent and the nature of the changes which have been introduced, can have few parallels in universal legal history; and undoubtedly the most significant and striking aspect of it has been the progressive improvement in the legal status of women. Daughters have been freed from their father's traditional power to contract them in compulsory marriage. Wives are no longer subject, to the same extent as before, to the patriarchal institutions of polygamy and unilateral repudiation of the marriage by the husband, and now have a much wider facility to obtain their release, by judicial divorce, from an unhappy union. This

[1] In this chapter I have drawn freely from the article of my colleague and mentor, J. N. D. Anderson: "Recent Reforms in the Islamic Law of Inheritance", *The International and Comparative Law Quarterly*, April 1965.

[2] Kemal Faruki, "Orphaned Grandchildren in Islamic Succession Law", *Islamic Studies*, Journal of the Central Institute of Islamic Research, Karachi, vol. IV, no. 3, 1965.

emancipation of women is an essential concomitant of the new emphasis upon the smaller family group, and it is against this broad background of reform in the family law that recent changes in the law of succession must be viewed. For these changes all point in the same direction and have been inspired by the same basic social purpose – namely, the strengthening of the rights of succession of those relatives who form the nuclear as opposed to the tribal family.

2. The juristic basis of reform

For Islamic jurisprudence, however, social need or desirability does not *per se* provide an adequate justification for legal reform. Insofar as Sharī'a law is the expression of divinely ordained, and therefore eternally valid and immutable, standards of conduct, it is for the law to prescribe and determine social purpose and not for social purpose to mould and fashion the law. Law, in the Islamic concept, does not grow out of society but is imposed upon society from above. Where, therefore, there arises in fact in modern times a social situation which makes a change in the law desirable, such a change will represent a legitimate expression of Sharī'a law only if it can be shown to be in conformity with the accepted dictates of the divine will of Allāh; in other words if it rests upon a juristic basis which does not contradict the fundamental Islamic ideology of law.

Clearly, then, the scope for legal reform, given a social impetus therefor, depends basically upon the extent to which the terms of the traditional law are deemed to constitute binding and incontrovertible expressions of the divine will. From mediaeval times until *circa* 1946 (the reason for the selection of this date, as will be apparent later, is an Egyptian law enacted in that year), the general view was that the legal manuals authoritative in each school constituted a final and perfect expression of Sharī'a law; in sum, that each and every rule of law recorded therein bore the stamp of a divine ordinance. This view went under the name of the doctrine of *taqlīd* (lit. "imitation"), by which judges and jurists alike were bound to adhere to the law as expounded in the authoritative manuals. Any deviation therefrom was regarded, in strict theory, as a contradiction of the divine law and therefore inadmissible.

It was the apparently insuperable strictures of the doctrine of *taqlīd* which forced the Turkish government of the 1920s to abandon the Sharī'a entirely and adopt in its place Western codes as the only practical means of achieving reform in the family law. But such a total break with Islamic tradition, at least in the sphere of family law, proved unacceptable to the other Muslim countries of the Near and Middle East, where means were found to adapt the Sharī'a law, as applied through the courts, to the changing circumstances of society.

2.1. The doctrine of *siyāsa*

As long as jurisprudential thought was dominated by the doctrine of *taqlīd*, the only acceptable juristic basis for reform lay in the principle of *siyāsa* (lit. "governmental administration"). According to the traditionally authoritative treatises on Islamic public law, this means that the political authority, while he certainly has no legislative power as such, has nevertheless the power to make administrative regulations to effect the proper application of Sharī'a law through the courts. As interpreted by the modern reformers, this doctrine of *siyāsa* enabled the political sovereign to issue directives to his courts designed to achieve one of two principal purposes. First, he might restrict the jurisdiction of his courts by denying them the competence to entertain cases which did not meet prescribed evidential requirements. The courts might thus, for example, be precluded from hearing claims which were not supported by documentary evidence. Second, the sovereign could define the jurisdiction of his courts in the sense that he could direct them to apply one view, in the case of divergence among the traditional authorities, to the exclusion of all other variants. Naturally, the view from among the traditional authorities which would be chosen for application by the courts would be that variant deemed best suited to contemporary social needs. Although this process of selection is justified on the ground that the variant doctrines of the different Sunnī schools are equally authoritative expressions of Sharī'a law, it was developed by the modern reformers to an extent which at least was never visualised by traditional jurisprudence. For the reformers in the Middle East did not limit their choice to authoritative variants within the Ḥanafī school or to the dominant doctrine of another Sunnī school. They selected opinions which could claim only the tenuous authority of some individual jurist of bygone days and which had traditionally been regarded as superceded by the general consensus of opinion. In a limited number of cases the only authority which could be adduced for the view selected lay outside the corpus of Sunnī doctrine altogether in the law of the sectarian school of the Shī'a. Finally, by a process termed *talfīq*, or "patching up", elements from the views of different schools and jurists were combined to form a composite legal rule for which no single school or jurist provided explicit authority.

2.2. The doctrine of *ijtihād*

But even when pursued to these extremes the doctrine of *siyāsa* provided only a limited potential for reform, and from 1946 onwards the fundamental doctrine of *taqlīd* itself has been ever more openly challenged. Support has grown for the view that the authority of the doctrine expounded in the mediaeval legal manuals is not absolute and infallible. Jurists of today, of course, admit to being bound by the dictates of the Qur'ān and the *sunna* just as their predecessors were. But they claim not to be bound by the interpretations which their predecessors placed upon those texts. On the contrary, they assert the right of *ijtihād*, or "independent interpretation" of the texts in the light of present social circumstances. It is on this basis that the most striking reforms of the traditional law have been effected. For in practice this modern *ijtihād* means not only that a proposed reform may be justified by a fresh interpretation of a specific text of the Qur'ān or *sunna*, but also that a novel rule may be considered a legitimate expression of Allāh's law because it is not contrary to any specific text of the Qur'ān or the *sunna*. It may be that this modern *ijtihād* is a subjective process inasmuch as it is used to justify a legal rule preconceived by the reformers on straightforward grounds of social need; but this, in fact, is to say little more than that the jurists of today are proceeding in the same way as their predecessors in the early centuries of Islam.

3. Relevant legislation

Examples of the use of each of the juristic media mentioned above to effect reform in the law of succession will be observed in this chapter and in those that follow. It must not be supposed, however, that there has yet emerged any uniform approach in Islam to the subject of legal reform. Just as the social impetus for reform varies from country to country, so does the attitude towards the permissible juristic basis of reform. And even within the ambit of a single modern legal enactment all the different juristic media may appear in support of this provision or that. This situation has inevitably produced a growing diversity in current Islamic legal practice, as will be apparent from the terms of the modern law relating to the particular topics considered in this chapter. The principal relevant modern enactments are:

Egypt: The Law of Inheritance, 1943. The Law of Testamentary Dispositions, 1946.

Syria: The Law of Personal Status, 1953.

Tunisia: The Law of Personal Status, 1956, and a Supplement thereto, 1959.

Morocco: The Code of Personal Status, 1958.

Iraq: The Law of Personal Status, 1959, with an Amendment thereto, 1963.

Pakistan: The Muslim Family Laws Ordinance, 1961.

4. The spouse relict

4.1. *Radd* in India, Pakistan, and the Sudan: the "acknowledged kinsman"

Under traditional Sharī'a doctrine, where the spouse relict is the only legal heir, the residual estate is inherited by (Mālikī law), or escheats to (general Sunnī law) the Public Treasury.

For some considerable time, however, the practice in India, as now carried over into Pakistan, has been that the spouse relict should take the residual estate by way of *radd* in the absence of any other legal heir. In 1925 the same rule was adopted in the Sudan, through the usual machinery of legal reform recognised in that country – a judicial circular emanating from the Grand *Qāḍī*.

In both these areas, however, the claim of the spouse relict to *radd* is postponed to that of "the acknowledged kinsman". Traditional Sunnī law maintains that in the absence of any known relative of the inner or the outer family, residual rights of succession belong to a person with whom the deceased has formally acknowledged a relationship (other than one of paternity which is subject to special rules). Such a person, acknowledged by the deceased as, for example, his brother, nephew, uncle or cousin, is an entitled residuary heir provided he is of unknown parentage. If his parentage is known and proved to be other than the one alleged in the acknowledgment, the acknowledgment is demonstrably false and therefore constitutes no ground for rights of succession; while if his parentage is known to be the one alleged in the acknowledgment, the acknowledgment itself is superfluous and the person will inherit as a genuine member of the deceased's family.

4.2. *Radd* in Egypt and Syria

Egypt and Syria have both adopted the rule of *radd* to the spouse relict in the absence of any surviving blood relative, but here the claim of the spouse to *radd* precedes that of any "acknowledged kinsman". Apparently, the acknowledged kinsman is no longer regarded as an heir proper because his relationship with the deceased is not in fact established. Where he does succeed, in the absence of any blood relative or spouse relict, he does so more as a legatee than a legal heir – as the Egyptian Law puts it: "out of respect for the will of the deceased and in fulfilment of his desires concerning his property".

The only juristic authority which could be adduced by the Egyptian reformers in support of the rule of *radd* to the spouse relict lay in the view of a few individual jurists of the eighth century that the spouse relict should participate in *radd* on an equal footing with other Qur'anic heirs. On a strict analysis, therefore, the rule is an example of *talfīq*, inasmuch as it combines this minority view (in the circumstance of there being no other surviving relative) with the majority view that the spouse relict is debarred from *radd* (in the circumstance of there being any other surviving relative).

4.3. *Radd* in Tunisia

Tunisia has gone considerably further than any of the countries previously mentioned in improving the position of a widow or widower in this regard. Prior to 1959 the law generally applicable was the Mālikī law, which does not recognise *radd*. *Radd*, however, was not altogether unknown in Tunisia; for since Ottoman times Ḥanafī law had been applied through the official courts to a fraction of the urban population which professed allegiance to this school. The Law of 1959 adopted the general doctrine of *radd*, but in so doing made no explicit distinction between the spouse relict and other Qur'anic heirs. With Roussier,[1] "one can assume that this is not a case of inadvertence", and the reform has two principal effects. First, the spouse relict will participate in *radd* along with other Qur'anic heirs, provided no male agnate, daughter or agnatic granddaughter survives (p. 142 below). Second, since Tunisia still holds to the general Mālikī rule that members of the outer family have no rights of succession, the spouse relict will not be debarred from *radd* in the presence of any such relative of the outer family, as would certainly be the case under the law of all the other Sunnī schools and is still the case in all the other countries which have adopted the rule of *radd* to the spouse relict.

[1] Jules Roussier, "Dispositions Nouvelles dans le Statut Successoral en Droit Tunisien", *Studia Islamica*, fasc. xii, 1960, p. 138.

5. Daughters

In Iraq and Tunisia, the rights of the immediate family, when in competition with relatives of the extended tribal group, have been recognised to the extent of allowing a daughter of the deceased to exclude from succession the deceased's brothers and sisters and *a fortiori* more remote male agnates.

5.1. Iraq: the application of the Shīʿī system of *qarāba*

In Iraq this was the result of the adoption in the Law of 1963 of the Shīʿī order of priorities in succession, under which any lineal descendant totally excludes all collaterals. Revolutionary though this step might appear from the general standpoint of Sunnī Islam, it was not so in the particular context of Iraq, where approximately half the population are Shīʿīs.

However, the Iraqi Law confines itself to laying down the bare order of priorities by class under the Shīʿī system and then enacts that: "With due regard to the foregoing, the distribution to the heirs by relationship of their entitlement and their shares shall be according to the rules of the Sharīʿa which were followed before the enactment of the Law of Personal Status." Apparently, the courts have interpreted this provision to mean that the detailed rules of Shīʿī law apply only to cases of succession concerning Shīʿīs, and that as far as Ḥanafī cases are concerned the traditional Ḥanafī principles of distribution still apply, subject only to the statutory order of priorities.

It is apparent that this interpretation of the Law will result in considerable divergence as regards the class of lineal descendants. Since the Shīʿī system applies the strict rule of priority by degree within this class, a daughter will totally exclude any grandson or granddaughter in a Shīʿī case. But in a Ḥanafī case an agnatic granddaughter will take a basic Qur'anic portion of one-sixth along with a daughter, and an agnatic grandson will take the residue of the estate after the daughter has taken her Qur'anic portion of one-half. Again, in a Shīʿī case of a competition between a father, mother and daughter, the distribution will be: father one-fifth, mother one-fifth, daughter three-fifths (all taking Qur'anic portions increased by *radd*). But the same case in a Ḥanafī court will result in the father being allotted one-third (one-sixth as a Qur'anic portion and one-sixth as the agnate residuary), the mother one-sixth and the daughter one-half. Finally, in a Shīʿī case, a daughter's child will take one-third when in competition with a son's child who will take two-thirds (according to the Shīʿī principle of representational entitlement), but in a Ḥanafī case the son's child will totally exclude the daughter's child.

No doubt it is sound social policy at the present time to allow the courts a latitude of discretion in interpreting the provisions of the new law. This certainly seems to have been the intention of the framers of the Law of Personal Status in regard to other important reforms introduced in the field of matrimonial law. But even when the law of succession is thus restrictively interpreted as far as the Sunnī population is concerned, it nevertheless still succeeds in promoting the interests of the nuclear family as against the agnatic collateral heirs of the tribal group. It was indeed precisely because the Shī'ī system gives obvious and consistent priority to the immediate family as against the tribal heirs that it appealed to the ethos of contemporary Iraqi society, at least in an urban milieu. In fact, prior to the reform of the law, it was not apparently unknown for Sunnī Iraqis in the twilight of their years, who had daughters but no sons, to profess conversion to the Shī'ī beliefs simply to prevent succession to a considerable part of their estate by some distant agnate.

5.2. Tunisia: the daughter's preferential right to *radd*

In Tunisia, reform was effected formally under the doctrine of *radd*. The relevant provision reads: "As for the daughter, whether one or many, or the son's daughter, how low soever, she shall take the residue of the estate by *radd* even in the presence of a male agnate, like a brother or an uncle, or the Public Treasury." The proper interpretation of this provision appears to be that it is the daughter or the agnatic granddaughter alone who is entitled to take the surplus of the estate by *radd* when she is in competition with other Qur'anic heirs. In effect, therefore, the daughter or granddaughter virtually becomes a residuary heir in her own right, not only excluding all collaterals from inheritance but also restricting the mother or grandmother to their basic Qur'anic portions of one-sixth. It seems reasonably certain, however, that the reform was not intended to prejudice the residual rights of succession of male agnate ascendants as distinct from collaterals. Since the father, or agnatic grandfather, in competition with a daughter is entitled to take both a Qur'anic portion of one-sixth and any surplus after the satisfaction of other Qur'anic portions as residuary heir, there is no occasion for *radd* and the daughter will accordingly be restricted to her basic Qur'anic entitlement of one-half.

From the way in which the reform was effected it is certain that the Tunisian Law is not the result of any conscious preference for Shī'ī principles. Nor was any express attempt made to justify the daughter's priority, as indeed it might well have been, by reference to the Qur'anic verse which states that a brother or sister is an heir only "if the deceased dies without a child". It may be observed that the reforms of family law effected by the Tunisian Law of 1956 were far more extreme than in any other Muslim country, particularly in the realm of divorce where husband and wife were put on a footing of exact parity. And it seems to be the case, in Tunisia at any rate, that the new functional approach to the role of law in society, which emerged with the initial break from the doctrine of *taqlīd*, has now developed to the point where the broad goal of emancipating women from their disabilities under the traditional law is in itself sufficient justification for reform.

In point of substance it may be that the Tunisian Law does not recognise the claims of the nuclear as opposed to the agnatic family in the same comprehensive way or to the same systematic extent as the Iraqi Law, even as restrictively interpreted in Sunnī cases. A daughter will not, for example, exclude the paternal grandfather completely as she will in Iraq. More particularly, in Tunisia the children of a predeceased daughter (although provided for in another way – see pp. 145–50 below) do not exclude agnatic collaterals from succession. Even so it may be observed that a daughter or agnatic granddaughter is sometimes more favourably treated under the Tunisian than under the Iraqi Law. In competition with the mother of the praepositus, for example, she will receive three-quarters of the inheritance in Iraq, but five-sixths in Tunisia. And, of course, in Tunisia just as in Iraq, once a daughter has taken the inheritance to the exclusion of her uncles or cousins, it will normally be lost for ever from the deceased's agnatic family, since it will pass to the daughter's children upon her decease.

6. Orphaned grandchildren

6.1. The social problem

Under traditional Sharī'a law the rule of priority in succession by degree means that a son of the praepositus excludes not only his own children but also his nephews and nieces, the children of other predeceased sons of the praepositus. Within the tribal agnatic family this rule did not occasion any real injustice, since the bond of *'aṣabiyya* welded all the sons and agnatic grandsons of the praepositus into one compact group, and the passing of the inheritance to the son of the deceased was consonant with his position as the new head of the family and the responsibilities he had for the family as a whole. But with the growing breakdown of the ties of the extended family in contemporary society the rule is no longer so readily supportable.

It is not primarily a question of the orphaned grandchildren of the deceased being in particular need, physically, of provision from his estate. They may be adequately provided for, either through the inheritance they have already received from their deceased parent, or through their other surviving parent and his or her relatives, or indeed through their own personal resources, since they are not necessarily helpless minors. Nor, of course, does the decay of tribal solidarity mean that in practice an uncle will ignore the manifest need of his nephews or nieces whom he has excluded from succession to their grandfather's estate. Inheritance, from the point of view of the heir, is not a matter of need but of right, and from the point of view of the praepositus it is the fulfilment of a responsibility towards his surviving relatives simply because they are his relatives. In the compact tribal group the responsibilities of the deceased towards his lineal descendants were fulfilled by the passing of the inheritance *en bloc* to the first degree of his issue. But today the different lines of the deceased's issue, through his several sons, form separate families to each of which the deceased owes an individual responsibility. Accordingly, it now appears that the responsibilities of the deceased are not properly fulfilled if the succession rights of one family line are to be totally extinguished, because of the chance occurrence of the predecease of its immediate link with the ancestor, and are to pass to another family line where the immediate link with the ancestor happens still to survive.

The broad social purpose of reform, therefore, was to make suitable provision in succession law for the orphaned grandchildren of the praepositus. Three principal questions were entailed. First, what precisely would constitute a reasonable provision for the children of a predeceased son? Second, should similar provision be made for the children of a predeceased daughter? Although such grandchildren would not ordinarily be legal heirs under the traditional Sunnī system where they were relatives of the outer family, they are now nevertheless part of the nuclear family of contemporary society. Third, upon what juristic basis could the desired reform be rested? Clearly the answers to the first two questions will depend to a large degree on the answer to this last, and the questions have been variously answered in the five countries which to date have tackled this problem – Egypt, Syria, Tunisia, Morocco and Pakistan.

6.1.1. Syria and Morocco

To summarise the position first. In Syria and Morocco the children of a predeceased son or agnatic grandson, who would be excluded from succession under the traditional law, are now entitled to either the share of the inheritance their father would have received had he survived the praepositus or one-third of the net estate, whichever is less. No provision is made for children of the deceased's daughter.

6.1.2. Egypt and Tunisia

In Egypt and Tunisia the children of a predeceased son or daughter, who would be excluded from succession under the traditional law, are entitled to the share their parent would have received had he or she survived the praepositus, within the maximum limit of one-third of the net estate. In Egypt, but not in Tunisia, the children of an agnatic grandson or granddaughter, how low soever, benefit from the same rule.

6.1.3. Pakistan

Pakistan has adopted a systematic and comprehensive scheme of representational succession by lineal descendants. Section 4 of the Muslim Family Laws Ordinance, 1961, reads:

> In the event of the death of any son or daughter of the *propositus* before the opening of succession, the children of such son or daughter, if any, living at the time the succession opens, shall *per stirpes* receive a share equivalent to the share which such son or daughter, as the case may be, would have received, if alive.

6.2. The rule of obligatory bequest in the Middle East

6.2.1. Grandchildren as legatees

While the law of the Middle Eastern countries clearly rests on the view that orphaned grandchildren should be allowed to claim a share in their grandparent's estate as representatives of their deceased parent, the fixing of the upper limit of their entitlement at one-third of the net estate is due to the fact that they formally receive their entitlement as a bequest and not as inheritance; and bequests, of course, may not in principle consume more than one-third of the net estate. This indirect approach was dictated by juristic considerations. The reform was first introduced in Egypt in 1946, and it was felt at that time that there was no legitimate ground for directly upsetting the settled principle of intestate succession that the nearer in degree excludes the more remote. The only satisfactory juristic basis upon which reform could be effected lay in the principles of testamentary disposition.

6.2.2. The juristic basis of obligatory bequests

A verse of the Qur'ān (Sūra 2, verse 180), generally known as "the verse of bequests", enjoins Muslims to make "bequests in favour of parents and close relatives". Although the great majority of jurists considered that this verse had been completely abrogated or repealed by the later Qur'anic rules of inheritance, a small but respectable minority (including the father of Muslim jurisprudence himself, al-Shāfi'ī) held that the verse was repealed only in respect of those close relatives who actually received a share of inheritance, and that it was still desirable at least for bequests to be made in favour of other close relatives. A few jurists, notably the prolific author Ibn Ḥazm, a representative of the now extinct Ẓāhirī school, went further and insisted that the Qur'anic verse implied a definite legal obligation to make bequests in favour of close relatives who were not legal heirs, and that if the deceased had failed in his duty to make this obligatory bequest the court should make it for him.

In relying upon this construction of the verse of bequests, the Egyptian reformers could claim, formally at any rate, that they were not contradicting the doctrine of *taqlīd*. But then an element of novel interpretation (*ijtihād*) creeps in with the specification of orphaned grandchildren as the only "close relatives" who are entitled to such an obligatory bequest, and with the determination of the *quantum* of their entitlement.

6.2.3. Legal incidents of the obligatory bequest

The substance of the law, then, is that where the deceased has failed to make a bequest in favour of his orphaned grandchildren who are not his legal heirs to the extent either of their predeceased parent's notional entitlement or the bequeathable third, whichever is less, the court must act as though such a bequest had in fact been made and had been duly accepted by the legatees. Against this determined entitlement must be offset any smaller bequest in fact made to the grandchildren or any gift delivered to them *inter vivos* by the deceased. The obligatory bequest will have complete precedence over any other bequests the deceased may have made. Where there are two or more entitled grandchildren to share the bequest, the male will take twice the share of the female.

6.2.4. Methods of applying the law

6.2.4.1. The court system

The application of the law, however, has not proved as simple a matter as it might at first sight appear. Initially, the courts adopted the all too obvious method of distributing the estate as though the predeceased parent of the grandchildren were in fact alive, and then passing this ascertained share, or one-third of the net estate, whichever was less, to the grandchildren. But the varying effect that this method may have upon the position of the other heirs will be apparent from three examples.

(i) P is survived by four daughters, a germane sister and a son's daughter. Assuming the predeceased son to be alive, he will exclude the germane sister and convert the daughters into residuary heirs. They will each take one-sixth of the inheritance and the son will take one-third, which latter share will pass to the granddaughter. But if P had actually made a bequest of one-third to his granddaughter, the daughters would have received two-thirds, and the germane sister (inheriting as accompanying residuary with them) one-third *of the inheritance*, i.e. four-ninths and two-ninths respectively of the whole estate.

(ii) P is survived by her husband, germane sister, uterine sister and daughter's daughter. Assuming the predeceased daughter to be alive, the husband will take one-quarter, the daughter one-half and the germane sister one-quarter. The uterine sister will be excluded by the daughter. When the daughter's share of one-half is necessarily reduced to one-third for transmission to her child, the surplus of one-sixth will go to the germane sister as residuary heir. But if P had actually made a bequest of one-third to his granddaughter, then the husband, germane sister and uterine sister would all have been entitled as Qur'anic heirs to three-sevenths, three-sevenths and one-seventh respectively *of the inheritance*, i.e. $\frac{6}{21}$, $\frac{6}{21}$ and $\frac{2}{21}$ of the whole estate.

(iii) P is survived by his father, mother, son, daughter and the daughter of a predeceased son. Assuming the predeceased son to be alive, the father will take one-sixth, the mother one-sixth, the son four-fifteenths, the daughter two-fifteenths, and the son's daughter her father's share of four-fifteenths. But if P had actually made a bequest of four-fifteenths to his granddaughter, then the shares of the other heirs, expressed as fractions of the whole estate, would have been: father ($\frac{1}{6} \times \frac{11}{15}$), $\frac{11}{90}$; mother, $\frac{11}{90}$; son ($\frac{4}{9} \times \frac{11}{15}$), $\frac{44}{135}$; daughter, $\frac{22}{135}$. In short, each of the heirs would have borne a proportionate share of the burden of the bequest. But under the courts' method of distribution the burden falls exclusively upon the son and the daughter, the Qur'anic portions of the parents being unaffected.

The result of this method of applying the law, then, is that the entitlement of the grandchildren is not at all in the nature of a bequest. On the contrary it amounts to inheritance by direct representation. And since the interference with the rights of the legal heirs which this causes was precisely what the law of obligatory bequests was designed to avoid, the decisions of the courts based upon this system of distribution have been rightly quashed on appeal.

6.2.4.2. The Muftī's system

An alternative system, which was backed by the authority of a formal opinion (*fatwā*) from the Chief Muftī of Egypt, was to regard the entitlement of the grandchildren as a bequest of a sum "equivalent to the share" of a son or daughter of the praepositus according to the sex of the predeceased parent. The institution of a bequest "equivalent to the share of" a specified relative was well known to Islamic legal practice and the traditional authorities lay down a fixed arithmetical method of calculating it. The entitlement of the legal heirs is first ascertained and expressed in fractions with a common denominator. The legatee is then allotted a fractional entitlement, the numerator of which is the same as that of the share of the heir to whose entitlement the bequest is to be equivalent and the denominator of which is the sum of the numerators of his own and the heirs' fractions. Finally, the denominator of the heirs' fractions is increased to this same figure.

P dies leaving a father (two-sixths), mother (one-sixth), daughter (three-sixths) and a daughter's daughter. The entitlement of the granddaughter, as a bequest equivalent to the share of a daughter, will be three-ninths. The shares of the inheritance now become: father two-ninths, mother one-ninth, daughter three-ninths.

Here the Muftī's system (*a*) does not affect in any way the relative priorities of the actual legal heirs, whose proportionate rights in the estate less the bequest remain precisely the same, and (*b*) gives the granddaughter exactly what her mother would have taken as a legal heir had she survived. But while (*a*) is always the result of the Muftī's system, (*b*) is not.

P is survived by her husband (one-quarter), son (two-quarters), daughter (one-quarter) and son's daughter. The obligatory entitlement of the son's daughter will be two-sixths. But while the proportionate rights of the husband, son and daughter will remain the same (respectively one-sixth, two-sixths and one-sixth of the whole estate), the granddaughter's deceased father, had he survived, would in fact have taken six-twentieths of the inheritance.

Since the Muftī's system, in cases like this, has results which are directly contrary to the express terms of the Law of 1946, it cannot be correct. And the basic reason why it is not correct is really simple enough. The bequest to the grandchild envisaged by the law is not "a bequest equivalent to the share of my surviving son or daughter", but "a bequest of the share my deceased son or daughter would have received". These can be two very different things.

6.2.4.3. Abū Zahra's system

The one sound method of applying the law of obligatory bequests is that formulated by Shaykh Muḥammad Abū Zahra.[1] The estate is first appor-

[1] Professor of Islamic law at the University of Cairo, in his *Aḥkām-al-Tarikāt wa'l-Mawārīth* (Cairo, 1963), pp. 284ff.

tioned as if the predeceased child were an entitled heir, and his or her share, or the bequeathable third, whichever is less, is taken out of the estate and allotted to the grandchild or grandchildren as a bequest. The remainder of the estate is then re-apportioned between the actual legal heirs. This method consistently ensures both that the grandchildren receive what their predeceased parent would have taken, within the limit of the bequeathable third, and that the rights of the actual legal heirs *inter se* (in respect of the estate left after the deduction of the bequest) are not affected. Its application to the four cases considered above to illustrate the defects of the court system and the Muftī's system has the following results:

(i)	Four daughters	$(\frac{2}{3})$	$(\frac{2}{3} \times \frac{2}{3})$	$= \frac{4}{9}$
	Germane sister	—	$(\frac{1}{3} \times \frac{2}{3})$	$= \frac{2}{9}$
	Son's daughter	$(\frac{1}{3})$		$\frac{1}{3}$
(ii)	Husband	$(\frac{1}{4})$	$(\frac{3}{7} \times \frac{2}{3})$	$= \frac{6}{21}$
	Germane sister	$(\frac{1}{4})$	$(\frac{3}{7} \times \frac{2}{3})$	$= \frac{6}{21}$
	Uterine sister	—	$(\frac{1}{7} \times \frac{2}{3})$	$= \frac{2}{21}$
	Daughter's daughter	$(\frac{1}{2})$		$\frac{1}{3}$
(iii)	Father	$(\frac{1}{6})$	$(\frac{1}{6} \times \frac{11}{15})$	$= \frac{11}{90}$
	Mother	$(\frac{1}{6})$	$(\frac{1}{6} \times \frac{11}{15})$	$= \frac{11}{90}$
	Son	$(\frac{4}{15})$	$(\frac{4}{9} \times \frac{11}{15})$	$= \frac{44}{135}$
	Daughter	$(\frac{2}{15})$	$(\frac{2}{9} \times \frac{11}{15})$	$= \frac{22}{135}$
	Son's daughter	$(\frac{4}{15})$		$\frac{4}{15}$
(iv)	Husband	$(\frac{1}{4})$	$(\frac{1}{4} \times \frac{14}{20})$	$= \frac{7}{40}$
	Son	$(\frac{6}{20})$	$(\frac{1}{2} \times \frac{14}{20})$	$= \frac{7}{20}$
	Daughter	$(\frac{3}{20})$	$(\frac{1}{4} \times \frac{14}{20})$	$= \frac{7}{40}$
	Son's daughter	$(\frac{6}{20})$		$\frac{6}{20}$

6.2.4.4. The effect of other bequests on the distribution

In the above illustrations it is assumed that the deceased has not made any other valid bequests. But if he has in fact done so, then it seems certain that these bequests must be taken into account when calculating the entitlement of the predeceased child. In sum, the entitlement of the predeceased child must be expressed as a fraction of the whole net estate (the estate less funeral expenses and debts) and not simply as a share in the property available for inheritance.

P, for example, is survived by his wife, son (S^1), and the son of a predeceased son (S^2), and has validly bequeathed one-third of his net estate to the local mosque. The share *of the inheritance* S^2 would have received had he survived would have been seven-sixteenths. But it would be wrong to hold that, since seven-sixteenths is greater than one-third, the grandson's entitlement will be one-third. For his father would actually have received $\frac{14}{48}$ of the whole net estate, and it would be contrary to the explicit terms of the law if the grandson were to receive more than this. $\frac{14}{48}$ is therefore the proper entitlement of the grandson in this case and $\frac{2}{48}$ of the estate will remain as partial satisfaction of the bequest in favour of the mosque.

6.3. The rule of representational succession in Pakistan

6.3.1. The juristic basis of representation

In adopting the rule of representational succession by lineal descendants as an integral part of the laws of inheritance, the Pakistani Muslim Family Laws Ordinance, 1961, effects a clean and total break with traditional Sharī'a doctrine, orthodox or sectarian.

One line of argument adopted by the supporters of this reform has been the criticism of traditional Sunnī doctrine, on intrinsically legal grounds, for its failure to recognise the principle of representational succession by grandchildren. Thus, the report of a Pakistani Commission, which was appointed in 1955 to advise upon possible reform of the family law and which advocated this particular reform of representational succession, stated that traditional doctrine recognises the principle of representation in regard to ascendants, inasmuch as the grandfather takes the place of the father in the latter's absence, and that therefore the same principle ought to apply to the grandchild in the absence of the child, for "the Islamic law of inheritance cannot be irrational and inequitable".[1] The fact is, of course, that the traditional law does apply the same principle both to ascendants and descendants; but it is the principle of substitution, not representation. In the absence of the father, the grandfather succeeds simply as the nearest ascendant, just as the grandson, in the absence of any son, will succeed as the nearest descendant.

Kemal Faruki[2] pursues the same erroneous course of reasoning. There are, he states, exceptions in the traditional law to the rule that the nearer in degree excludes the more remote – namely that (i) a maternal grandmother is not excluded by the father; (ii) a son's daughter is not excluded by a daughter; and (iii) a uterine brother or sister is not excluded by a germane brother or sister. Then he concludes: "Now if the rule of the nearer in degree excluding the more remote is powerless to exclude (the relatives in the above cases), how much more powerful should be the

[1] An analysis of the Commission's report is the subject of my article: "Reform of Family Law in Pakistan", *Studia Islamica*, fasc. vii, 1957, pp. 135ff.

[2] Faruki, *Islamic Studies*, IV, no. 3, 1965, pp. 264ff.

claims by right of an orphaned grandchild." It is difficult to imagine a more blatant instance of a *non sequitur*. The cases cited (to which numerous others could be added, as, for example, the fact that a germane sister does not exclude a consanguine brother's agnatic grandson), have nothing whatsoever to do with the rule of degree as understood by traditional law. There it operates, systematically and without exception, as the rule that a male agnate excludes more remote agnate relatives of the same class.

This attempt to discredit the traditional law, on the broad ground of its inconsistency, is without any real foundation. Such recognition as was afforded by the traditional law to the general principle of representation did not undermine in any way the rule of exclusion by degree. Shaybānī's doctrine of *per stirpes* distribution among relatives of the outer family, and the general Shī'ī doctrine of representational entitlement, apply only after priorities have been determined, *inter alia* by the rule of degree. And even the Shāfi'ī and Ḥanbalī doctrine of *tanzīl*, which is the most extreme example of representation in the traditional law inasmuch as it determines both priorities and *quantum* of entitlement, involves the consistent observance of the rule that the nearer in degree excludes the more remote.

Kemal Faruki is on much more solid ground when he argues that to "strengthen the Islamic social ideal it may prove desirable or necessary to revise our interpretations of Islamic principles as they find expression in rules of positive law". More particularly, he goes on, "there is no Qur'anic statement excluding such grandchildren" and

> to mechanically interpret [the precedent of the Prophet which states that residual rights of succession belong to the nearest male agnate] in such a way that the very object of strengthening the immediate family is nullified in some lines of descent would not be in consonance with Islamic principles and would constitute an unwarranted interpretation of these principles for the given social situation.

In sum, he sees the reform as the result of independent interpretation, or *ijtihād*, under which a socially desirable rule finds its juristic justification in the fact that it is not contrary to any explicit ruling of the Qur'ān or *sunna*.

Whether such *ijtihād* is a legitimate basis for reform or not is, of course, entirely a question of religious conviction, and as such totally outside the competence of the external observer. But it is arguable whether Kemal Faruki is right in going on to suggest, as he does, that the present Pakistani Law is more correct in principle than the traditional law. He refers to the traditional rule of no representation as "merely a discordant by-product of a classical construction" of the *sunna*, and to the modern law as "exposing a lacuna, even contradiction in the classical rules of interpreting" the Qur'ān and the *sunna*. This is reminiscent of the arguments of the 1955

Commission, which regarded the rule of no representation as a rule of pre-Islamic practice wrongly perpetuated by the mediaeval jurists and completely contradictory to the general spirit of the Qur'ān – particularly those verses which show great concern for the protection and welfare of orphans. Since this is not a question of inner religious faith, but one of the interpretation of external legal rules and their role in society, a non-Muslim might be permitted to suggest that the interpretation of the Qur'ān and the *sunna* adopted by the traditional law appears as valid in the context of traditional Islamic society as the modern interpretation does in the context of present-day Pakistani society. It may also be suggested that if the reform does rest upon the right of contemporary society to depart from the interpretations of the traditional authorities, then those intrinsically legal arguments which seek to establish the inconsistent and irrational nature of the traditional law in the matter of representation are as unnecessary as they are unconvincing.

6.3.2. The substantive effect of representation

Because the Pakistani rule of representational succession by lineal descendants is absolute in its application and not confined to cases where the grandchildren would otherwise be excluded from succession, it brings about radical changes in the structure of inheritance, affecting not only the heirs' *quantum* of entitlement but also their priorities.

In effect, the rule both adds to and subtracts from the traditional list of Qur'anic heirs entitled to fixed portions. The child of a predeceased daughter, who would not have inherited at all before, now takes a Qur'anic portion exactly as a daughter would do. He or she restricts the mother and spouse relict to their minimal shares, cuts down the entitlement of all competing collaterals and excludes uterine brothers and sisters altogether. Agnatic grandchildren derive even greater benefit from the rule, particularly the son's daughter, who now loses her character of a Qur'anic heir and becomes a primary residuary. She will take twice the share of a daughter of the deceased and will exclude all collaterals. So, too, the son's son is no longer liable to *de facto* exclusion. In competition, for example, with the deceased's father, mother and two daughters he will now take one-third of the inheritance.

6.3.3. A comparison with Shī'ī law

Where the only surviving lineal descendants are grandchildren, their position under the Pakistani Law often approximates to that they would have under Shī'ī law. The major differences that obtain between the two systems in regard to lineal descendants are due to the Shīʿī rule of class, under which any lineal descendant excludes any collateral, and, of course, where any immediate child survives, the Shīʿī rule of priority by degree.

		Ḥanafī law	Shīʿī law	Pakistani law
(i)	Daughter's son	—	21/32	21/32
	Wife	1/4	1/8	1/8
	Mother	1/2	7/32	7/32
	Uterine sister	1/4	—	—
(ii)	Son's daughter	1/2	3/4	3/4
	Husband	1/4	1/4	1/4
	Germane brother	1/4	—	—
(iii)	Daughter's daughter	—	3/4	1/2
	Mother	2/5	1/4	1/6
	Germane sister	3/5	—	1/3
(iv)	Daughter	1/2	All	1/3
	Son's daughter	1/6	—	2/9
	Son's son	1/3	—	4/9

6.4. The systems of representation and obligatory bequests compared

The purpose of this brief comparative note is not to assess the legitimacy or the validity of the juristic justification for the Middle Eastern and the Pakistani reforms respectively, since the only competent arbiter in this matter is the Muslim religious conscience. And because it is primarily the accepted juristic basis for reform which determines the degree to which the substance of the traditional law is changed, it follows that the extent to which one system or the other is more or less disruptive of the traditional law is not, for the present purpose, a relevant comparative consideration. Certainly, it is the Pakistani reform which is the more extreme in this regard. And it may be that this was due, in part at least, to the developments in the philosophy of Islamic legal reform which had taken place in the fifteen years which followed the promulgation of the Egyptian Law of Obligatory Bequests. Several years prior to the Pakistani Law, in fact, an attempt was made to introduce direct representational succession in Lebanon, but it had to be abandoned, at least as far as Muslims were concerned, because of strong opposition from traditionalist elements. However, the sole question here is that of the intrinsically legal merits of the reforms. How far do the rules of obligatory bequests and representational succession, respectively, provide an effective and equitable remedy for the social problems they were designed to solve?

Clearly it was considered reasonable provision for orphaned grandchildren, both in the Middle East and in Pakistan, that they should receive the notional share of their predeceased parent (subject to the upper limit of one-third in the Middle East). Equally clearly, while Syria and Morocco were concerned only with the position of agnatic lineal issue, the intention in Egypt, Tunisia and Pakistan was that daughters' children should enjoy similar benefits. Now this necessarily implies the intention to preserve the traditional superiority of males, as legal heirs, over females, in the broad sense that a male or his issue should receive twice the share of a female or her issue. This is consistently the result of the Pakistani Law. In the Middle East it is also the result, generally speaking, where the only surviving issue are grandchildren or where all the grandchildren are excluded from inheritance by the survival of a son. But where a daughter or daughters of the deceased survive, the position of the grandchildren is often anomalous.

6.4.1. The anomalies of the system of obligatory bequests

Even under the limited form of obligatory bequests applicable in Syria and Morocco an agnatic grandson may find himself in the curious position of benefiting from the presence of a greater, rather than a lesser, number of other entitled heirs, while an agnatic granddaughter may take more than a grandson would take in similar circumstances. In Egypt and Tunisia more serious anomalies result from the inclusion of daughters' children within the ambit of the rule. Daughters' children may find themselves in a more favourable position than sons' children even when in direct competition with them. These obviously unsystematic results are all occasioned by the rule that an agnatic grandchild does not rank as an obligatory legatee if he or she is entitled to receive *anything* as a legal heir. Six illustrations of such anomalies follow, the distribution in each case being based on Abū Zahra's method (the only correct method) of applying the rule of obligatory bequests.

(i) In competition with a mother and two daughters, a son's son will take one-sixth of the estate as a residuary heir. But if the father of the deceased survived as well the son's son would take one-third as an obligatory legatee. In Pakistan the grandson will take five-twelfths in the first circumstance and four-twelfths in the second.

(ii) In competition with a wife, mother and two daughters, a son's son will take $\frac{1}{24}$ of the estate as residuary heir, whereas a son's daughter in competition with the same heirs will take one-third as an obligatory legatee.

In Pakistan the son's son or the son's daughter will take $\frac{17}{48}$.

(iii) Where the praepositus is survived by a husband and two daughters, a son's son will take one-twelfth of the estate as a residuary. A daughter's son in competition with the same heirs would take one-quarter of the estate as an obligatory legatee.

In Pakistan the son's son will take three-eighths and the daughter's son two-eighths.

(iv) Where the praepositus is survived by a daughter, a son's daughter and a daughter's daughter, the son's daughter takes one-sixth as a Qur'anic heir and the daughter's daughter one-third as an obligatory legatee.

In Pakistan the son's daughter takes one-half and the daughter's daughter one-quarter.

(v) In a competition between a husband, mother, father, daughter, son's daughter and daughter's daughter, the son's daughter takes $\frac{22}{225}$ of the whole estate as a Qur'anic heir and the daughter's daughter $\frac{60}{225}$ as an obligatory legatee.

In Pakistan the son's daughter takes $\frac{10}{48}$ and the daughter's daughter $\frac{5}{48}$.

(vi) Where the praepositus is survived by a husband, two daughters, a son's son and a daughter's son, the son's son will receive $\frac{7}{108}$ of the whole estate as residuary heir and the daughter's son $\frac{24}{108}$ as an obligatory legatee.

In Pakistan the son's son takes six-twentieths and the daughter's son three-twentieths.

6.4.2. A possible solution of the anomalies

In these and similar cases, then, it is clearly the Pakistani Law which makes the more consistent and equitable provision for orphaned grandchildren. Under the Middle Eastern principle of obligatory bequests, a possible way to iron out the anomalies and achieve the same systematic results as the Pakistani Law would be to regard *any* orphaned grandchild as potentially an obligatory legatee, to the extent that an agnatic grandchild who is a legal heir should be entitled to such a share of the estate as he or she would receive as an obligatory legatee if this would be greater.

This would mean that where the only surviving grandchildren are in fact legal heirs, they will be entitled by way of bequest to such an additional amount as is necessary to make up their share of the estate to the notional entitlement of the predeceased parent, within the maximum of one-third; and that where there are other grandchildren entitled as obligatory legatees, the collective entitlement of all the grandchildren, by way both of inheritance and bequest, will be redistributed among them on the basis of the notional entitlement therein of their respective predeceased parents and the rule of double share to the male.

In case (i) above, for example, the son's son would take one-third whether the deceased's father survived or not; in case (iv) the son's daughter would take one-third and the daughter's daughter one-sixth; and in case (vi) the son's son would take twice the share of the daughter's son in their collective entitlement of 31/108.

This solution might offend the settled rule of traditional Sunnī law that a bequest in favour of a legal heir is *ultra vires* – a rule based on the ground that the balance between the claims of the different relatives established by the law of inheritance ought not to be upset. But such an objection is no longer relevant in the case of Egypt at least, where the Law of 1946 abandoned the traditional rule and gave a testator freedom to make bequests to his legal heirs within the normal limit of the bequeathable third.

6.4.3. The restriction of testamentary liberty under the obligatory bequest system

There remains, however, a further and more fundamental objection to the system of obligatory bequests which is most persuasively argued by Kemal Faruki in his vigorous championship of the Pakistani system of representational succession. This is the fact that the obligatory bequest system may often result in a person being "deprived of dealing with one-third of his estate in complete violation of the spirit of legacies".[1] Testamentary dispositions may be intended by the deceased to fulfil a personal duty which he conceives to be of considerable importance and which would not be fulfilled by the rules of inheritance, such as a bequest for the performance of religious duties omitted by the deceased during his lifetime, or a bequest in favour of his Jewish or Christian wife who cannot inherit from him because of their difference in religion, or a bequest in favour of a particularly needy and deserving relative who is not his legal heir. Under the Pakistani system the deceased's testamentary liberty in this respect remains unimpaired. But in the Middle East the rule that the obligatory bequest takes complete precedence over any other that has been made may occasion injustice.

> Suppose, for example, that P has made a bequest of one-third of his estate to his orphaned and disabled nephew who is in great need of financial aid, and that P is survived by his son and an orphaned grandson, the latter having acquired a considerable fortune from his own profession and the inheritance he received from his father. Under the obligatory bequest system the legacy to the nephew will fail and the grandson will take one-third of the estate.

Ideally, perhaps, any legal system should recognise and give effect to the two distinct criteria of succession by right and succession in case of need; and traditional Islamic law catered for the former by the compulsory

[1] Faruki, *Islamic Studies*, IV, no. 3, 1965, p. 259.

rules of inheritance and for the latter by allowing the deceased testamentary liberty over one-third of his estate. In the Middle East no less than in Pakistan, succession by orphaned grandchildren is in fact regarded as a matter of right and not of need. Juridically, therefore, the Pakistani Law is much sounder in principle because it regulates the position of the grandchildren in a systematic fashion and at the same time preserves the balance between the criteria of right and need by leaving the deceased's testamentary freedom intact.

6.4.4. The anomalous position of a daughter under the Pakistani Law

The one question-mark, however, that must hang over the Pakistani Law is whether the effect that the representational rule has upon the scheme of inheritance rights as a whole is in conformity with the notion of family ties and responsibilities to which present-day Pakistani society subscribes. Perhaps the most obvious result of the law is the remarkable improvement in the position of an agnatic grandchild, who will now always take twice as much of the inheritance as the deceased's own daughter. Furthermore, the agnatic granddaughter will exclude from succession any brother or more remote male agnate whereas the deceased's own daughter will not. It is at least arguable that it is not in line with the present concept of ties within the nuclear family for such a premium to be placed upon the agnatic tie that the traditional rule of priority by degree is almost completely reversed and a daughter is in a much worse position than a granddaughter.

The moral is, perhaps, that the question of the rights of orphaned grandchildren ought not to be treated as an isolated issue. It ought to be answered within the context of a broader and systematic review of the laws of inheritance which decides, *inter alia*, precisely what priority is to be given to the nuclear as opposed to the extended family, and whether any priority, not necessarily total, is to be given to a relative, male or female, who is nearer in degree to the deceased. A final illustration of the position of orphaned grandchildren in this wider context will indicate the varied state of the law as it stands at present in different countries.

	Syria and Morocco	Iraq	Egypt	Pakistan	Tunisia
Daughter	$\frac{1}{2}$	All	$\frac{1}{3}$	$\frac{1}{3}$	$\frac{2}{3}$
Daughter's son	—	—	$\frac{1}{3}$	$\frac{1}{3}$	$\frac{1}{3}$
Agnatic cousin	$\frac{1}{2}$	—	$\frac{1}{3}$	$\frac{1}{3}$	—

7. A grandfather in competition with collaterals

For the great majority of Muslim countries and communities the traditional law of the school prevailing in the area concerned still applies. Thus, for example, the courts in Pakistan and India apply the Ḥanafī doctrine, under which the grandfather totally excludes all collaterals, as also do the courts in Jordan, where the Law of Family Rights, 1951 introduced no changes at all as regards priorities in succession. Similarly, the codifications of family law in Tunisia and Morocco have confirmed the application of traditional Mālikī law in this regard, under which agnatic brothers and sisters are not excluded by the grandfather.[1]

7.1. The Sudan, Egypt and Syria

In the Sudan, Egypt and Syria, however, the Ḥanafī law traditionally applicable has been superceded by a system which admits brothers and sisters to succession along with the grandfather – the reforms resting upon the general juristic basis that a Ḥanafī political authority may order his courts to apply authoritative opinions from the general body of Sharī'a doctrine other than the dominant Ḥanafī view where this appears to be in the public interest.[2]

Although the Sudan took the first step in this direction in 1939, when it was decreed that cases involving a competition between the grandfather and the collaterals should henceforth be regulated in accordance with Zaid's doctrine,[3] it is the Egyptian Law of Inheritance, 1943, which provides the focal point of attention in this regard; for this law was adopted *verbatim* by the Sudan in 1943 and with one important refinement by Syria in her Law of Personal Status, 1953.

[1] In Tunisia, however, the practice of the courts was not to recognise the two particular refinements of the *Mālikiyya* and the *Shibh al-Mālikiyya*. This practice was confirmed by article 145 of the Tunisian Code of Personal Status, which expressly allots one-sixth of the estate to the grandfather and one-sixth to the germane or consanguine brother(s) in both these cases.

[2] For a discussion of this principle of legal reform and its application to the present problem, see my *A History of Islamic Law* (Edinburgh, 1964), pp. 195ff. The statement there that under Ḥanbalī law the grandfather excludes all collaterals is incorrect.

[3] Among the supporters of Zaid's doctrine were the early Ḥanafī jurists Abū Yūsuf and Shaybānī, and it was, appropriately enough, to the authority of these two scholars that the Sudanese Judicial Circular introducing the reform specifically referred. See J. N. D. Anderson, "Recent Developments in Sharī'a Law VII", *Muslim World*, April 1952, pp. 135ff.

7.1.1. The Egyptian Law of Inheritance (Law no. 77 of 1943)

7.1.1.1. The practical reasons for reform

The particular mischief which the Egyptian reform was designed to remedy is explained in the preamble to the law and may be best appreciated by a simple diagram.

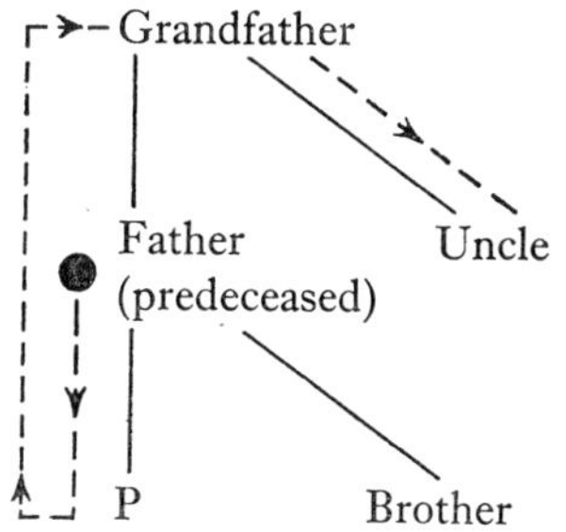

In these circumstances, which the explanatory memorandum states to be of frequent occurrence, the property which the praepositus P had inherited from his father would, under Ḥanafī law, go to P's grandfather and then upon the latter's death to P's uncle. Such a situation, in the eyes of the reformers, occasions injustice to P's brother, who is in effect ousted from a considerable part of his father's estate by his uncle. Accordingly, a suitable remedy was deemed to lie in allowing him to succeed to P's estate along with his grandfather. In short, the broad motive which inspired the Egyptian Law was the protection of the interests of children in their parent's estate. Thus the Egyptian reform falls naturally into line with all the other steps taken to strengthen the rights of inheritance of the nuclear family.

7.1.1.2. 'Alī's doctrine preferred except in one case

Under the Law of 1943 a competition between the grandfather and collaterals is to be resolved strictly in accordance with the principles laid down by 'Alī in all but one particular case. This exception is the case of a competition between the grandfather and a sister or sisters, when the deceased is also survived by a daughter or a son's daughter (or a plurality thereof). Here, according to 'Alī, the grandfather takes one-sixth as a Qur'anic heir and the sisters inherit as "accompanying residuaries". According to the Egyptian Law, however, the grandfather will take as a residuary heir, entitled to twice as much as a sister, where this is more advantageous to him than his Qur'anic portion.

Although actual distribution under the Egyptian Law in this case is the same as it would be under Zaid's doctrine (the provision is in fact formally justified on this basis), this is not the result of an adoption of Zaid's rule of *ta'ṣīb* but of a novel approach which may fairly claim to be even more systematic and correct in principle than 'Alī's doctrine. The grandfather does not, under the Egyptian Law, convert the sister into a residuary heir. She is already, in the presence of a daughter or son's daughter, an "accompanying residuary", and the grandfather then simply inherits along with her in what is, in fact, his normal capacity. For the grandfather, like the father, is basically a residuary heir whose Qur'anic portion is designed to safeguard his position where a superior residuary heir is present or where the portions of other Qur'anic heirs would exhaust the estate. Furthermore, in addition to his rights as a Qur'anic heir, he retains his character as a residuary in the presence of a daughter so that he is entitled to any residue available. It therefore seems eminently logical that he should inherit as a residuary in the present case where it is to his advantage.

7.1.2. The Syrian variation

To the provisions of the Egyptian legislation, which it adopts *in toto*, the Syrian Law of Personal Status, 1953, adds a unique proviso – namely, that *wherever* it is to his advantage the grandfather "shall be regarded as a quota-sharer with a share of one-third".[1] The far-reaching effect of this extension of Zaid's advantage rule to cover cases in which other heirs are present in addition to the grandfather and the collaterals is obvious. In a great number of instances the grandfather will receive double the share in the inheritance that he would obtain under either of the traditional systems.

7.1.3. Illustrations of modern variations

A hypothetical case will serve to summarise the effect of these novel elements superimposed upon 'Alī's doctrine by the Egyptian and Syrian legislation.

In competition with the praepositus' wife, daughter, germane sister and consanguine sister, the grandfather will:

(*a*) under 'Alī's doctrine take his Qur'anic portion;

[1] J. N. D. Anderson, "The Syrian Law of Personal Status", *Bulletin of the School of Oriental and African Studies*, vol. XVII, no. 1, 1955, p. 48.

(*b*) under Zaid's doctrine take as a residuary with the consanguine sister counting against him in the distribution on the "Computation" principle;

(*c*) under the Egyptian Law take as a residuary without the "Computation" principle applying;

(*d*) under the Syrian Law take one-third as a quota-sharer.

Leaving aside the intermediate arithmetical calculations, the final distribution of the estate, expressed in parts of $\frac{1}{48}$, will be as follows:

	'Alī	Zaid	Egyptian Law	Syrian Law
Wife	6	6	6	6
Daughter	24	24	24	24
Germane sister	10	9	6	2
Consanguine sister	0	0	0	0
Grandfather	8	9	12	16

7.2. Iraq

In Iraq the Ḥanafī system of intestate succession as a whole is no longer applicable. Unification of the law on a national basis presented particular problems in a country whose population is approximately evenly divided between the Ḥanafī school and the Ithnā 'Asharī branch of the Shī'a; and the Law of Personal Status, 1959, adopted a "neutral" system of succession which owed nothing to traditional Sharī'a law and under which, in fact, any brother or sister of the praepositus totally excluded the grandfather.[1] But this system was short-lived, for it was abolished by a Law of February 1963, which laid down a basic order of priorities identical with that of Shī'ī law. Under this statutory order of priorities the grandfather and all collaterals belong to Class II and will be totally excluded by any parent or lineal descendant. But, as has been observed (p. 141 above), within each class of heirs the courts in Sunnī cases determine priorities and distribution upon traditional Ḥanafī principles. It seems, therefore, that the traditional Ḥanafī principle that the grandfather excludes all collaterals must continue to apply to the Sunnī population of Iraq.

8. The outer family

Apart from those particular reforms which have greatly improved the position of daughters' children of the praepositus – the system of obligatory

[1] J. N. D. Anderson, "A Law of Personal Status for Iraq", *The International and Comparative Law Quarterly*, October 1960, pp. 559ff.

bequests in Egypt and Tunisia, and the rule of representational succession in Pakistan – the major change in this sphere of the law has taken place in Iraq.

8.1. Iraq

Because the statutory order of priorities of the Law of 1963 covers all relatives, the traditional Ḥanafī law has ceased to apply to the estates of Sunnī Iraqi Muslims, insofar as the claims of the outer family will no longer be wholly deferred to those of any member of the inner family. Although the effect of the interpretation of the law adopted by the Sunnī courts is that within each class of heirs any relative of the traditional inner family will exclude any relative of the outer family, nevertheless, where the only representative of one class is a member of the outer family, he or she must now totally exclude any member of a lower class. A daughter's child, for example, will exclude a germane brother, and a uterine sister's daughter will exclude an agnatic uncle or cousin.

It is noteworthy, however, that where no member of the inner family survives, the order of priorities and mode of distribution among relatives of the outer family under the Law of 1963 (as interpreted by the Sunnī courts) will be precisely the same as under the Ḥanafī system of *qarāba*. Lineal descendants (Class I) will exclude ascendants (Class II), who in turn will exclude descendants of the parents (Class II), who in turn will exclude descendants of the grandparents (Class III).

8.2. Egypt and Syria

Further minor changes in the traditional law of succession by the outer family have taken place in Egypt and Syria. In Ḥanafī jurisdictions generally the courts have consistently favoured the *per stirpes* doctrine of Shaybānī as opposed to the *per capita* doctrine of Abū Yūsuf, and this is still the case in India and Pakistan. But the Egyptian Law of Inheritance, 1943, and the Syrian Law of Personal Status, 1953, provided that the doctrine of Abū Yūsuf should henceforth be applied. These two laws, however, embody one variation from the generally accepted doctrine of Abū Yūsuf. This concerns the system of priorities applying to relatives of Class IV – the issue of uncles and aunts of the praepositus.

Here, according to the classical version of Abū Yūsuf's view, the rule of the strength of blood-tie – that germanes exclude consanguines who in turn exclude uterines – applies before the rule that the children of male agnates exclude others. But under the Egyptian and Syrian Laws the rule that children of male agnates exclude others is applied before the rule of the strength of blood-tie, just as is the case where the heirs are the issue of nephews and nieces of the praepositus. Thus, in a competition between the daughter of a germane paternal aunt and the daughter of a consanguine paternal uncle, the latter alone will now succeed, whereas under the classical version of Abū Yūsuf's doctrine she would be excluded by the former.

10. DUAL RELATIONSHIPS

The coincidence of both a paternal and a maternal connection between relatives is a not uncommon feature of Islamic society. It arises from a variety of factors – from the institution of polygamy, the frequency of divorce and remarriage of divorcees, and particularly, in the context of traditional society, from marriages within the closely knit family group. Lines of paternal and maternal relatives may be linked, for example, by the marriage of cousins, or the marriage of a woman with the brother of her former husband, or the marriage of a man with the stepdaughter of his mother or his father. Succession law is therefore naturally concerned to regulate the effect of such a dual relationship with the praepositus, which may occur either in a relative of the inner family or, in an inevitably greater number of instances, in a relative of the outer family.

1. The rule of succession in a dual role

The basic principle, common to all versions of Sharī'a law, is that each aspect of a dual relationship constitutes a separate and individual title for the purposes of succession. The relative concerned may therefore succeed under both titles in appropriate circumstances – i.e. where he or she is not excluded in one title by the other title or by other heirs competing.

Because of the fundamentally different rules of priority obtaining under Sunnī and Shī'ī law, the effect of the application of this basic principle varies in the two systems. The illustrations of the rule which follow are based on the Sunnī classification of heirs with the solution of Shī'ī law being noted in each case.

1.1. Relatives of the inner family.

There are three principle instances of succession in a dual title by relatives of the inner family.

1.1.1. Spouse and blood relative

Cousins are not within the prohibited degrees of marriage. A husband, therefore, who is the son of his wife's germane or consanguine paternal uncle, may be as such her nearest agnatic heir. A wife who is the cousin of her husband can never be his agnatic heir, although she may be entitled to succeed under the rules applicable to relatives of the outer family in the absence of any other Qur'anic or agnatic heir.

1.1.2. Agnatic and uterine relative

There is no bar to marriage between a divorced or widowed woman and the brother of her former husband. Where a woman does so marry the germane or consanguine brother of her former husband, the male children of the second union are at once the uterine brothers and the agnatic cousins of the children of the first union.

1.1.2.1. The rule illustrated

The effect of both the above types of dual relationship may be illustrated by the following hypothetical case:

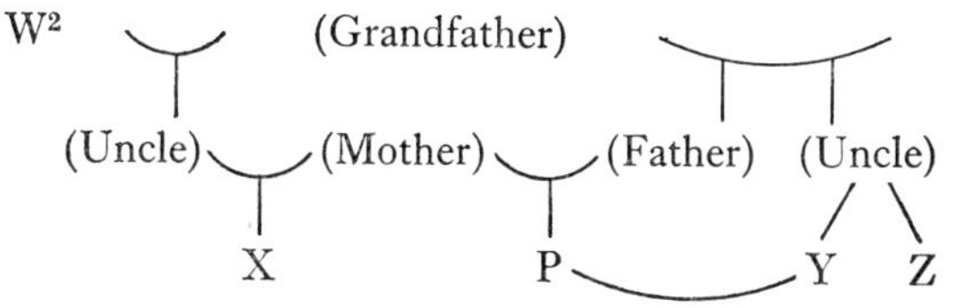

The paternal grandfather of the deceased woman P had three sons, two by his wife W¹ and one by his other wife, W². After the death of P's father, P's mother married his consanguine brother. P's sole surviving relatives are her three agnatic cousins X, Y and Z. X is her consanguine paternal uncle's son and at the same time her uterine brother; Y is her husband and her germane paternal uncle's son; Z is her germane paternal uncle's other son.

X and Y will therefore be entitled to the Qur'anic portions of a uterine brother and husband respectively. X, Y and Z are all agnatic relatives of equal degree, but the strength of blood-tie rule – that the full blood is superior to the half blood – will operate to exclude X, so that Y and Z will each be entitled to a moiety of the residue. Accordingly, distribution of the estate will be:

X	(Qur'anic)	$\frac{1}{6}$
Y	$\frac{1}{2}$ (Qur'anic) + $\frac{1}{6}$ ($\frac{1}{2}$ of residue)	$\frac{4}{6}$
Z	$\frac{1}{2}$ of residue	$\frac{1}{6}$

1.1.2.2. Shī'ī law

A uterine brother excludes any cousin of the praepositus. Z is therefore totally excluded. Y takes one-half as a husband but is excluded as a cousin. X takes one-sixth as a uterine brother and the residue of the estate by *radd*.

1.1.3. Paternal and maternal grandmother

Where the praepositus is the child of a marriage between cousins, his maternal great grandmother (his mother's mother's mother) will also be his paternal great grandmother (either his father's father's mother or his father's mother's mother). Such a grandmother may be, under Ḥanafī, Shāfi'ī, Ḥanbalī and Shī'ī law, in competition with another paternal grandmother of equal degree.[1] The question therefore arises whether she benefits from this dual connection and, being entitled both as a paternal and maternal grandmother, takes twice as much of the grandmothers' portion as her competitor.

Ḥanafī and Shāfi'ī law answer this question in the negative. A grandmother who is connected with the deceased through both his father and mother cannot claim to inherit on both accounts any more than a germane brother of the deceased can claim to inherit under the two titles of a consanguine and a uterine brother.

1.1.3.1. Ḥanbalī law

The Ḥanbalīs argue, however, that some advantage must always derive from the coincidence of a paternal and maternal connection.[2] It results either in a priority of entitlement – as germane brothers or sisters have priority over consanguines – or in succession in a dual role – as where a person is at once the cousin and uterine brother of the deceased. Since, therefore, a grandmother connected on both the paternal and maternal sides has no priority as such over a grandmother connected on one side only, she is entitled to claim a grandmother's share in both respects.

1.1.3.2. Shī'ī law

Shī'ī law recognises the right of a grandmother connected on both sides to succeed under both titles. Accordingly, where she is in competition with another paternal great grandmother, the rule of allotting two-thirds

[1] Such a competition cannot arise under Mālikī law, where only one paternal grandmother can be an entitled heir – the father's mother or direct female ascendant thereof (p. 61 above).

[2] The Ḥanafī jurist Shaybānī also subscribed to this view, which does seem to have the greater logical appeal.

to paternal and one-third to maternal grandparents will apply. The paternal great grandmother will take one-third of the estate and the grandmother connected on both sides two-thirds (one-third as one of two competing paternal grandmothers, and one-third as the sole maternal grandmother).

1.2. Relatives of the outer family

As has been observed, succession by these relatives is a matter of considerable controversy. Under Mālikī law they have no rights of inheritance. Under Shāfi'ī and Ḥanbalī law they succeed on the principle of representation (*tanzīl*). Ḥanafī law adopts the principle of relationship (*qarāba*) as applied by the two variant doctrines of Abū Yūsuf and Shaybānī respectively. Shī'ī law integrates these relatives within its general scheme of priorities. While the varying results of these different doctrines will be noted, the following illustrations of the incidence of a dual relationship are based upon the Ḥanafī method of dividing such relatives into four classes, within each of which there may be relatives who succeed in a dual title.

1.2.1. Descendants

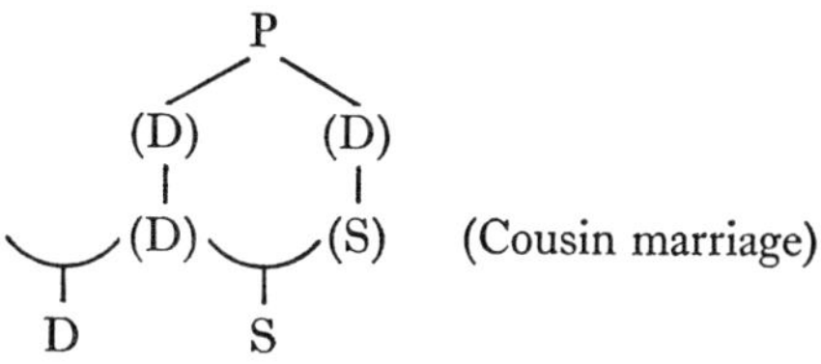

S = Son, D = Daughter.

Here the two great grandchildren are uterine brother and sister, the children of successive marriages on the part of their mother. D succeeds as a daughter's daughter's daughter, S as both a daughter's daughter's son and a daughter's son's son.

1.2.1.1. Abū Yūsuf

Per capita principle. D: 1/5, S: 4/5.

1.2.1.2. Shaybānī

Distribution *per stirpes*, intermediate granddaughter taking two shares because there are two claimants through her.

D: 1/6 (1/3 × 1/2), S: 5/6 (2/3 × 1/2 = 2/6 + 1/2).

1.2.1.3. *Tanzīl*

Share of each daughter (one-half) distributed among claimants through her, double share to the male in Shāfi'ī but not in Ḥanbalī law.

D: $1/6$ $(1/3 \times 1/2)$, S: $5/6$ $(2/3 \times 1/2 = 2/6 + 1/2)$.

1.2.1.4. Shī'ī law

Precisely the same principles as under *tanzīl*. D: $1/6$, S: $5/6$.

1.2.2. Ascendants

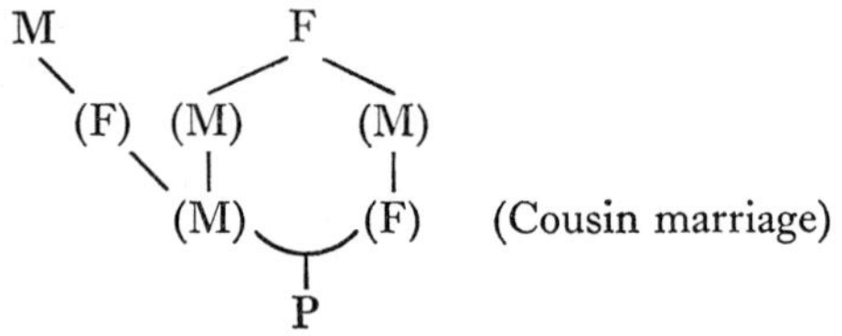

F = Father, M = Mother.

F is entitled to succeed both as a paternal and a maternal great grandfather.

1.2.2.1. Abū Yūsuf and Shaybānī

Under either title F, as the father of a Qur'anic heir, totally excludes M. Ḥanafī jurists who deny such priority (p. 99, n. 1) would distribute:

M: $1/9$ $(1/3 \times 1/3)$. F: $8/9$ $(2/3 \times 1/3 = 2/9 + 2/3)$.

1.2.2.2. *Tanzīl*

Under either title F is nearer to the ordinary heir he represents (the mother's mother or father's mother) than M, who is therefore totally excluded from succession.

1.2.2.3. Shī'ī law

Maternal grandparents share equally in one-third and paternal grandparents share two-thirds, double share to males.

M: $1/6$ $(1/2 \times 1/3)$, F: $5/6$ $(1/2 \times 1/3 = 1/6 + 2/3)$.

1.2.3. Nephews and nieces

There is, of course, no bar to marriage between a person's consanguine brother and his uterine sister, since they are the children of totally different unions. In the following case, where P is survived by his three nieces, Y is both a maternal and paternal relative of P.

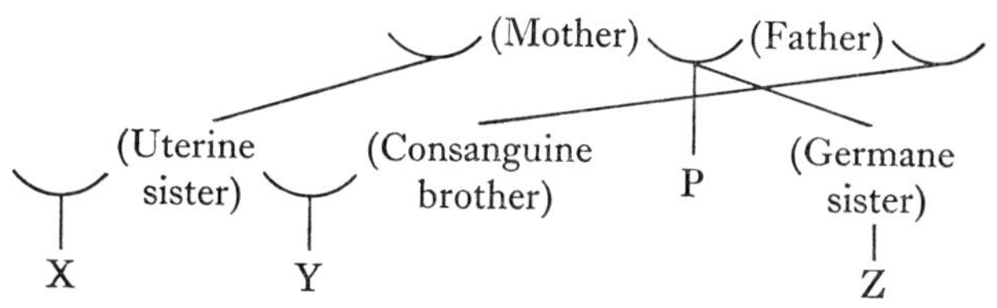

1.2.3.1. Abū Yūsuf

By virtue of the strength of blood-tie rule Z, as the child of a germane collateral, excludes both X and Y as the children of uterine and consanguine collaterals.

1.2.3.2. Shaybānī

Under his *per stirpes* principle the notional distribution is between a germane sister, a consanguine brother and two uterine sisters. Y then takes half of her mother's notional Qur'anic portion and the notional residual share of her father. X: 1/6, Y: 1/6+1/6, Z: 3/6.

1.2.3.3. *Tanzīl*

Z takes the germane sister's share, X and Y divide between them the uterine sister's share, and Y takes the residue as the representative of the consanguine brother. X: 1/12, Y: 1/12+4/12, Z: 6/12.

1.2.3.4. Shī'ī law

Under the principle of representation Y, as the representative of the consanguine brother, will be excluded by Z, who represents the germane sister. The uterine sister's portion will be divided between her daughters, and the germane sister's daughter will take a portion of one-half and the surplus of the estate by *radd.* X: 1/12, Y: 1/12, Z: 10/12.

If, in this illustration, Y was the daughter of a marriage between the consanguine sister of the praepositus and his uterine brother, the distribution of the estate would be precisely the same under Shī'ī law. According to Abū Yūsuf, Z would again exclude X and Y because of his rule that the children of sisters of the full blood exclude the children of sisters and brothers of the half blood. Under Abū Yūsuf's doctrine, therefore, relatives of this class can never succeed under both of two titles. According to Shaybānī, and under the doctrine of *tanzīl*, Y would inherit under both titles. Apportionment by *tanzīl* would be as between a germane sister (three-fifths), a consanguine sister (one-fifth) and a uterine brother (one-fifth) – i.e. Qur'anic entitlement increased by *radd* – and their shares would then go to their respective issue. Thus:

X: 1/10, Y: 1/10+2/10, Z: 6/10.

Shaybānī, notionally counting two uterine brothers, would distribute:

X: 1/6, Y: 1/6+1/6, Z: 3/6

1.2.4. Uncles, aunts and cousins

An uncle or aunt of the praepositus will be connected on both the paternal and maternal sides when such uncle or aunt is the child of a marriage between the praepositus' maternal grandmother and paternal grandfather. In the following case Y is the germane maternal aunt of the praepositus. Z is at once his uterine maternal aunt and his consanguine paternal aunt.

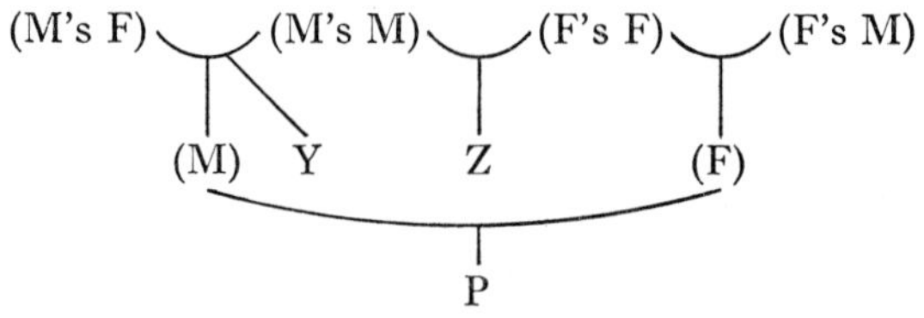

1.2.4.1. Abū Yūsuf and Shaybānī

Z inherits under her paternal title only. In her maternal title she is, as an aunt of the half blood, excluded by Y, an aunt of the full blood. Y: 1/3. Z: 2/3.

1.2.4.2. *Tanzīl*

Z takes two-thirds as the sole representative of the praepositus' father. Y and Z inherit the mother's portion of one-third as a germane sister and a uterine sister respectively.

Y: 1/4 (3/4 × 1/3), Z: 3/4 (2/3 + 1/12 (1/4 × 1/3)).

1.2.4.3. Shī'ī law

The same principles of representational succession apply, but Z is restricted to a share of one-sixth of the mother's one-third, being, as a uterine sister, excluded from *radd* by the germane sister.

Y: 5/18 (5/6 × 1/3), Z: 13/18 (1/18 (1/6 × 1/3) + 2/3).

Under Shī'ī law, which accords no priority to male agnate relatives as such, there is obviously a greater possibility of succession in a dual title by uncles of the praepositus than there is under Sunnī law. If, for example, Z in the above illustration were a male (the consanguine paternal uncle and uterine maternal uncle of P), the distribution of the estate would be exactly the same in Shī'ī law. But in Sunnī law Z would be the sole heir as a member of the inner family.

2. Modern law in Egypt

One limited modification of the traditional Sharī'a law in this regard is contained in the Egyptian Law of Inheritance, 1943. Under this law succession in a dual title by relatives of the outer family is confined to those who are both paternal and maternal relatives of the praepositus. This provision, therefore, directly affects only the class of descendants, who now may not succeed in a dual title.[1] But this same Egyptian Law, as has been noted (p. 162 above), regulates succession by relatives of the outer family according to the doctrine of Abū Yūsuf, under which the issue of the praepositus' brothers and sisters can never inherit by a dual title (p. 169 above). It is only, therefore, in the two classes of (*a*) ascendants, and (*b*) uncles and aunts and their issue, that a dual relationship will now give rise in Egypt to succession in a dual title.

[1] Certain traditional authorities state that Abū Yūsuf did not allow *any* relative of the outer family to succeed in a dual title. The Egyptian Law applies this alleged variant view to the class of descendants and the normal Ḥanafī doctrine to all other classes.

11. IMPEDIMENTS TO INHERITANCE

In its strict technical sense an impediment to inheritance is a personal act or attribute which disqualifies from succession an individual who would otherwise be an entitled heir on the ground of either marriage or blood relationship with the praepositus. Three such causes of disqualification are recognised by contemporary Islamic law – homicide of the praepositus by the heir, a difference of religion between the heir and the praepositus, and a difference of domicile between the heir and the praepositus.

1. Slavery

Under traditional Sharī'a law the status of slavery constituted a further impediment to inheritance, since the slave, as a general rule, was not capable of owning property. But the rule clearly has no practical relevance today, and for this reason was omitted from the bars to succession listed in the Egyptian Law of Inheritance, 1943. It is noteworthy, however, that the relevant section of that law begins with the words: "Among the impediments to inheritance are..."; and this form of words, according to the Explanatory Memorandum to the law, was deliberately used to indicate that the terms of the section were not exhaustive, "lest it might be thought that the purpose of the omission [of slavery as an impediment] was to change a rule of the Sharī'a which was the subject of a consensus of all Muslims".

2. Illegitimacy

Although there are no mutual rights of inheritance between a father and his illegitimate child, illegitimacy is not, technically, an impediment to inheritance in the same way as homicide or difference of religion. The blood relationship, or *nasab*, which grounds a right of inheritance, must be a legal relationship; and since there is no legal tie of *nasab* between a father and his illegitimate child, or between their respective "legal" relatives, the root cause of inheritance simply does not exist. Just as the partners in an invalid marriage are not "husband" and "wife", so a person and his illegitimate offspring are not "father" and "child" for the purposes of inheritance. This chapter, however, seems to be the most appropriate point at which to deal with the law relating to the illegitimate person, both as a claimant heir and as the praepositus.

2.1. Disqualified heirs are totally ignored

Spouses or blood relatives debarred from inheritance by reason of an impediment do not adversely affect the position of other surviving relatives in any way, neither excluding them nor restricting their shares. For all practical purposes of succession disqualified relatives are nonexistent in the eyes of the law. Disqualification by impediment, therefore, differs from exclusion under the system of priorities since relatives who are themselves excluded from inheritance may nevertheless partially or totally exclude others. The obvious example is the case of agnatic brothers who restrict the mother's Qur'anic portion to one-sixth even when they themselves are excluded by the father of the deceased. If the brothers, on the other hand, were disqualified from succession because, say, of their difference of religion with the praepositus, they would not so restrict the mother.[1]

2.2. Inheritance by illegitimate persons

2.2.1. Sunnī law

Under Shī'ī law the illegitimate child has no legal relationship with either its father or its mother. No mutual rights of inheritance therefore exist between an illegitimate person and his or her parents, nor between the issue of the illegitimate person and the blood relatives of either the father or the mother.

Sunnī law, on the other hand, while accepting that there is no ground for inheritance between an illegitimate person and his or her father, or between their respective blood relatives, does recognise the existence of a legal relationship between an illegitimate child and its mother for all purposes. An illegitimate person may therefore inherit from his mother, from her children, legitimate or illegitimate, as a uterine brother and, in appropriate circumstances, from her other relatives as a member of the outer family.

[1] An exception to this settled principle of traditional Sharī'a law is contained in article 392 of the current Civil Code of Iran, which provides that the mother's share is restricted by brothers who are disqualified because they have caused the death of the praepositus, though not by brothers disqualified because of their difference of religion with the praepositus. It has been explained (p. 116 above) that in Shī'ī law the restriction of the mother by the brothers is seen as a rule designed for their ultimate benefit, inasmuch as they will subsequently inherit from the father whose share is increased by this rule and in the absence of whom the rule does not apply. Presumably the reasoning behind the provision of the Iranian Code is that the brothers will still eventually inherit from the father despite their killing of the present praepositus (assuming the offence not to be a capital one), whereas their difference of religion will disqualify them from eventual inheritance from the father.

2.2.2. Indian case law

Decisions of the Indian courts appear somewhat inconsistent in this regard. For example, in the Calcutta case of *Bafatun* v. *Bilaiti Khanum* (1903), 30 Cal. 683, an illegitimate person inherited half the estate of his mother's sister, a Ḥanafī woman whose only other surviving relative was her husband. On the other hand, in the Allahabad case of *Rahmatullah* v. *Maqsood Ahmad*, 1950 I.L.R. All. 713, an illegitimate person was not regarded, for purposes of inheritance, as the uterine brother of his mother's legitimate son.

2.3. Inheritance from illegitimate persons

2.3.1. General Sunnī law: maternal relatives take on normal principles

Where the praepositus is an illegitimate person there is a divergence of view in Sunnī law as regards the rights of inheritance of the maternal relatives. According to the majority – the Mālikī, Ḥanafī and Shāfi'ī schools – the mother and her relatives inherit upon normal principles. Subject to the rules of total or partial exclusion, the mother herself, her own mother and her children (the uterine brothers or sisters of the praepositus) will succeed as Qur'anic heirs, while her other relatives will inherit only as members of the praepositus' outer family. Thus, an illegitimate person who is not survived by his own son or son's son will have no agnatic residuary heirs.

2.3.2. Ḥanbalī law: residual succession by maternal relatives

Ḥanbalī law, on the other hand, holds that the male agnate relatives of the mother are to be considered, for purposes of succession, as the male agnate relatives of her illegitimate child, on the ground that these relatives shoulder the burden of responsibility for the tortious actions of the illegitimate child which entail the payment of compensation and are therefore entitled, in return, to rights of succession.[1] The mother's male agnate relatives will, of course, be excluded by any true male agnate of the illegitimate praepositus himself – i.e. a son or son's son how low soever – but will otherwise succeed as his residuary heirs. The application and effect of this Ḥanbalī rule may be illustrated by the following hypothetical cases.

[1] A variant Ḥanbalī view, though of weak authority, is that the mother herself is a residuary heir of her illegitimate child, and as such excludes from succession all her own male relatives.

2.3.3. Illustrations

(*a*) Illegitimate praepositus survived by:

	Germane maternal aunt	Consanguine maternal aunt	Consanguine maternal uncle
Mālikīs	—	—	—
Ḥanafīs	All	—	—
Shāfiʿīs	$\frac{1}{2}$	$\frac{1}{4}$	$\frac{1}{4}$
Ḥanbalīs	—	—	All

In Mālikī law these three relatives of the outer family are excluded from succession in favour of the Public Treasury; in Ḥanafī law the normal rules of *qarāba*, and in Shāfiʿī law the normal rules of *tanzīl*, apply, but in Ḥanbalī law the mother's brother ranks as a residuary heir and totally excludes the mother's sisters. Residual succession is therefore strictly confined to the mother's *male* relatives, and the brother does not here turn his sister into a residuary heir.

(*b*) Illegitimate praepositus survived by:

	Mother's father	Mother	Uterine sister	Uterine brother
Mālikīs	—	$\frac{1}{6}$	$\frac{1}{6}$	$\frac{1}{6}$
Ḥanafīs	—	$\frac{1}{3}$	$\frac{1}{3}$	$\frac{1}{3}$
Shāfiʿīs	—	$\frac{1}{3}$	$\frac{1}{3}$	$\frac{1}{3}$
Ḥanbalīs	—	$\frac{1}{6}$	$\frac{1}{6}$	$\frac{4}{6}$

After satisfaction of the Qur'anic portions of the mother, uterine brother and sister, the residue goes: in Mālikī law to the Public Treasury; in Ḥanafī and Shāfiʿī law to the Qur'anic heirs by way of *radd*; in Ḥanbalī law to the uterine brother as residuary heir. Although the mother's father is, in Ḥanbalī law, potentially a residuary heir, he is here excluded by a superior residuary heir – the mother's son. And it is because the rights of the mother's relatives in no way interfere with normal succession by the true Qur'anic heirs, but only attach to the residue left after the deduction of the Qur'anic portions, that the uterine brother here inherits in a dual capacity.

(*c*) Illegitimate praepositus survived by:

	Mother	Daughter	Uterine brother	
Mālikīs	$\frac{1}{6}$	$\frac{1}{2}$	—	(Residue to Treasury)
Ḥanafīs	$\frac{1}{4}$	$\frac{3}{4}$	—	(Shares increased
Shāfiʿīs	$\frac{1}{4}$	$\frac{3}{4}$	—	by *radd*)
Ḥanbalīs	$\frac{1}{6}$	$\frac{1}{2}$	$\frac{1}{3}$	(Residue)

Under Ḥanbalī law a daughter, or son's daughter, of the illegitimate praepositus will not exclude the mother's male relatives from succeeding to any residue. This must therefore represent the only occasion in Islamic law when a uterine brother will inherit along with the daughter of the praepositus.

3. Homicide

All schools of Islamic law accept the general principle that a killer does not inherit from his victim, for the obvious reason, as expressed by the Shāfi'ī jurist al-Ramlī (*Nihāyat al-Muḥtāj*, v, 23), that "the public interest requires that the killer be debarred from inheritance since, if he did inherit, killing would accelerate inheritance and lead to universal chaos". There is, however, considerable divergence among the schools as to the precise circumstances in which homicide does constitute a bar to inheritance, and it is therefore necessary to begin with a brief account of the nature of the offence of homicide in traditional Sharī'a law.

3.1. General: classification of homicides

In traditional Sharī'a law homicide is essentially a private wrong or tort rather than a public wrong or crime. Homicide is a crime in the technical sense that the State prosecutes the offence and exacts the punishment therefor in a limited number of cases – where, for example, it is committed in the course of highway robbery or in furtherance of other crimes such as rape or theft. But generally it is a tort inasmuch as it is the right of the victim's family to decide whether to prosecute or not and, in the event of a successful prosecution, to determine the penalty. They may, in cases of deliberate homicide, insist upon the death penalty by way of retaliation (*qiṣāṣ*), or they may opt to take blood-money (*diyya*), or they may pardon the offender altogether, although in this last event the State reserves a power of discretionary punishment of the offender. In cases of accidental homicide the only remedy available to the victim's relatives is the exaction of blood-money.

3.1.1. Actionable and non-actionable homicide

As an actionable offence homicide does not necessarily involve any element of intent to kill. Nor, indeed, does it necessarily involve any degree of culpability through negligence, since the basic purpose of the law is to recompense the tribe or family of the victim for the loss of one of its members. The law here comes very close to the notion of absolute liability, inasmuch as a person will generally be held responsible for a death caused directly by his act, however involuntary or innocent such act may be.

Cases of non-actionable homicide are therefore rare and broadly confined to circumstances where the homicide results from the exercise of a definite legal right or duty. Four principal categories of homicides which do not constitute a legal offence may be distinguished.

(*a*) The execution of a lawful sentence of death.

(*b*) The killing of an outlaw, i.e. a person who is not legally protected, such as an apostate from Islam, a rebel or a heretic.

(*c*) Killing in the legitimate exercise of the right of self defence. Homicide is regarded as justifiable where it is the only means by which a person may protect himself or his property, or the person or property of someone else, from an unlawful attack.

(*d*) Death resulting from a *bona fide* act intended to benefit the health of the deceased and performed at his request, such as "the administering of medicine...or the lancing of an abscess or the removal of a leech" (*al-Mughnī*, VI, 292).

3.1.2. Deliberate and accidental homicide

The actual presence or absence in the mind of the accused of a deliberate intent to kill is, of course, a matter known only by the accused himself. A court can only infer the intent of the accused from his external conduct or from his own or others' testimony as to his state of mind. Moreover, the particular question arises in cases of homicide as to whether the accused should be held responsible for a deliberate killing when the court is prepared to ascribe to him the intention to hurt or to wound, but not to kill, his victim. These principal difficulties led to a divergence of view among the different schools as to the circumstances in which a homicide should be classified as deliberate. The classification is primarily related to the sanction for the offence, only the deliberate killer being liable to the death penalty by way of retaliation; but it is also directly relevant in Mālikī and Shī'ī law to the question of the killer's right of inheritance.

3.1.2.1. Mālikī law

In Mālikī law a person is guilty of deliberate homicide if he causes the death of another by any intentional act or omission, directed against a human being, which is either hostile or intrinsically likely to kill. This is the widest definition of deliberate homicide in traditional Sharī'a law, since it includes death caused by any potentially lethal conduct, however innocent the intention, and death caused by any behaviour which is hostile, however unlikely it is that such behaviour will cause death.

3.1.2.2. Shīʿī law

Under Shīʿī law a person is guilty of deliberate homicide if he causes the death of another by deliberately acting towards him in a way which is intrinsically likely to kill, or in a hostile manner which would not normally cause death, provided, in this latter circumstance, there is acceptable evidence that he intended to kill. If, therefore, a person throws a pebble at someone else, intending only to hurt but in fact killing him, he will be guilty of deliberate homicide under Mālikī, but not under Shīʿī, law.

3.1.2.3. General Sunnī law

Under Ḥanafī, Ḥanbalī and Shāfiʿī law the presence or absence of homicidal intent is determined exclusively by the means used to kill. Only where the act or omission is deliberately directed against a human being and is intrinsically likely to kill will it constitute deliberate homicide. Where the deliberate act is not such as normally results in death, the offence is classified as "quasi deliberate" homicide and the offender is not subject to the death penalty.

Outside such limits an actionable homicide is broadly classified as accidental, although Sunnī jurisprudence generally distinguishes several different types of accidental homicide. Homicide through "mistake in the purpose", for example, arises when a person shoots at and kills something which he believes to be an animal but which is in fact a human being. An instance of homicide through "mistake in the performance" is when a person shoots at a target but misses and kills someone. In both these cases, of course, the act is deliberate and intrinsically likely to kill, but it is not directed against a human being. If it were and someone other than the intended victim were killed, either through mistaken identity or inaccurate shooting, it would be a case of deliberate homicide.

Where the act which causes death is wholly involuntary and therefore involves no mistake in its purpose or performance, the homicide is classified as "quasi accidental". This is the case, for example, if a person falls from a height upon another person and kills him, or if a driver loses control of his vehicle through mechanical failure and kills a pedestrian.

3.1.2.4. Minors and lunatics

Within the above definitions a minor or a lunatic may be guilty of deliberate homicide, but because they are not legally capable of forming a criminal intent they are not subject to the death penalty. There is the same strict illogicality here as in the "guilty but insane" verdict of English criminal law. Following the normal principals of tort, however, liability to pay blood-money is incurred when any actionable homicide is committed by a minor or a lunatic.

3.1.3. Direct and indirect homicide

All schools of Islamic law except the Mālikīs draw a distinction between a direct killing (*qatl bi'l-mubāshara*) and an indirect killing (*qatl bi'l-tasbīb*). This classification is based on a theory of causation which cuts right across the two previous classifications inasmuch as any homicide, actionable or non-actionable, deliberate or accidental, may be either direct or indirect. Cases of direct homicide are strictly confined to death caused directly and exclusively by the killer's physical assault upon his victim, with or without a weapon, e.g. by strangulation, stabbing or beating to death. Outside these narrow limits a homicide is classified as indirect whenever there intervenes between the act of the killer and the death of the victim any other contributory cause of death. Among the many instances of indirect but deliberate homicide cited, for example, by the authoritative Shīʿī text, *Sharāʿi al-Islām*,[1] are the following.

(*a*) Where the killer uses a mechanical means of attack, such as "an arrow shot from a bow or a stone from a catapult".

(*b*) Where the killer's assault is not in itself the ultimate cause of death, as where the victim is thrown into a fire and burns to death, or is thrown into water and drowns, or is incarcerated and dies from starvation.

(*c*) Where the behaviour of the victim is a contributory cause of his death, as where he consumes poisoned food or falls into a death trap prepared by the killer.

(*d*) Where the killer contrives the death of his victim by hiring an assassin or setting a vicious dog upon him.

(*e*) Where the killer gives false testimony in court against his intended victim which results in the latter's conviction and execution.

[1] See the French translation of A. Querry, under the title *Droit Musulman* (Paris, 1872), II, 542ff.

3.2. Homicide as a bar to inheritance

3.2.1. Shāfi'ī law

In Shāfi'ī law the principle that the killer does not inherit from his victim is of absolute application and covers every case of homicide from wilful murder to lawful execution. A person does not inherit from one whose death he has caused simply because he has unnaturally accelerated the process of succession. Hence, in the Shāfi'ī view, such considerations as legal responsibility for homicide, criminal intent and causation have no relevance in this context.

3.2.2. Ḥanbalī law

In Ḥanbalī law any actionable homicide, deliberate or accidental, direct or indirect, raises the bar to inheritance. The reason why non-actionable homicide (e.g. lawful execution or killing in self defence) does not constitute an impediment is explained by Ibn Qudāma (*al-Mughnī*, VI, 293) as follows:

> Inheritance is prohibited to avoid encouraging unlawful killing and to deter people from taking the lives of protected persons. It would be contrary to this basic purpose to prohibit inheritance in these cases [of non-actionable homicide], for this would hinder the application of necessary penalties and the exercise of legal rights, while the absence of a bar to inheritance in these cases in no way encourages unlawful homicide.

3.2.3. Ḥanafī law

Ḥanafī law rests firmly upon the criterion of causation in homicide and holds that only a direct, unlawful killing of the praepositus by the heir is a bar to inheritance. A direct killing may, of course, be deliberate or accidental, although the incidence of the latter must be rare because of the strict definition of direct homicide. Minors and lunatics, however, are not debarred from inheriting from a praepositus whom they have killed directly. This exception is commonly said to rest upon the ground that there is no "sin" or "guilt" in a homicide committed by a minor or a lunatic. But there is equally no sin or guilt in a purely accidental, though direct, homicide committed by a sane adult, and he is denied the right to inherit from the victim. A contemporary Egyptian jurist, 'Umar Abdallāh, attempts to explain the exception by regarding minors and lunatics as a special category of persons outside the ambit of the general law.

> The impediment to inheritance is a punishment for a killing which is legally forbidden. But it is not technically correct to describe the acts of minors or

lunatics as legally forbidden, for these persons are not subject to the law inasmuch as the commands and prohibitions of the Law-giver are not addressed to them.[1]

The fact remains, however, that a homicide committed by a minor or a lunatic is an actionable or unlawful homicide, often equated in other spheres of the law to accidental homicide and sanctioned, like the latter, by the payment of blood-money. The exemption, therefore, of minors and lunatics from the bar to inheritance on the ground that they have no guilty or criminal intent is strictly inconsistent with the general Ḥanafī criterion of causation in this regard.

3.2.4. Mālikī law

Under Mālikī law the bar to inheritance is raised by any actionable homicide which is deliberate within the broad Mālikī definition of this term. Somewhat illogically, minors and lunatics are also barred from inheritance when they have committed deliberate homicide, although they are not liable to the penalty of retaliation because of the lack of any criminal intent.

Accidental homicide does not constitute an impediment to succession but the killer does not inherit any part of the blood-money which is payable in respect of the death and which forms part of the victim's estate.

> P is killed accidentally by his brother Zaid. He is survived by a second brother, 'Umar, and by his mother. Of the general estate of P, the mother takes a Qur'anic portion of one-sixth (due to the presence of two brothers), and Zaid and 'Umar share the residue equally. Of the blood-money the mother takes a Qur'anic portion of one-third (following the principle that an heir who is debarred from inheritance is ignored, there is only one brother, 'Umar, competing with the mother) and 'Umar takes the residue.

3.2.5. Shī'ī law

Shī'ī law consistently bases the bar to inheritance upon the presence of criminal intent. Only a deliberate homicide, according to the Shī'ī definition of that term, constitutes an impediment, and minors and lunatics cannot be held guilty of deliberate homicide under Shī'ī law because the necessary criminal intent cannot be ascribed to them. As in Mālikī law, the accidental killer is debarred from inheriting any share of the blood-money.

[1] 'Umar Abdallāh, *Aḥkām al-Mawārīth fi'l-Sharī'a al-Islāmiyya* (3rd ed., Alexandria, 1960), p. 81.

3.3. Modern law

3.3.1. Egypt and Syria

The traditional Islamic law of homicide, based upon the notion of the offence as a private wrong within the context of a tribal society, was clearly unsuited to the developing social and political order of the emergent modern Muslim states, and during the latter part of the nineteenth century jurisdiction in cases of homicide was formally removed from the Sharī'a tribunals in most Middle Eastern countries and transferred to secular courts which applied modern penal codes derived from European sources. The Penal Code promulgated in Egypt in 1875, for example, was based on French law, while the later Egyptian Criminal Code of 1937 directly adopted Italian law. Since family law, including succession, remained the undisputed province of the Sharī'a courts, this development created a dichotomy in the general administration of law which involved, in particular, the recognition of two distinct doctrines of homicide. In the secular courts homicide, broadly, was a capital offence only where the killer intended to kill or to do an act likely to cause death. But in the Sharī'a courts applying Ḥanafī law a person was debarred from inheritance if he killed the praepositus directly, however accidental his act or innocent his intention, while the indirect killer (by shooting or by poison) suffered no such bar however criminal his intention may have been.

The Egyptian Law of Inheritance, 1943, which was closely followed by the Syrian Law of Personal Status, 1953, set out to remove this dual standard by providing that a homicide would raise a bar to inheritance by the killer from his victim when it amounted to the capital offence of murder under the Criminal Code.

Section 5 of the Egyptian Law accordingly enacts: "Among the impediments to inheritance is the intentional killing of the praepositus, whether the killer acted as principal or accessory or as a false witness whose testimony led to a sentence of death and its execution, provided the killing was unlawful and without excuse and provided the killer was sane and at least fifteen years of age. Among excuses is to be counted the case of one who exceeds his legal right of self-defence."

3.3.1.1. The juristic basis of the reform

Although the provisions of section 5 are remarkably close to traditional Shī'ī law, they are formally represented as an amalgam, by way of *talfīq*, of the Mālikī principle that any deliberate homicide, direct or indirect creates a bar to inheritance and of the Ḥanafī principle that a minor or a lunatic killer is not debarred from inheritance. It is clear, however, that the real inspiration for the reform lies in the Criminal Code of 1937. In the first place, the intentional killing envisaged by section 5 is certainly a killing where there is the intention to kill or at least to do an act likely to cause death as opposed to the very much wider definition of intentional killing that in fact obtains in Mālikī law. In the second place, when the Explanatory Memorandum elaborates upon the modes of killing and the degrees of complicity etc. which will raise the bar to inheritance, it makes detailed reference to the provisions of the Criminal Code rather than to the traditional Mālikī authorities. This is the case when the memorandum expressly excludes from inheritance the person who commands another to commit a homicide, or leads the way to it, or shares in it, or keeps watch while it is done.

3.3.1.2. Homicide under the influence of drugs or alcohol

Two points of substance call for brief comment. Normal Islamic doctrine is preserved in the rule, as laid down in the Explanatory Memorandum, that one who kills in temporary loss of reason as the result of a drug taken under compulsion or in ignorance of its nature is not to be regarded as a sane killer; for this implies that the bar to inheritance will be raised by a homicide committed under the influence of a drug or intoxicant knowingly and willingly taken. Because voluntary intoxication through alcohol or drugs is itself a crime under traditional Islamic law, loss of reason due to drunkenness or the effect of drugs is not a defence to a charge of wilful homicide.

3.3.1.3. Excusable homicide

The final sentence of section 5 clearly indicates that excusable homicide is not confined to the case of a person who exceeds his lawful right of self defence – i.e. uses more force than is absolutely necessary to repel an attack and kills when his intention is not to kill but merely to defend himself or his property. The original draft of the law in fact expressly included as a case of excusable homicide a husband's killing of his wife when he caught her in the act of adultery. In the debate on the clause, however, it was generally agreed that a person who caught his mother, daughter or sister in the act of adultery had even greater excuse for killing her, since he could not, like the husband, wipe out the stigma on the family's honour by the simple expedient of divorce. Hence the law as finally enacted deliberately refrained from specifying all the categories of excusable homicide so that cases of the type mentioned (and presumably others) might be brought under this head in appropriate circumstances.

3.3.2. Tunisia

Article 88 of the Tunisian Code of Personal Status, 1956, provides: "Deliberate homicide is one of the impediments to inheritance. The killer does not inherit, whether he acted as principal or accessory or was a false witness whose testimony led to a sentence of death against the praepositus and its execution." Unlike the Egyptian legislation, therefore, the Tunisian Law does not expressly make the exclusion of the killer from inheritance dependent upon his majority and sanity. Since the same Tunisian Law does make express reference to these conditions of majority and sanity when it deals with homicide as a bar to testamentary succession (p. 230 below), it seems that the omission here was deliberate and that the traditional Mālikī doctrine, which excludes even the minor or lunatic killer from inheritance, still applies.

3.3.3. Iraq

The Iraqi legislation of 1959 states simply that a killer, without further definition, is barred from inheriting from his victim. It seems, therefore, that traditional Sharī'a doctrine continues to apply in Iraq in this regard, since the practice is to interpret the terms of the legislation according to the traditional Ḥanafī or Shī'ī authorities (pp. 141–2 above).

3.3.4. India and Pakistan

There has never existed in India and Pakistan the same dichotomy in the court system as obtained in the Middle East with the separate jurisdictions of the secular and the Sharī'a courts. Sharī'a law has always been administered in the sub-continent as the law of personal status for Muslims through the unified system of courts which applies the criminal and the general civil law. Hence, with the introduction of the Indian Penal Code in 1860 (English criminal law codified for export), the traditional Ḥanafī law of homicide ceased to have any application at all, both in criminal and civil cases, and since that time homicide has constituted an impediment to succession only if it amounts to a criminal offence under the terms of the Penal Code.

A recent decision of the Pakistani High Court, however, has greatly extended the effect of criminal homicide as an impediment to succession. Under the traditional Islamic law of all schools it is only the killer who is debarred from succession to the estate of his victim. But according to this decision a homicide may result in persons other than the actual killer being debarred from succession to estates other than that of the victim.

In *Beguman* v. *Saroo*, P.L.D. (1964), Lah. 451, the facts were as follows. In 1948 one Dara was convicted and hanged for the murder of his two nephews, the only sons of his brother Rehman and his wife Beguman. When Rehman died in 1951 his nearest surviving relatives were his wife Beguman, his two daughters and his two nephews, Saroo and Manak, the sons of the murderer Dara.

It was decided by the court of first instance, correctly according to Ḥanafī law, that Beguman was entitled to one-eighth, the two daughters to two-thirds and the two nephews, as agnatic residuary heirs, to 5/24 of Rehman's estate. Against this decision Beguman appealed, claiming that the nephews were not entitled to any share of the inheritance since it was only through their father's murder of Rehman's sons that they had been let in as the nearest residuary heirs.

The High Court allowed this appeal for the sins of the father to be visited upon the children and observed:

> Under the principles of justice, equity and good conscience, a murderer or his progeny cannot be allowed to benefit by his crime of murder. The murderer may be the father alone but if the descendants claim through him even though not merely from him their title becomes tainted, as the source or the channel through which the inheritance has to flow becomes blocked and extirpated by reason of the crime committed by that source.

4. Difference of religion

4.1. The relevant circumstances

Sharīʿa law naturally pays considerable attention to the legal status of those non-Muslim minorities whose security in the practice of their faith was guaranteed by the Muslim State in return for tribute. Strict theory may have confined such legal recognition to the Jewish and Christian communities on the ground that, as distinct from paganism and idolatry, these religions were based on revealed scriptures, but in historical fact Muslim States tolerated the existence of other non-Muslim communities. Broadly speaking, the protected non-Muslim minorities had the right to the jurisdiction of their own community courts in matters of personal status. Cases involving Muslims and non-Muslims, however, were justiciable by the Sharīʿa courts, and here it was perhaps inevitable that the law should, in certain particulars, place the non-Muslim in an inferior position to the Muslim.

In cases of homicide, for example, the blood-money payable for a Jewish or Christian victim is half that due for a Muslim victim; while only the Ḥanafī school allows a Muslim to be put to death for the deliberate homicide of a non-Muslim. Mixed marriages are permissible under Sharīʿa law to the extent that a Muslim male may marry a Jewish or Christian woman, although a Muslim woman cannot validly marry any but a Muslim husband. But while, in general, a husband owes precisely the same marital duties, particularly in the matter of maintenance and support, towards his non-Muslim as he does towards his Muslim wife, the non-Muslim wife suffers certain disabilities. Her right of custody, for example, over the children of the marriage is not so extensive as that of a Muslim mother, because of the undesirable influence that her different religion might have upon the Muslim child. But more particularly, a non-Muslim wife has no right of inheritance from her Muslim husband. Since the law of inheritance is designed to distribute property among surviving relatives within the community of Muslims, naturally enough the difference of religion between Muslim and non-Muslim, seen as a difference of communal allegiance, constitutes a general bar to inheritance.

In the context of the traditional Sharīʿa law of inheritance it is necessary to distinguish three principal cases of difference of religion. First, there is the difference of religion between the person who is non-Muslim, by birth or by conversion from paganism or some religion other than Islam, and his relative who is, by birth or conversion, a Muslim. Secondly, there is the particular case of the apostate who has, by free choice, renounced the religion of Islam. Such defection from the community of Muslims entails forfeiture of all civil rights and puts a person outside the protection of the law. Apostasy is a crime punishable by death in the case of males, and imprisonment in the case of females, if the apostate refuses the command to return to Islam. The position of an apostate, therefore, both as praepositus and claimant heir, is subject to special considerations and differs from that of one who has never been a Muslim. Finally, the jurisdiction of the Sharīʿa courts might be invoked to deal with cases of succession among relatives who are not Muslims but belong to different non-Muslim religions.

In modern times, with the growing tendency of Muslim countries to unify their law on a national basis, the law relating to non-Muslims has become a matter of more direct concern, particularly as regards succession. For although, in general, non-Muslims in Muslim states continue to be governed by their own personal law in family matters, the Egyptian Law of Inheritance, 1943, and the provisions concerning inheritance in the Syrian Law of Personal Status, 1953, apply equally to non-Muslim and Muslim nationals of the two countries.

4.2. Muslims and non-Muslims

Although difference of religion is not a bar to taking a bequest, there is no exception in traditional Sunnī law to the rule that a non-Muslim does not inherit from a Muslim and a Muslim does not inherit from a non-Muslim.

The rule remains unchanged in current Islamic law both in the Middle East and in the Indian sub-continent. In *Chandrashekharappa* v. *Government of Mysore*, A.I.R. (1955), Mysore 26, for example, a Muslim widow, who had been converted before her marriage from Hinduism to Islam, died intestate and without issue. Since it was held that Islamic law applied, her Hindu brother's claim to be her legal heir failed on the ground of his different religion.

4.2.1. The Ḥanbalī rule

According to the Sunnī majority the impediment arises, and cannot be removed by any subsequent events, if the difference of religion exists at the moment succession opens, i.e. the time of the praepositus' death. Under Ḥanbalī law, however, a relative who is not a Muslim at the time of the Muslim praepositus' death becomes entitled to inherit if he is converted to Islam at any time before the actual distribution of the inheritance. Ibn Qudāma (*al-Mughnī*, VI, 300) attempts a systematic explanation of this doctrine by arguing that rights and obligations may accrue to a deceased's estate as a result of events that happen after his death. If, for example, the deceased has set a snare during his lifetime, animals caught by it after his death belong to his estate. So, too, the deceased's estate will be liable to pay compensation for the injury or death of a person who falls, after the deceased's death, into a well which the deceased dug during his lifetime. On the same principle, concludes Ibn Qudāma, a relative's conversion to Islam after the praepositus' death transforms his latent right of succession, existing by virtue of his relationship, into an effective one. It would appear, however, that the real ground for the doctrine is to be found in Ibn Qudāma's final remark that to allow inheritance in these circumstances is "also an impetus and incitement to accept Islam".

4.2.2. The Shī'ī rule

Shī'ī law not only accepts this same doctrine of subsequent conversion but also weights the scales much more heavily in favour of Islam. For it holds that while non-Muslims do not inherit from Muslims in any circumstances, Muslims do inherit from non-Muslims and are even given priority over closer non-Muslim relatives. Thus, according to the Sharā'ī al-Islām,[1] where a non-Muslim dies survived by his minor children and nephews who were born Muslims because of the conversion to Islam of their parents (predeceased), a Shīʿī court having jurisdiction in the case must grant the inheritance to the nephews, subject to their duty to maintain and support the minor children, who may subsequently claim the inheritance if, on attaining majority, they profess conversion to Islam.

4.3. Apostates

All schools hold it to be part of the punishment for his crime that an apostate is barred from inheritance from anyone, whether Muslim, non-Muslim or other apostate. If, for example, a father and son become apostates from Islam, a Sharīʿa court having jurisdiction will rule that neither inherits from the other, regardless of whether they have become converts to no other, or the same, or different religions.

Following their same variant doctrine in the case of non-Muslims by birth, the Ḥanbalīs and the Shīʿa maintain that the return of an apostate to Islam before the actual distribution of his deceased relative's estate removes the bar to inheritance.

4.3.1. General Sunnī law

With the exception of the Ḥanafīs, the Sunnī schools hold that the Muslim relatives of an apostate do not inherit from him, in accordance with the basic principle that Muslims do not inherit from non-Muslims. All the property of the apostate, whether acquired before or after the act of apostasy, is classified as booty taken from an alien enemy and belongs to the Public Treasury.

4.3.2. Ḥanafī and Shīʿī law

According to the Ḥanafī and the Shīʿī schools, an apostate differs from a non-Muslim by birth inasmuch as he is subject to Sharīʿa family law until his act of apostasy. At this moment he becomes dead in the eyes of the law, since he loses legal protection and may be killed with impunity if he does not accept the invitation to return to Islam. Accordingly, his Muslim relatives inherit the property of which he "dies" possessed – i.e. the property he has acquired before the act of apostasy which opens succession to his estate. Any property subsequently acquired by the apostate is classified as booty and belongs to the Public Treasury.

A Muslim woman, however, does not lose the protection of the law by

[1] See Querry, *Droit Musulman*, II, 331.

her act of apostasy. Because of her sex she is not considered to be an alien enemy of Islam; she is not subject to the death penalty but is to be imprisoned until she recants. Succession to her estate, therefore, does not open until her actual death, when her Muslim relatives will inherit all her property, whether acquired before or after her apostasy.[1]

4.3.3. The effect of apostasy on marriage

Apostasy by a spouse terminates the marriage *ipso facto*, the divorce being classified as final and irrevocable (*bā'in*). In Mālikī, Shāfi'ī and Ḥanbalī law, following the principle that there is no inheritance between Muslims and non-Muslims, neither spouse inherits from the other. But in Ḥanafī and Shī'ī law, where Muslims in principle may inherit from apostates, the normal rule that mutual rights of inheritance between spouses cease immediately upon a final divorce is modified in the case of a spouse's apostasy. In no circumstance will the apostate spouse inherit from the spouse who remains Muslim. But an apostate husband, like any other convicted criminal awaiting the death penalty, is deemed in law to be a person in his death-sickness (Chapter 15 below). Accordingly, the final divorce effected by his act of apostasy does not have the particular result of immediately extinguishing the wife's right to inherit from him. Following the normal principles of final divorce during death-sickness, the wife's right of inheritance will continue formally for the duration of her *'idda* period in Ḥanafī law and for the stipulated period of one year in Shī'ī law. But these periods of time have no particular significance as far as her right of inheritance is concerned, since the commencement of her *'idda* and the opening of succession to her husband's estate take place at the time of the apostasy.

An apostate wife, on the other hand, cannot be deemed to be in her death-sickness by reason solely of her apostasy because she is not liable to the death penalty. Her husband will not, therefore, inherit from her if she dies during her *'idda* period, unless she qualifies as a dying person on other grounds at the time of her apostasy. In this latter event the husband's

[1] Although this distinction between male and female apostates is the Shī'ī and the most authoritative Ḥanafī view, the two Ḥanafī jurists Abū Yūsuf and Shaybānī were of the opinion that all the property of a male as well as a female apostate constitutes inheritance for his Muslim relatives. They based this opinion on the grounds: (*a*) that as long as the apostate is alive he is subject to the law of Islam, since he is only to be put to death if he cannot be persuaded to recant, and (*b*) the apostate is as effectively the legal owner of property acquired after, as of property acquired before, his apostasy. The personal view of the jurist al-Shāfi'ī also did not distinguish between male and female apostates, but he held that only property acquired before apostasy passed to the Muslim relatives as inheritance.

right of inheritance will continue during her *'idda* because the law negates the purpose which it ascribes, however artifically, to the wife's apostasy, namely, that of disinheriting her husband by effecting a final divorce.

4.3.4. Current law in India and Pakistan

In India and Pakistan the traditional Sharī'a law concerning apostates has been substantially superceded by the Caste Disabilities Removal Act, 1850, which provided that

> So much of any law or usage...as inflicts on any person forfeiture of rights or property, or may be held in any way to impair or affect any right of inheritance by reason of his or her renouncing or having been excluded from the communion of any religion...shall cease to be enforced as law...

Apart, therefore, from apostasy being no longer a criminal offence, no bar to mutual rights of inheritance now exists between an apostate from Islam and his Muslim blood relatives. Nor does the Public Treasury have any claim to the property of apostates.

4.3.4.1. Apostasy of the spouse: uncertain effect of Indian legislation

The Act, however, was not construed as overriding the substantive rule of Sharī'a matrimonial law that apostasy from Islam by a spouse *ipso facto* dissolves the marriage. The rule was recognised, for example, by the High Court of Madras in *Narantakath* v. *Parakkal* (1922), 45 Mad. 986. A Muslim wife, whose Ḥanafī husband had embraced the tenets of the heterodox Ahmadiyya sect, married a second husband and defended a prosecution for bigamy on the ground that her husband's conversion to the Ahmadiyya sect was apostasy and therefore her first marriage was dissolved. Her defence succeeded in the lower court, but the High Court held that she had committed bigamy, ruling that the Ahmadiyya was a Muslim movement and that her first husband accordingly was not an apostate.

However, since the passing of the Dissolution of Muslim Marriages Act, 1939, apostasy by a wife no longer ends her marital tie. Section 4 of the Act provides: "The renunciation of Islam by a married Muslim woman or her conversion to a faith other than Islam shall not by itself operate to dissolve her marriage."

It is expressly stated in the preamble to the Act that the purpose of this section was "to remove doubts as to the effect of the renunciation of Islam by a married Muslim woman on her marriage tie". Apparently these doubts stemmed from the principle laid down in the Caste Disabilities Removal Act, 1850, that apostasy should not entail any "forfeiture of rights". For while there was a sound reason for maintaining that a Muslim husband forfeited his marital rights by apostasy – namely, the substantive Sharī'a rule that a Muslim woman cannot be validly married to a non-Muslim – there was no such ground for maintaining that a Muslim wife forfeited her marital rights by apostasy, at least if she embraced a scriptural religion which did not, according to the Sharī'a, constitute a bar to a valid marriage between her and a Muslim husband.

Curiously enough, however, this section of the Dissolution of Muslim Marriages Act was designed to protect the position of the husband rather than that of the wife. Prior to the Act, when the courts applying Ḥanafī law recognised no doctrine of judicial dissolution of marriage for matrimonial offences committed by the husband, Muslim wives had apparently resorted to apostasy as a means of getting rid of an unwanted husband. The primary purpose of the section, therefore, was to abolish this practice which was prejudicial both to the general interests of the religion of Islam and to the marital rights of an innocent husband. The Act provided liberal grounds upon which a Muslim wife might obtain a judicial dissolution of her marriage, and these grounds were expressly made available to an apostate wife. Included among these grounds (under the broad head of cruelty) is the fact that the husband "obstructs her in the observance of her religious profession or practice". In the event of his wife's apostasy, of course, a Muslim husband desirous of ending the marriage may always avail himself his power to terminate the marriage unilaterally by *ṭalāq*.

It must be admitted that the current law relating to a spouse's apostasy, as a result of its rather haphazard development, is far from being wholly clear or systematic. It seems, for instance, that the combined effect of the Caste Disabilities Removal Act and the Dissolution of Muslim Marriages Act is that an apostate Muslim wife will not lose her right of inheritance from her Muslim husband, whether she professes to be an atheist or embraces a scriptural religion, while an apostate Muslim husband certainly loses all his marital rights, including that of inheritance from his wife. What is sauce for the goose, here, is not sauce for the gander.

4.3.4.2. Possible means of resolving the uncertainty

It seems questionable, therefore, now that apostasy has ceased to be a crime and does not in principle entail any "forfeiture of rights", whether there is any real value in retaining the distinction between non-Muslims by birth and apostates, at least in the context of matrimonial law. And it may be, if Muslim personal law is to continue to apply, that the most equitable and systematic solution would be to apply, in all cases of apostasy by a spouse, the fundamental Sharī'a principles relating to difference of religion.

If this were so, then the marriage of an apostate Muslim husband, and with it his right of inheritance, would terminate not solely or directly by reason of his renouncing his religious belief, but because of the basic rule that there is an impediment to a valid marriage between a Muslim woman and a non-Muslim. In the case of apostasy by a Muslim wife, her marriage would remain valid if she embraced a scriptural religion but not otherwise; and in any event she would have no right of inheritance from her husband, again, not solely because of the change in her religious belief but because of the substantive rule that bars inheritance between a Muslim and his non-Muslim wife.

4.3.5. Traditional law in the Middle East

In the Middle East, and generally elsewhere in the Muslim world, apostasy is no longer a capital criminal offence, but the apostate is still subject to the civil disabilities imposed by traditional Sharī'a law. In its draft form, the Egyptian Law of Inheritance, 1943, contained a clause which stated that an apostate had no right of inheritance from anyone; that the property of an apostate, male or female, which had been acquired before apostasy passed as inheritance to his or her Muslim relatives; and that the property acquired by the apostate after apostasy belonged to the Public Treasury. This, in substance, represented the personal view of al-Shāfi'ī. In the debate on the law, however, there was considerable support for the view that these provisions offended against the constitutional guarantee of freedom of personal religious belief. As a result the clause was dropped, on the understanding that a comprehensive law concerning apostates would shortly be drafted. Such a law has not yet materialised and therefore traditional Ḥanafī law still in theory obtains, in accordance with the principle laid down in the Explanatory Memorandum to the Law that "in cases not regulated by the Law the Courts shall apply the most preferable Ḥanafī opinion".

4.4. Non-Muslims

When the jurisdiction of Sharī'a courts is invoked to decide cases of succession between non-Muslims, the doctrine of the Ḥanafī, Shāfi'ī and Shī'ī schools is that no bar to inheritance is raised by any difference of religion. In sum this majority view regards all non-Muslims, for purposes of inheritance, as one "faith" or "community". This same rule is adopted by the Egyptian Law of Inheritance, 1943, and the Syrian Law of Personal Status, 1953.

At the other extreme, Ḥanbalī law regards all the different faiths as different communities with a bar to inheritance existing between them.

Mālikī law adopts a middle course by holding that there are three "communities" of non-Muslims between which there is a bar to inheritance – namely, Jews, Christians and "others".

5. Difference of domicile

In the contemplation of traditional Sharī'a law the world was simply divided between "the abode of Islam" (*Dār al-Islām*) and "the abode of war" (*Dār al-ḥarb*). *Dār al-Islām* consisted of those territories or states which were ruled by a Muslim political authority. All other territories made up the *Dār al-ḥarb*, against which the Muslim community was committed to wage war to establish the ultimate goal of the universal supremacy of Islam, although temporary peace treaties might be concluded with individual states in the *Dār al-ḥarb*.

5.1. Ḥanafī and Shāfi'ī law

Difference of domicile or national allegiance, seen in these terms, does not as a general rule create any impediment to inheritance in Sharī'a law. Mutual rights of inheritance exist between Muslim relatives who are domiciled in different States, Islamic or non-Islamic, and between non-Muslim relatives (subject to the rules relating to difference of religion) who are domiciled in different Islamic states. The only exception to the general rule is in Ḥanafī and Shāfi'ī law where there are no mutual rights of inheritance between non-Muslim relatives if one is the subject of an Islamic state and the other is the subject of a non-Islamic state, whether the latter is in treaty relationship with Islam or not. In the context of traditional Islamic polity this rule is nothing more than the modern equivalent of the barring from rights of succession of an alien enemy.

5.2. Current law in Egypt and Syria

The traditional Ḥanafī rule was abandoned by the Egyptian Law of Inheritance, 1943, with the purpose, according to the Explanatory Memorandum, of "establishing parity between Muslims and non-Muslims in this matter". Difference of domicile is no longer a bar to inheritance between non-Muslim relatives, where one is the national of a Muslim state and the other is a national of a non-Muslim state, unless the law of the non-Muslim state concerned bars foreigners from inheriting from its own nationals.

Formally, the juristic basis of the law is the principle of *talfīq*, or combination of authoritative doctrines. The view of the Mālikī and Ḥanbalī schools, that difference of domicile is not a bar to inheritance between non-Muslims, is adopted in cases where the law of the non-Muslim state concerned allows reciprocal treatment, while the Ḥanafī view is maintained in cases where the relevant foreign law does not allow reciprocal treatment. But the combined effect of this provision of the law and the provision that no bar to inheritance between non-Muslims arises from any difference of religion is to allow a right of inheritance in cases where the doctrine of no single Sunnī school of traditional Sharīʻa law would allow it.

Under the new Law, for example, a Russian Jew would inherit from his deceased relative who was an Egyptian national of the Christian faith. According to traditional Sunnī law he would be barred from inheritance, in the Mālikī and Ḥanbalī schools because of the difference of religion, and in the Ḥanafī and Shāfiʻī schools because of the difference of domicile. Shīʻī law, however, would have the same results as the Egyptian Law in this case.

The Syrian Law of 1953, which generally follows the Egyptian Law very closely, also abandons the Ḥanafī rule that difference of domicile is a bar to inheritance between non-Muslims. But it takes the principle of reciprocity, and incidentally the principle of parity between Muslims and non-Muslims, much further by applying it to succession by Muslims as well as non-Muslims. Any foreigner, Muslim or non-Muslim, is barred from inheritance from a Syrian national unless the law of the foreigner's domicile allows reciprocal treatment.

12. CONDITIONS OF INHERITANCE

As the transfer of property from the dead to the living, inheritance depends upon two fundamental and rather self-evident conditions – the decease of a praepositus and the survival of an heir. Positive proof that these conditions have been fulfilled may, however, be lacking. It may be uncertain whether a person is dead or not, or whether one who is potentially an heir is alive or not, or, finally, whether an alleged heir was alive or not at the time of the praepositus' death. Such uncertainty arises in the three principal cases of (*a*) missing persons, whose death or survival cannot be established as a fact; (*b*) persons dying in circumstances where the precise time of death cannot be ascertained; and (*c*) children in the womb.

In these situations the interests of other parties require a resolution of the uncertainty and an answer to the question of whether a succession has opened, and if so in favour of whom. This involves the law in a twofold task. First, in the absence of factual evidence, the decision as to whether the basic conditions of inheritance have been fulfilled must rest upon the best evidence available – namely, that provided by legal presumptions. The relevant presumptions must therefore be determined and the scope of their application defined. Secondly, the final resolution of the uncertainty by such presumptions must often await a future date or event. The law, therefore, aims at making due provision for this future event without thereby occasioning unnecessary prejudice to the present and established rights of the other parties involved.

1. Death of the praepositus

1.1. Judicial decree of death of missing persons

The principal problem raised by this first condition of inheritance is the case of a missing person (*mafqūd*), concerning whom there is no reliable information to establish whether he is alive or dead. In what circumstances will such a person be deemed dead in law so that succession to his estate may take place?

All schools recognise that the basic evidential presumption to be applied here is that of "continuance", or *istiṣḥāb*. Where no factual evidence of present circumstances is available, it is presumed that the circumstances known to have existed previously continue to exist. At the same time the law will naturally recognise that human life cannot continue indefinitely.

Hence, the basic doctrine common to all the schools is that a judicial decree of the death of a missing person may be obtained when what is recognised as his life-span has passed; but until such decree issues the missing person is, by the presumption of *istiṣḥāb*, deemed to be alive.

1.1.1. Circumstances in which the decree may be obtained: expiry of recognised life-span

Variations between the several schools in the application of this basic doctrine occur in two major respects.

Firstly, the life-span to be observed by the courts is defined by Ḥanafī law as a period of ninety years and by Mālikī law as a period of seventy years.[1]

Shāfi'ī, Ḥanbalī and Shī'ī law, however, hold that the determination of the period is a matter for the discretion of the court in each case.[2]

1.1.2. Mālikī and Ḥanbalī law: disappearance in circumstances raising presumption of death

Secondly, while the majority apply the criterion of the human life-span in all cases, the Mālikīs and Ḥanbalīs introduce an important exception. Where the missing person has disappeared in circumstances which give rise to a reasonable apprehension of his death, the court may proceed to issue a decree of death after a period of search and enquiry has failed to provide any indication that the missing person is still alive.

Ḥanbalī law gives as examples of circumstances which raise a presumption of death: disappearance during a battle or some such calamity as an earthquake or shipwreck; disappearance in a community or locality which is struck by plague or fatal epidemic, and unaccountable absence, such as failure to return from a visit to the local mosque or market as distinct from, say, failure to return from a mercantile or professional venture abroad. In all these cases, due search and enquiries having been made, a judicial decree of death may be obtained when four years have elapsed since the date of disappearance.

Mālikī law recognises three specific situations in which a decree of death may be obtained prior to the expiry of the missing person's recognised life-span of seventy years.

[1] These periods represent the dominant view in the respective schools, although individual jurists prescribed other periods. Abū Ḥanīfa, for example, favoured 120 years, Shaybānī 110 years, and Abū Yūsuf 105 years.

[2] As far as Shī'ī law is concerned this, again, appears to be the dominant view, although certain authorities maintain that a judicial decree of death may be obtained when a person has been missing without trace for a specified period – ten years according to some jurists and four years according to others.

(i) In the case of disappearance during a battle between Muslim forces, a judicial decree of death may be obtained at the conclusion of hostilities.

(ii) A person who is missing after a battle between Muslim and non-Muslim forces may be pronounced dead in law when a period of one year has elapsed since proper enquiries concerning him were undertaken.

(iii) Where a person disappears in Islamic territory during a fatal epidemic or at the time of a disaster or calamity, a decree of death may be obtained, after due search and enquiries, when one year has passed since the date of disappearance.[1]

1.1.3. The nature of the decree

A judicial decree of death is in no sense declaratory of an actual death: it is the legal instrument which causes a purely legal death. The expiry of the life-span, or the existence of circumstances raising an apprehension of death, do not in themselves prove actual death but simply serve to rebut the presumption of the continued life of the missing person and thus enable the court to proceed to its act of judicial homicide. This type of judicial decree must therefore be clearly distinguished from cases in which the court finds, on the basis of acceptable evidence, that a person is in fact dead and that he died from a particular cause or at some particular time. Death by operation of law is confined to persons concerning whom there is no acceptable factual evidence and cannot by its nature be held to occur at any time prior to the judicial act which causes it.

1.1.4. The effect of the decree

Succession to the estate of missing persons, therefore, opens at the time the decree is given and, even where the decree is first obtained some considerable time after the expiry of the missing person's life-span, is confined to those relatives of the missing person who are alive at that time. Relatives who have died during the period between the missing person's disappearance and the issue of the decree of death have not, in law, survived him.

A judicial decree of death naturally ceases to be effective if the missing person is subsequently found to be alive. Such a person may recover any properties of his estate which are still in the possession of his "heirs", but he has no claim against them, the court or third parties for property which has been consumed or alienated.

[1] These rules clearly reflect basic concepts of the mediaeval Islamic law of international relations – the division of the world into two areas, that which is controlled by an Islamic political authority and that which is not, and the constant state of hostility between Islam and the unbelievers.

1.2. Decree of putative widowhood

The marriage of a missing person is naturally terminated by the judicial decree of his death, and his surviving wife is free to remarry after the *'idda* of widowhood has been observed. Under the law of dissolution of marriage, however, the wife of a missing person has the right, apart from any other grounds of divorce which may exist, to petition the court for a declaration that she is a widow. Such a decree of putative widowhood, in certain schools at least, does not of itself open succession to the husband's estate and may be granted in circumstances where a judicial decree of death properly so-called could not be obtained. The two types of decree, therefore, are to be carefully distinguished.

In Shāfi'ī and Shī'ī law, where a judicial decree of death can only be obtained after the expiry of the life-span, a wife may obtain a decree of putative widowhood where her husband has been missing without trace for a period of four years. Mālikī law observes the same rule in the case of a wife whose husband has disappeared in circumstances which do not raise a presumption of his death.

In Ḥanafī and Ḥanbalī law, however, no separate doctrine of putative widowhood exists. The court will only declare the wife of a missing person to be a widow where the conditions for a decree of his death are satisfied. Thus a judicial pronouncement of death, under the respective rules obtaining in these two schools, is effective for all purposes.

2. Survival of the heir

Sunnī law generally requires positive evidence of the fulfilment of this condition. In the various circumstances where it is uncertain whether a relative of the praepositus was alive or not at the time of the latter's decease, such a relative will not be entitled as a legal heir. In Shī'ī law, however, the survival of an heir may in certain circumstances be presumed under the principle of "continuance", or *istiṣḥāb*.

2.1. Missing persons

2.1.1. Reservation of a missing heir's share

Where a relative of the praepositus is a missing person at the time of decease, the share of the inheritance which he would have taken if present is reserved for him. If it is subsequently established that he survived the praepositus, he or his heirs will be entitled to the property so reserved, while if it is established that he predeceased the praepositus, the reserved portion will revert to the praepositus' estate and be distributed among his entitled heirs.

2.1.2. Present heirs take minimal entitlement

The fact that the missing relative proves to be an entitled heir may affect the position of a relative who is present in a variety of ways. He or she may be totally excluded from succession, reduced to a smaller share or, in some circumstances, entitled to a larger share. In all cases the rule is that relatives present take either the share they would receive in the event of the missing person's survival, or the share they would receive in the event of his predecease, whichever is less.

P dies leaving a net estate of £72. Her known surviving relatives are her husband, her mother and her germane sister. Her germane brother is a missing person.

If the germane brother proves to be an entitled heir the distribution of the estate will be:

Husband (Qur'anic portion of $\frac{1}{2}$)	£36
Mother (Qur'anic portion of $\frac{1}{6}$ in presence of brother and sister)	£12
Germane sister ($\frac{1}{3}$ of the residue)	£8
Germane brother ($\frac{2}{3}$ of the residue)	£16

If the germane brother proves not to be an entitled heir, the distribution of the estate will be:

Husband	Qur'anic portions of	$\frac{1}{2}$	reduced by *'awl* to:	$\frac{3}{8}$	£27
Mother		$\frac{1}{3}$		$\frac{2}{8}$	£18
Germane sister		$\frac{1}{2}$		$\frac{3}{8}$	£27

Here, the survival of the brother would reduce the shares of the mother and sister but increase that of the husband. The mother and sister therefore take the amount they would receive in the event of the brother's survival – £12 and £8 respectively – and the husband the £27 he would receive in the event of the brother's predecease. The sum reserved from distribution is £25. If it is duly established that the brother survived the praepositus, he will be entitled to £16 of this sum and the remaining £9 will go to the husband; while if it is established that the brother predeceased the praepositus, £6 of the reserved sum will go to the mother and the remaining £19 to the sister.

Since, however, £9 of the reserved sum is destined in any event for one or other of the heirs present, the husband, mother and sister may come to a valid settlement as to the apportionment of this sum between them and thus secure its immediate distribution.

2.1.3. Sunnī law: evidence of survival required

In Sunnī law the missing relative, or his heirs, will not be entitled to the reserved portion of the estate unless positive evidence that he survived the praepositus is forthcoming. Where no such evidence materialises and a judicial decree of the missing person's death is eventually obtained, the reserved share will be distributed among the original heirs of the praepositus. In contemplation of law, therefore, the date of a missing person's death, for purposes of succession to his own estate, is the date of the judicial decree, while for the purpose of his succession to the estates of others it is the date of his disappearance. The presumption of continuance may serve as a shield for the missing person, to protect his own estate from the claims of his heirs, but it does not serve as a sword to enable him to succeed to the estates of others.

2.1.4. Shī'ī law: survival presumed

In Shī'ī law, however, the presumption of continuance serves both as a shield and a sword. Unless evidence of the fact that the missing person predeceased the praepositus is forthcoming, he will be presumed alive until a judicial decree of his death is obtained and will therefore inherit the share of the estate reserved for him. In Shī'ī law the date of his death, for all purposes, will be the date of the judicial decree.[1]

> P's only relatives are his three sons, Ahmad, Bashir and Hasan, and a grandson Ibrahim, the son of Ahmad. In 1958 Ahmad and Bashir become missing persons. In 1960 P dies leaving a net estate of £300. Evidence subsequently adduced shows that Bashir died in 1959. In 1965 the court issues a decree of Ahmad's death.

Upon P's death Hasan will inherit £100, and shares of £100 each will be reserved for Ahmad and Bashir. When it is found that Bashir predeceased his father, £50 of his share will go to Hasan and the other £50 will be reserved for Ahmad.

Following the judicial decree of Ahmad's death in 1965 the share of £150 reserved for him from P's estate will go to Hasan under Sunnī law, while under Shī'ī law it will, as part of Ahmad's estate, go to Ibrahim.

[1] This doctrine was in fact held by Shāfi'ī and Aḥmad b. Ḥanbal, but is not supported by the later authoritative manuals of the schools they founded.

2.2. Concurrent deaths of mutual heirs

Where two relatives with mutual rights of succession die simultaneously, neither inherits from the other because neither has in fact survived the other. Again, where two such relatives, A and B, die at approximately the same time and the precise moment of decease can be established in the case of A but not in the case of B, B will in effect be treated as a missing person. A will not inherit from B because there is no evidence that B predeceased A. Neither, in Sunnī law, will B inherit from A because there is no evidence that B survived A. But in Shīʿī law B will inherit from A because there is no evidence that B predeceased A.

2.2.1. No evidence of precise time of either death

The particular problem, therefore, with which this section is concerned is the death of two or more relatives in circumstances where the precise moment of neither death is known. Of the variety of situations in which this can occur the most obvious and perhaps the most common example is death in the same calamity – natural disaster, epidemic, battle or accident.

In these cases the law must, for purposes of succession, fix the order of decease, and the rights of surviving relatives may obviously be affected according as to whether one death is deemed to have preceded the other or both deaths are deemed to have occurred simultaneously.

A woman and her son perish in a fire which destroys their home. Both leave estates of £60. The only two surviving relatives are H, the husband of the woman and father of her son, and B, the woman's germane brother.

If the woman is deemed to have died before her son, H will inherit the whole of both estates. The heirs of the woman are her husband and her son (who excludes the brother), and the sole heir of the son is his father.

If the son is deemed to have died before his mother, she will inherit one-third of his estate and the father two-thirds. The heirs of the mother will then be her husband and her brother, each entitled to one-half of her estate. H therefore receives from both estates a total sum of £80 and B the sum of £40.

If the deaths are deemed to have occurred simultaneously, H receives £90 (the whole of his son's estate and one-half of his wife's estate) and B £30 (one-half of his sister's estate).

2.2.1.1. The general Sunnī rule: neither inherits from the other

With the exception of the Ḥanbalīs, the Sunnī schools hold that where relatives die in the same calamity, or in other circumstances where the order of their deaths is unknown, neither of them inherits from the other. Succession to their respective estates is confined to their other surviving relatives. This is because there is no evidence that either survived the other, and therefore the basic condition of inheritance has not been satisfied. There is no parallel in Islamic jurisprudence to the presumption of English law that the younger relative survives the elder.

2.2.1.2. The Shāfi'ī variant rule

Shāfi'ī law recognises one exception to the general rule. Where the fact that one relative died first is established, but it is not known which relative this was, distribution of the estate is suspended until either the identity of the relative who died first becomes known or the surviving heirs reach a valid settlement among themselves. This is apparently because the presumption that neither relative survived the other is illogical in such circumstances.

2.2.1.3. Shī'ī and Ḥanbalī law: each inherits from the other

In Ḥanbalī and Shī'ī law, the rule in these cases is that each relative inherits from the other.[1] The most usual instances given by the texts of the death of relatives in a common calamity are death by drowning and death from the collapse of a roof, in a mine for example. Certain authorities, in fact, appear to restrict the rule to these two particular cases, but the majority regard it as applicable to all cases in which it is uncertain which relative died first.

For the Shī'a the rule rests on the presumption of continuance. Each relative is known to be dead and the other is presumed to have survived him because there is no proof of his predecease. For the Ḥanbalīs the rule derives from an alleged precedent of the Caliph 'Umar, who is reported to have ruled that relatives who died during a plague in Syria should inherit from one another.

The Ḥanbalī jurist Ibn Qudāma is obviously embarrassed by the rule and accepts the view of the other Sunnī schools that it must always result in an error. The relatives concerned must have died either simultaneously or one before the other. Therefore, if the former is the case, there is a double error in holding that the relatives inherit from each other because neither in fact survived the other; while if the latter is the case, then one who has in fact predeceased the praepositus is allowed to inherit from him. The rule of the Sunnī majority, on the other hand, is at least correct if the deaths were in fact simultaneous. Ibn Qudāma, however, limits himself

[1] This is also the rule adopted by the current Civil Code of Iran.

to the suggestion that each relative should inherit from the other only where the other surviving heirs agree that the order in which the relatives died is uncertain. If, on the other hand, some of the heirs assert that relative A died first and others assert that relative B died first, each side denying upon oath the claim of the other, then neither the survival of A by B, nor the survival of B by A is established. Accordingly neither should inherit from the other.

2.2.2. Variant rules illustrated

Amr and his brother Zaid are drowned at sea. They are survived only by their respective wives and their paternal uncle. Amr leaves a net estate of £32 and Zaid a net estate of £64.

According to the Sunnī majority the sole heirs to both the estates of Amr and Zaid will be a wife, entitled to a Qur'anic portion of one-quarter, and a paternal uncle, entitled to the residue of three-quarters.

Entitlement of:	from A's estate	from Z's estate	Total
A's wife	£8	—	£8
Z's wife	—	£16	£16
Uncle	£24	£48	£72

Under Shī'ī and Ḥanbalī law, Amr and Zaid inherit from each other and take the residue of each other's estate after deduction of the wife's portion, the paternal uncle being excluded when in competition with a brother. The share that Amr inherited from Zaid's estate is then distributed to Amr's heirs, i.e. his wife and paternal uncle. Zaid does not inherit from this share, for this would not only lead to an infinite series of fractional divisions of an ever decreasing sum, but would also involve the absurdity of Zaid inheriting something which had already been inherited from him. The share that Zaid inherited from Amr's estate is distributed in the same fashion. Thus,

Entitlement of:	From A's estate	From A's share in Z's estate	From Z's estate	From Z's share in A's estate
A's wife	£8	£12	—	—
Z's wife	—	—	£16	£6
Uncle	—	£36	—	£18
Amr	—	—	(£48)	—
Zaid	(£24)	—	—	—

as opposed to the result of the rule of the Sunnī majority, A's wife now takes a total share from both estates of £20, Z's wife £22 and the paternal uncle £54.

2.3. Children in the womb

2.3.1. The legal existence of a child in embryo

For the purposes of succession a child who is born alive is deemed by law to have been alive, and therefore to have possessed rights of inheritance, from the time of its conception. Accordingly, where a female relative of the praepositus claims to be pregnant at the time of decease with a child who is potentially an heir of the praepositus, provision must be made for the rights of such a child pending the determination of its existence or otherwise. Its existence will subsequently be established if it is born alive within such a period as indicates that it was conceived prior to the death of the praepositus.

2.3.2. Reservation of the share

2.3.2.1. The general rule: other heirs take minimal shares

According to Mālikī law distribution of the estate is wholly suspended until it is established whether the alleged pregnancy existed or not at the time of the praepositus' death. The other schools, however, hold that this occasions unnecessary prejudice to the rights of the other heirs. Only where all the other heirs may be totally excluded by the child will no distribution take place, as, for example, where the praepositus is survived only by brothers and sisters and his deceased son's wife who claims to be pregnant. Otherwise, the heirs present are entitled to take their minimal shares as in the case where one of the heirs is a missing person.

As distinct from the case of a missing person, however, the sex and number of the potential heir(s) is here unknown, and the rights of the other heirs may obviously be affected according to whether the subsequent birth is of a boy or a girl or twins or triplets.

2.3.2.2. Factors relevant in the reservation of the share: sex and number of the children to be born

In some circumstances the child will not be an heir at all unless it is male, as where the pregnant woman is the wife of the deceased brother of the praepositus. But while the share of a male child will usually be greater than that of a female this is not always so. Where, for example, it is the mother of the praepositus who is pregnant, by a husband other than the praepositus' father, the share of a female child (the uterine sister of the praepositus) will be the same as that of a male child. There are also a limited number of cases where a son's daughter, germane sister or consanguine sister, inheriting as a Qur'anic heir in competition with other relatives, will take more than the corresponding male relative – son's son, germane or consanguine brother – would take. For instance, where a deceased woman is survived by her husband and her mother who is pregnant by her predeceased father, the child, if male, will take one-sixth of the estate as a residuary heir, but if female will take three-eighths – the Qur'anic portion of a germane sister reduced in these circumstances by *'awl*.

The fact that more than one child results from the pregnancy will naturally diminish the shares of those heirs who belong to the same class as the children, and may diminish the shares of other heirs. The mother of the praepositus, for example, will be reduced to one-sixth by the birth of twins to a wife of the praepositus' father, even though the twins themselves are not legal heirs. Other heirs may obviously be affected by the increased Qur'anic entitlement of a plurality of daughters or sisters.

To meet these possibilities, the following rules relating to reservation of a portion of the estate and immediate distribution to the other heirs are observed by the different schools.

2.3.2.3. Ḥanbalī and Shī'ī law

The assumption is that twin boys or twin girls will be born, and the other heirs are entitled to take the share they would receive in the one case or the other, whichever is less.

2.3.2.4. Shāfi'ī law

The assumption is that twin boys or twin girls will be born, and other heirs take their minimal shares accordingly. But there is to be no distribution to heirs of the same class as the unborn heir(s) until the result of the pregnancy is known.

2.3.2.5. Ḥanafī law

The assumption is that one boy or one girl will be born. Other heirs take their minimal shares accordingly, but appropriate security is to be taken from those heirs whose entitlement will be diminished by the birth of two or more children.[1]

[1] Ḥanafī law here follows the view of Abū Yūsuf. Abū Ḥanīfa himself, along with certain scholars of other schools, maintained that the law should assume that the pregnancy would result in the birth of four boys or four girls.

2.3.3. The differences between the schools illustrated

P dies survived by his father, his mother, his daughter and his wife who claims to be pregnant. He leaves a net estate of £1,080.

Here the entitlement of all the heirs will vary according as to whether the heir subsequently born is male or female, but only the daughter will be affected by the birth of more than one child.

If the pregnancy results in the birth of a boy, or in the birth of more than one child including a boy, distribution of the estate will be as follows:

Wife		$\frac{1}{8}$		£135
Father	Qur'anic heirs	$\frac{1}{6}$		£180
Mother		$\frac{1}{6}$		£180
Daughter	Residuaries	$\frac{13}{24}$	(£585)	£195
(Son)				£390

If, on the other hand, the wife of the praepositus gives birth to a daughter or daughters, distribution will be as follows:

Wife	$\frac{1}{8}$		$\frac{3}{27}$	£120
Father	$\frac{1}{6}$	Qur'anic portions	$\frac{4}{27}$	£160
Mother	$\frac{1}{6}$	reduced by *'awl*	$\frac{4}{27}$	£160
Daughter	$\frac{2}{3}$	to:	$\frac{16}{27}$	£320
(Daughter)				£320

On this basis the different schools of law adopt the following solutions.

2.3.3.1. Mālikī law

Distribution is completely suspended until the birth of the child or until it is established by the passage of time that the wife was not in fact pregnant at the time of the praepositus' decease.

2.3.3.2. Ḥanbalī and Shī'ī law

£468 (the share of two sons) is reserved for the embryo. The daughter takes £117, which will be her share of the residue if two sons are in fact born. The wife, father and mother take the lesser shares they would receive in the event of the birth of a daughter. Any necessary adjustments will be made when the pregnancy terminates or is shown not to have existed at the time of decease.

2.3.3.3. Shāfi'ī law

The wife, father and mother take their minimal shares as above. There is no distribution to the daughter until the result of the pregnancy is known.

2.3.3.4. Ḥanafī law

The wife, father and mother take their minimal shares. The daughter takes £195, which will be her share if a son is born, and must provide security for the necessary reduction in her share in the event of more than one son being born.

2.3.4. The child must be born alive

The first condition that must be met before the child is entitled to take the reserved portion of the estate is that it must be born alive. In the majority view this means that the child must live,[1] for however brief a period, after delivery has been completed; and delivery is apparently regarded as completed when the child has fully emerged from the mother's body, even though it may still be attached to the mother by the umbilical cord. Traditional Ḥanafī law, however, allows the child to inherit if it lives when the process of birth is *substantially* completed – i.e. when, as the texts express it, the greater part of the child's body has emerged from the mother.

To this rule that a child born dead does not inherit there is one exception in traditional Ḥanafī and Ithnā 'Asharī law. This is the case of a fully formed child stillborn as a result of an assault suffered by the mother during her pregnancy.

2.3.4.1. The *ghirra* rule: blood-money for destruction of embryo

As part of the system of compensation payable in cases of homicide and physical injury, it is an established rule of Sharī'a law that the person responsible for the destruction of a child in embryo is bound to pay, over and above any liability he may bear for injury to the mother, a special sum known as *ghirra*, which amounts to 5% of the blood-money normally due in cases of homicide. It is accepted by all schools of law that this *ghirra* belongs to the stillborn child and must therefore pass to its heirs.

[1] There is considerable debate in the texts as to how the child's life may be proved. Some jurists hold that the only certain sign of life is a cry or some other noise and that physical movement by itself does not necessarily establish life. Nowadays cases of doubt will obviously be resolved by expert medical opinion.

2.3.4.2. Ḥanafī and Ithnā ʻAsharī law: extension of the *ghirra* rule

The Ḥanafīs and the Ithnā ʻAsharīs then argue that, since blood-money is only payable in the case of offences against living persons, this rule must rest on the assumption that the child in embryo was alive prior to the assault. Accordingly, such a child should also be deemed alive for the purpose of any rights of inheritance that may belong to it. The other schools, however, do not accept this extension of the *ghirra* rule and maintain that in this case, as in all other cases of children stillborn, there is no evidence of the life of the child sufficient to establish its right to inherit.

2.3.5. The child must have been conceived before the death of the praepositus

The existence or otherwise of the embryo at the time of the praepositus' decease is established upon the birth of the child by the legal presumptions relating to the gestation period. As has already been observed (p. 23 above), the law recognises a minimum period of gestation – one below which it is held to be impossible that a child should be conceived and born alive – and a maximum period – one beyond which it is held that a pregnancy cannot be protracted. The agreed minimum period is six lunar months, while the maximum period differs in the various schools: in Ithnā ʻAsharī law it is ten lunar months, in Ḥanafī law two lunar years, in Ḥanbalī and Shāfiʻī law four lunar years, and in Mālikī law five lunar years. The application of these presumptions in the present context depends upon the status of the female relative of the praepositus who claims to be pregnant with a potential heir, and the law may be summarised as follows.

2.3.5.1. Married women: minimum period of gestation applied

Where the woman claiming to be pregnant is married at the time of decease, the child will inherit only if it is born within the minimum period of gestation – six months – from the time of the decease. Since there is a presumption of continuing sexual relations between a married woman and her husband, a child born after six months may have been conceived after the praepositus' death; and the general principle applies that there is no inheritance where there is doubt as to whether the basic conditions have been fulfilled. In this situation, however, the doubt is removed if the other legal heirs formally acknowledge the existence of the pregnancy at the time of decease, and the child then inherits if born within the maximum period of gestation from the time of decease. But it is, apparently, only the Ḥanbalī school which adds the eminently logical rider that the maximum period of gestation also applies where it can be established that there was no further sexual relationship between the woman and her husband after the time of decease.

Owing to the rules of exclusion the number of cases in which a married woman can claim to be pregnant with a potential heir are in practice extremely limited. If the father of the praepositus is alive he will exclude any child of the mother, whether his own or by another husband, from succession. Any other female blood relative of the praepositus will exclude her own child, and a female relative of the praepositus by marriage cannot give birth to an entitled heir if her husband, the blood relative of the praepositus, is alive, since he will exclude his own child.

Apart, therefore, from the situation where the mother of the praepositus, after the decease of the praepositus' father, is married to another husband and claims to be pregnant with a child who will be the uterine brother or sister of the praepositus, cases can only arise under this head if the parent by whom the child would normally be excluded is himself or herself debarred on some ground from succession.

2.3.5.2. Women observing the term of '*idda*: maximum period of gestation applied

Since the law assumes no further sexual relations on the part of a woman whose marriage has terminated, the '*idda*[1] of a divorcee or widow who claims to be pregnant may last for the maximum period of gestation recognised by the law, and a child born to her within this period will be presumed to have been conceived during her former marriage and therefore be the legitimate child of her former husband.

Legitimacy is an essential qualification for the child's right of succession where it is the praepositus' own wife, or the divorcee or widow of any male relative of the praepositus, who claims to be pregnant at the time of decease. In these cases, therefore, the law must be able to presume not only the existence of a child but the existence of a legitimate child at the time of decease. Accordingly the rule is that the child will be entitled to inherit if it is born within the maximum period of gestation, not from the time of decease, but from the commencement of the '*idda* of the woman concerned – i.e. from the death of her husband in the case of a widow and from the date of her divorce in the case of a divorcee.

[1] For the law relating to the '*idda*, see p. 14 above.

2.3.5.3. Unmarried women: illegitimate children

A child born to a woman who is not married or in her *'idda* period is illegitimate. An illegitimate child, however, has a legal relationship with its mother for all purposes, including that of succession, under Sunnī law, and accordingly may inherit from the estate of a deceased relative of its mother. Where, therefore, a female blood relative of the praepositus claims, at the time of decease, to be pregnant with a child who will inherit on this basis, the law is concerned only to establish whether or not the child was in existence at the time of decease; and it will be presumed to have been so if it is born within the maximum period of gestation from the time of the praepositus' decease.

For example, P's father predeceased P by four months. P's mother claims to be pregnant at the time of P's death.

If the child is born within the maximum period of gestation from the time of the death of P's father, it will inherit as a germane brother or sister. If it is born outside this term but within the maximum period of gestation from the death of P, it will inherit as a uterine brother or sister.

Apart from the child of the praepositus' mother, however, there is little likelihood of other cases occurring in this category; for the illegitimate child of any other female blood relative of the praepositus can only inherit as a member of the outer family, and even then only when the mother herself is debarred from succession.

3. Modern law

While the basic principles and procedures of traditional Sharī'a law still apply, certain significant changes have been introduced in the Indian sub-continent and the Middle East in the presumptions relating to missing persons and children in the womb.

3.1. Missing persons: judicial decrees of death

In the light of modern systems of communication and methods of search and enquiry, the Ḥanafī rule that a person could not be judicially pronounced dead until he had passed the recognised life-span of ninety years was felt to be impractical and occasion unnecessary hardship.

In India and Pakistan the rule has been superceded by the Indian Evidence Act, 1872, under the terms of which a judicial decree of death may be issued when, despite proper search and enquiry, a person has been missing without trace for a period of seven years.

As always, a greater concern was shown in the Middle East to effect reform on the basis of acceptable Islamic authorities, and the Egyptian Law no. 25 of 1929 in effect adopted Ḥanbalī law in this regard.[1] Where a person disappears in circumstances which raise a presumption of his death and due enquiries concerning him prove fruitless, a judicial decree of death may be issued when four years have elapsed since the date of disappearance. In all other cases the court may, at its absolute discretion, pronounce a decree of death when it is satisfied, taking into account the particular circumstances of the case and the results of enquiries, that the missing person can no longer be alive.

The adoption of these provisions, almost *verbatim*, by the Jordanian Law of Family Rights, 1951, is noteworthy, inasmuch as it constitutes the solitary instance of change in the traditional law of succession introduced by Jordan.

Adopting the same general approach, the Tunisian Law of Personal Status of 1956 declares that, where a person disappears during a battle or in other circumstances which make his death probable, the court shall fix a period not exceeding two years for the purpose of search and enquiry, after which, if no information is forthcoming, it may proceed to issue a decree of death. Other cases, as in Egypt, are a matter for the absolute discretion of the court.

The Shīʿī law embodied in the Civil Code of Iran appears as something of an amalgam of traditional authorities. A person may be judicially declared dead (*a*) when he has been missing without trace for ten years and would at the end of this period have reached the age of seventy-five, or (*b*) when he has been missing for three years where the circumstances of disappearance raise a presumption of death.

3.2. Children in the womb

3.2.1. Period of gestation: maximum restricted

The views of the mediaeval jurists on the subject of gestation have been abandoned in favour of modern medical opinion in Egypt, Syria, Tunisia and Morocco, where the law now holds the maximum period of gestation

[1] This Egyptian Law was a Law of divorce, it being particularly the hardship suffered by wives of missing husbands, who were for all practical purposes prevented from remarrying under the traditional Ḥanafī law, which provided the impetus for reform. This is one of many instances which show the debt of Egyptian reformers to Ḥanbalī jurisprudence. Explanatory memoranda and commentaries on the Law reproduce, on occasions almost *verbatim*, the reasoning and language of the Ḥanbalī scholar Ibn Qudāma.

to be 365 days, while traditional Ḥanafī law has also been superceded in the Indian sub-continent by the provisions of the Evidence Act, 1872, relating to paternity.[1] In appropriate circumstances, therefore, these new rules will determine the existence or otherwise of a child in embryo at the time of the praepositus' decease.

3.2.2. Rule of physical access between spouses

As opposed to traditional Sunnī law, proof of non-access between the spouses at any possible time of conception will now rebut the presumption of legitimacy under the Indian Evidence Act and modern legislation in the Middle East.[2] This may therefore defeat the claim of a child in embryo to inherit, at least where the basis of such claim is the legitimacy of the child.

3.2.3. Married women: normal period of gestation applied

Under the Egyptian Law of Inheritance, 1943, a child born to a married woman within 270 days of the decease of the praepositus will be presumed to have been in embryo at the time of decease. This rule replaces the period of six lunar months applicable in such cases under the traditional law and departs to some extent from the strict principle that there must be no doubt about the existence of a claimant heir at the time of decease. But the reformers argued with some point that the law should in these cases presume that gestation followed its normal, and not an exceptional course.[3] The same rule is adopted by the Tunisian Law of Personal Status, 1956.

3.2.4 Live birth

In Egypt, Syria and Tunisia, the Ḥanafī rule that the child inherits if it lives when the process of birth is substantially completed has been replaced by the view of the Sunnī majority that the child must live when delivery has been completed.

3.2.5. *Ghirra*

In Egypt and Tunisia, the Ḥanafī rule that a child stillborn as a result of an assault upon the mother is entitled to inherit has been abolished. Moreover, the *ghirra* itself no longer belongs to the stillborn child so as to pass to its own heirs, but is regarded as an additional sum of compensation payable to the mother for an injury caused to her.[4]

[1] For details see pp. 27–8 above.
[2] For details see pp. 27–8 above.
[3] The reform also claimed the authority, though somewhat tenuous and indirect, of the Ḥanbalī jurist Ibn Taymiyya.
[4] For this departure from the accepted view of all the schools the reformers claimed the authority of two Muslim scholars of the early eighth century (see my *A History of Islamic Law*, p. 195).

13. BEQUESTS

1. The original sources of the law of bequests

It is ordained for you that anyone who is at the point of death, and has goods to leave, should bequeath equitably to his parents and near relatives. This is an obligation upon the pious (Qur'ān, 2, 180).

Such of you as die leaving wives should bequeath to them maintenance for one year... (Qur'ān, 2, 240).

These Qur'anic verses, the first of which is generally known as "the verse of bequests", represent historically the first Islamic regulations on the subject of succession. They enjoin testamentary dispositions only, or at least primarily, as a means by which the deceased might make suitable provision for his surviving relatives; and for this reason the verses were generally held to be superseded and abrogated by the later Qur'anic texts which laid down the rules of inheritance. The Qur'anic rules of inheritance were never regarded as applying only in the case of persons who died wholly or partially intestate. The juristic consensus held that the general duty of the deceased to transmit his property to his relatives had become particularised; a permissive and discretionary system of succession to property at death had now been replaced by mandatory rules which prescribed the entitlement of the different relatives in terms of a fixed fractional share of the estate.

At the same time the Qur'ān itself clearly still allowed some power of testamentary disposition inasmuch as the shares of inheritance that it allotted were specifically described as portions of the residual estate left "after the payment of any bequests and debts". Hence the fundamental problem, unanswered by the Qur'ān itself, was that of the relationship between the two systems of voluntary and compulsory devolution of property. What limits, if any, were to be set upon testamentary dispositions in order to safeguard the scheme of inheritance?

2. The limits of testamentary power

Muslim jurisprudence finds the solution of this problem in the precedents, or *sunna*, of the Prophet Muḥammad, which impose two principal restrictions upon testamentary power. The first restriction concerns the *quantum* of bequests, where the rule is that a person may not dispose by will of more than one-third of his property. The most popular version of the origin of this rule is the following report by the Prophet's companion Sa'd b. Abī Waqqās:

The Prophet came to visit me in the year of the farewell pilgrimage when I was afflicted with a severe illness. I said to him: "O Prophet, you see how ill I am. I have property and no heir except my daughter. Shall I then give away two-thirds of my property as alms?" He replied "No." I said "A half then?" He still said "No." I then asked "A third?" He replied: "A third. And a third is much. It is better that you leave your heirs rich than that you should leave them destitute, begging from their neighbours."[1]

In similar vein, another companion of the Prophet, Sa'd b. Mālik, reports:

When I was very sick the Prophet visited me and asked: "Have you made a will?" I replied "Yes. I have bequeathed all my property to the poor and for pious purposes." The Prophet then advised me: "Bequeath only a tenth part of it." I replied "But my estate is vast and my heirs are rich..." Eventually the Prophet said: "Then bequeath a third. A third is much."

The second limitation upon testamentary power recognised by Sunnī law concerns the recipients of bequests, where the rule is that a testator may not make a bequest in favour of any of his legal heirs. Abū Imāma reported: "I heard the Prophet say: 'Allah has already given to each entitled relative his proper entitlement. Therefore, no bequest in favour of a legal heir.'"

3. The general attitude to bequests

As a result of these precedents of the Prophet, Muslim, or at least Sunnī, jurisprudence sees the essence of succession law to lie in protecting the interests of the legal heirs and preserving the balance between their claims established under the sacrosanct scheme of inheritance. Bequests, however meritorious their purpose – in providing for cases of particular hardship, in fulfilling a charitable purpose, or in performing what the testator conceived to be a personal duty left outstanding during his lifetime – are not allowed to defeat the entitlement of the legal heirs to at least two-thirds of the estate. Furthermore, the limitation upon the *quantum* of bequests applies regardless of the small number or the affluent circumstances of the legal heirs; for their inheritance is a matter of right and not of need.

Ethical standards are as much the province of traditional Sharī'a doctrine as strictly legal rules. And on this broader plane traditional Sunnī

[1] As reported in Ibn Qudāma, *al-Mughnī*, VI, 1–4.

jurisprudence approves of bequests only where the residue of the testator's estate is substantial enough to constitute a real benefit for his legal heirs. If this is not the case, then bequests, even for charitable or other worthy purposes, are generally disapproved. According to one dictum, "No wealth brings greater reward than that which a man leaves for his children to make them independent of others" (*al-Mughnī*, VI, 3). Certainly, in the majority view, the duty to make a bequest as laid down in the earliest Qur'anic regulations had lapsed in all cases except where the bequest was designed to discharge a legal duty of the deceased – to pay a debt, for example, which could not otherwise be discharged because of the lack of legal proof. A minority of jurists, however, held that it was still a duty of the deceased, in accordance with the Qur'anic verse of bequests, to provide by way of bequest for those near relatives who were in need and were not legal heirs; and this view, as has been seen (pp. 145–6 above) in fact provided the juristic basis for recent reforms in succession law in the Middle East.

But whatever the moral standards that are applied to bequests, the law recognises the validity of testamentary power within the broad limits described. A detailed examination of the limits of testamentary power is the subject of the following chapter. The remainder of this chapter is concerned solely with the legal incidents of the transaction of bequest.

4. Declaration of bequest

A bequest, or *waṣiyya*, is a gift of property postponed until after the death of the donor. As such it is classified as a contractual transfer or property, or '*aqd*, and is completed by the offer (*ījāb*) of the transferor and the acceptance (*qabūl*) of the transferee. Accordingly, the first constituent element of the transaction is a valid offer or declaration by one who has the legal capacity so to dispose of his property gratuitously.

4.1. Formalities: traditional law

Traditional Sharī'a doctrine prescribes no special form for the declaration of a bequest. Any words, or indeed signs, may be used provided they clearly indicate the testator's intention that the property should pass to the legatee after his death. Ideally, perhaps, in accordance with a procedure specifically recommended by the Qur'ān itself, a bequest ought to be made in writing and witnesses called to its oral declaration; but a purely oral declaration of a bequest is perfectly valid. Moreover, a bequest, as a general rule, may be proved only by the testimony of witnesses, usually two male adult Muslims, who were present at its oral declaration. It is only the Mālikī and Ḥanbalī schools who recognise the validity of a written bequest, in the known handwriting or under the known signature of the testator, when there were no witnesses to any oral declaration or when witnesses were called to verify the fact that the document constituted a bequest by the testator but were ignorant of its contents.

4.2. Modern law: documentary evidence required

Recent legislation in many Muslim countries, however, requires bequests to be proved by documentary evidence. Under article 2 of the Egyptian Law of Testamentary Dispositions, 1946, for example, no disputed claim of a bequest will be entertained by the courts unless it is supported by official documents, by documents written and signed by the testator or by documents bearing the officially authenticated signature of the testator. The Syrian Law of Personal Status, 1953, closely followed the Egyptian Law in this respect, while article 176 of the Tunisian Code of Personal Status, 1956, similarly enacts: "A bequest can be proved only by an official document or by a document written, dated and signed by the testator." The relevant provisions of the Iraqi Law of Personal Status, 1959, are somewhat more detailed. Article 65 (i) of the Law provides that a bequest can be established "only by the evidence of a document signed by the testator or stamped with his seal or thumb print. But if the bequest is one of immoveable property, or one of moveable property which exceeds in value 500 dinars, the authentication of the document by a public notary is required." Article 65 (ii), however, goes on to state that a bequest "may be established by oral testimony where there exists a substantial obstacle to prevent the production of documentary evidence". According to one Iraqi writer,[1] this concession would apply, for example, where an illiterate testator was on his death-bed and no one to write the will could be found in time, or where a written will had been destroyed by fire or other unforseen event.

4.3. Capacity of the testator: the test is rational appreciation

As a general principle, a full legal capacity to engage in transactions, and particularly to dispose of property gratuitously, belongs, in the contemplation of traditional Sharīʿa doctrine, to those who have the quality

[1] Muḥsin Nājī, *Sharḥ Qānūn al-Aḥwāl al-Shakhṣiyya* (Baghdad, 1962), pp. 430 ff.

of "prudent judgment" (*rushd*). A person who lacks this quality and cannot be described as *rāshid*, because of immaturity or irresponsibility or mental deficiency, is said to be under interdiction (*hajr*). His affairs are managed by a guardian and any transactions entered into by the interdicted person will normally be either *ipso facto* void or at least subject to ratification by his guardian. The classes of persons subject to such interdiction include not only minors, lunatics and mental defectives, but also simpletons and prodigals, those who by carelessness or design tend to squander their property immoderately and to no good purpose.

However, this strict and somewhat paternalistic doctrine of legal incapacity is considerably relaxed as regards bequests, where the general test of the validity of the declaration is simply that it is made voluntarily by one who rationally appreciates what he is doing. All schools agree that a person who is adult in the sense that he has attained physical puberty – which the law conclusively presumes to be reached at the upper limit of the age of fifteen for both sexes – has the capacity to make a bequest. But Mālikī and Ḥanbalī law also recognise the validity of a bequest made by a minor who has reached the age of seven, and Shī'ī law that of a minor who has reached the age of ten, on the ground that this is the age of "discernment" (*tamyīz*). Bequests made by lunatics, mental defectives, persons acting under compulsion or in temporary loss of reason through, for example, intoxication, are void, but those made by simpletons or prodigals are valid. These last two classes of interdicted persons have a rational appreciation of what they are doing and the purpose of interdiction in their case, which is to protect their property during their lifetime, does not apply to dispositions which will be effective only after their death. It is broadly for the same reason that a declaration of bequest by another class of interdicted person, the bankrupt, is not *per se* invalid. The purpose of interdiction in this last case is to protect the interests of the creditors, and these cannot be prejudiced, either during the bankrupt's lifetime or after his death, by any declaration of bequest he may make.

4.4. Statutory ages under modern law

Modern legislation has generally raised the age of capacity for making a bequest. Under the terms of the Indian Majority Act, for example, as now applicable in India and Pakistan, it is eighteen, as it also is in Syria and Iraq. In Egypt the statutory age of majority is twenty-one and in Tunisia it is twenty, but in both these countries persons who have attained the age of eighteen may make a bequest with the consent of the court. The

Egyptian and Tunisian Laws also require the consent of the court in the case of bequests made by those under interdiction on account of their simplicity or prodigality.

5. The substance and terms of bequests

5.1. Bequest of the corpus (*'ain*) of property

Apart from those items which are declared by the Sharī'a to be illegal and prohibited (*ḥarām*), such as pigs and intoxicants, and which do not therefore constitute legal property (*māl*), any property which is owned by the testator and could be the subject of a valid contract *inter vivos* constitutes proper subject matter for a bequest.

5.1.1. Specific and general bequests

Just as is the case with the law of inheritance, the law of testate succession does not depend upon any distinction between real and personal property or between moveables and immoveables. The distinction of English law, for example, between a devise and a bequest has no parallel in Islamic law, so that the term bequest may be properly used in reference to all types of property. Accordingly, bequests may be simply classified as either specific or general.

A specific bequest consists of a particular item of property distinguished from other property of the same kind – e.g. "my law books", or "my farm known as Wadī Ḥimār".

A general bequest is a gift of property not so specifically distinguished. It may be a pecuniary legacy or a gift of property generally described, for example "two three-year-old camels", where the bequest will be satisfied by any two such camels, from the testator's herd or from elsewhere, or by providing the legatee with their market price.

A type of bequest popular in Muslim society because of its affiliation with the system of quota shares of inheritance is that of a fractional part of the testator's property. Such a bequest is to be classified as general if it consists of a share in the entirety of the testator's property or a share in a particular genus of his property – e.g. "one-third of my estate" or "one-quarter of my animals"; while it is a specific bequest if it consists of a share in a particular item of property or a species of property – e.g. "one-quarter of my goats".

The primary relevance of the distinction between a specific and a general bequest is that the former is held to refer to the testator's property at the time the bequest is made and the latter to his property as it exists at the time of his death. Accordingly, the subject-matter of a specific bequest must be in the ownership of the testator at the time of the declaration of bequest; otherwise the bequest fails on the broad ground of fundamental mistake. A general bequest, on the other hand, is effective if the property concerned is owned by the testator at the time of his death. It also follows, in the case of bequests of fractional shares of property, that the beneficiary of a specific bequest – e.g. "one-quarter of my goats" – is entitled to the stated fraction of the property as it exists at the time of the bequest, while the beneficiary of a general bequest – e.g. "one-quarter of my animals" – is entitled to the stated fraction of the property as it exists at the time of the testator's death.

5.1.2. Uncertainty

As a general rule testamentary dispositions do not fail on the ground of uncertainty or ambiguity in the subject matter of the bequest. Where, for example, a testator bequeathes "a share in my estate", or "the share of an heir", this will be construed as the bequest of an amount equivalent to the lowest fractional entitlement of any of the legal heirs. Similarly, if the testator simply bequeathes "something", or "a small gift", the legal heirs are allowed, but at the same time required, to specify what shall be given to the legatee.

5.1.3. Joint bequests

Where a bequest of a certain sum is made jointly to two or more beneficiaries, or for several different purposes, without any express apportionment of the sum between them, the general rule is that the different beneficiaries or purposes share equally in the bequest. To this rule there is one principal exception. Where such a bequest is made exclusively for various pious or charitable purposes, which include the performance on behalf of the testator of a religious duty (such as the pilgrimage) omitted by him during his lifetime, the performance of the religious duty takes precedence over the other pious or charitable purposes. This is, perhaps, only a natural construction of the testator's intention, since in a bequest of this nature he may be supposed to have had the performance of his religious duty primarily in mind and to have nominated the other charitable purposes simply as residual beneficiaries.

T, for example, bequeathes £200 "for the performance of the pilgrimage on my behalf and for the maintenance of the local mosque". If the cost of performing the pilgrimage is £150, the mosque will benefit only to the extent of £50.

The rule, however, is confined to a joint bequest made *exclusively* for pious or charitable purposes. If a non-charitable purpose is included in the bequest, the normal rule of equal apportionment applies.

T bequeathes £150 "for the performance of the pilgrimage, the local hospital and my friend Zaid". £50 will go to each of the three purposes, even though this sum should prove inadequate for the performance of the pilgrimage.

5.2. Bequest of the usufruct (*manfa'a*) of property

During the formative period of Sharī'a law certain jurists maintained that the future produce or income of property belonging to the testator was not property in existence at the time of his death and therefore could not properly be the subject of a bequest. From mediaeval times onwards, however, the settled doctrine of all the schools has been that a bequest of the future usufruct of property which is in existence at the time of the testator's death is valid, although Ḥanafī law is considerably more restrictive in this respect than the law of the other schools.

5.2.1. Traditional law: duration of usufructory interest

All schools agree that where the use or income of property is bequeathed permanently or without any express time limit to a general class of persons whose extinction is inconceivable, such as the poor or the sick, or to some other public charity, the legatees are entitled in perpetuity. But where a usufructory bequest is made in favour of a particular individual, or a limited group of particular individuals, its effect in Ḥanafī law is restricted by two principal rules.

There is first the Ḥanafī rule that a usufructory right is not inheritable. Hence, if T bequeathes to L "the produce of my orchard", expressly stating that the gift is "for ever" or omitting to set any time limit to it, in Ḥanafī law the right to the produce of the orchard will belong to L as long as he lives, but on his death it will revert to the owner of the orchard. According to the other schools the right to the orchard's produce will pass, on L's death, to his heirs in perpetuity. Similarly, if the produce is bequeathed for a fixed term of years and L dies before the term is complete, the right to the produce will revert to the owner of the orchard in Ḥanafī law, but will pass to L's heirs for the remainder of the stipulated term according to the other schools.

The second relevant rule of Ḥanafī law, which is also followed by the Shāfi'īs and the Ḥanbalīs, is the rule that a particular legatee – as opposed to a legatee of a general class like "the poor" – must be in existence at the time of the testator's death. Accordingly, a bequest of the income of property "to Zaid and his issue, generation after generation" will be effective only in favour of those children of Zaid who are alive at the time of the testator's death. Mālikī law, however, holds that bequests may validly be made in favour of persons who are not alive at the time of the testator's death but who are born subsequently. Hence, such a usufructory bequest is valid under Mālikī law in favour of an unrestricted number of generations or series of beneficiaries.

5.2.2. Current law in Egypt and Syria

A more permissive attitude towards usufructory bequests is one of the features of the Egyptian Law of Testamentary Dispositions, 1946, and the Syrian Law of Personal Status, 1953. On a relatively minor matter of construction, for example, the traditional Ḥanafī view was that a bequest of "fruit" meant such fruit as was in existence at the time of the testator's death and only entitled the legatee to future fruits if none existed at that time. This Ḥanafī view has now been abandoned in Egypt and Syria in favour of the view of other schools, and particularly the Shāfi'īs, that a bequest of "fruit" always includes the right to future produce.

On a more substantial issue, both the Egyptian and Syrian Laws adopt the Mālikī view and permit bequests, whether of the corpus or the usufruct, in favour of legatees who are not yet in existence, or some of whom are not yet in existence, at the time of the testator's decease. On this basis usufructory bequests in favour of "descendants" are declared to be valid, but only for two generations or series of beneficiaries under the Egyptian Law and for one generation under the Syrian and Tunisian Laws.[1] This last provision is an example of the process of reform termed *talfīq*, or the combination, within the ambit of a single legal rule, of the views of different schools of Sharī'a law. Where a usufructory bequest, for example, is made in favour of an indefinite number of generations of descendants, the validity of the bequest for the first two generations may be said to rest upon Mālikī authority, while its invalidity for subsequent generations may be said to rest upon Ḥanafī law, which does not allow bequests in favour of persons not in existence at the time of the testator's decease, or indeed upon the views of those early jurists who denied the validity of usufructory bequests altogether.

[1] This "rule against perpetuities" is closely parallel with Egyptian legislation of 1946 relating to family settlements under the *waqf* system. The right to enjoy the income of property constituted as *waqf* was restricted to two generations of descendants or two series of beneficiaries.

5.3. Contingent and conditional bequests

5.3.1. Contingent bequests

A contingent bequest, in the terminology of Sharī'a law, is one which is "suspended upon a condition" (*mu'allaq 'alā sharṭ*), that is to say the bequest is not to become operative unless and until a specified event takes place or a specified condition is fulfilled. As a general rule, the essence of transactions *inter vivos* under Sharī'a law is that they constitute an immediate disposition of property. A donor, for example, is someone who is prepared to relinquish ownership of the property concerned immediately and who signifies this, conventionally, by phrasing his offer or declaration of gift in the past tense – e.g. "I have given". As a result of this philosophy a promise to give *in futuro* is generally not binding; in other words a future or contingent gift is a nullity. The same considerations, however, do not apply to a bequest, which, by its nature, is a postponed transfer of ownership and which may be revoked by the testator at any time prior to his death. A testator who makes his bequest dependent upon an uncertain future event or condition is in fact merely indicating in advance the circumstances in which he would revoke the bequest. Hence the general rule is that contingent bequests are valid.

'Umar bequeathes his house to Zaid "if I die within the next year", and £1,000 to Fāṭima "if she is unmarried at the time of my death". The bequests will be good if, but only if, the specified conditions are fulfilled.

5.3.2. Conditional bequests

A conditional bequest is a bequest coupled with a condition which seeks to regulate either the manner in which the property bequeathed shall be enjoyed or the general conduct and activities of the beneficiaries. If the condition is deemed valid it will be enforced against the beneficiaries or, alternatively, its infringement will entail forfeiture of the bequest. But if the condition is deemed invalid the normal doctrine of severance will apply: the condition will be ignored and the bequest will remain valid.

A bequest of the corpus of property transfers full and absolute ownership to the legatee, and any condition which contradicts this essential legal effect of the transaction is a nullity. If, for example, a house is bequeathed on condition that the legatee does not sell it or let it, and that on his death it will revert to the testator's heirs, the conditions are void and the legatee takes the house as absolute owner. He may use it or alienate it as he sees fit and on his death it will pass to his own heirs or as he otherwise instructs.

Usufructory bequests, on the other hand, may be validly subject to restraints upon user and time limits. Ḥanafī law is particularly rigid in this regard. A bequest of "the use" of a house, for example, is construed as entitling the beneficiary to occupy the house himself but not to let it to anyone else. Shāfi'ī and Ḥanbalī law, however, would here allow the beneficiary to sub-let, and even where the testator had specified a particular mode of user would, as against the Ḥanafīs, allow the beneficiary to use the property in any other way he wished provided no damage was caused to the property thereby. The recent Egyptian and Syrian legislation has now abandoned the strict Ḥanafī rules in these respects in favour of the Shāfi'ī and Ḥanbalī law, on the broad ground that conditions which are beneficial to no one should be disregarded.

5.3.3. Current law in Egypt and Syria

Current Egyptian and Syrian law also adopts a more liberal attitude than that of the majority of traditional authorities towards the question of conditions which seek to make the entitlement of the beneficiaries dependent upon their following a specified course of conduct. Thus the Syrian Law, following the Egyptian Law almost *verbatim*, provides (article 210) that a condition attached to a bequest is valid and enforceable if it is "one in which there is some legal benefit to the testator or to the legatee or to some other person, and which is neither forbidden nor contrary to the purposes of the Sharī'a". Under this legislation, therefore, a condition that the legatee, in order to continue to enjoy a bequest of income or usufruct, should remain unmarried or should live in a specified place, would be held to be void, on the ground that restrictions upon the freedom to marry or to change one's place of residence are contrary to the purposes of the Sharī'a. According to the traditional doctrine of all the schools, however, such a condition would be valid, since the only void conditions in this context are those which attempt to impose something specifically forbidden by the law, such as a condition that the legatee should ignore the fast of Ramaḍān. But certain individual jurists of the Ḥanbalī school – particularly Ibn Taymiyya and Ibn al-Qayyim – had regarded conditions such as those in restraint of marriage as unduly oppressive, contrary to the general purposes of the lawgiver, and therefore void; and it was this view which provided the juristic authority for the Egyptian and Syrian legislation.

5.4. Void bequests

5.4.1. Illegal purpose

A bequest, whether of the corpus of property or its usufruct, is null and void if it is expressly devoted to an illegal purpose, such as the promotion of gambling or the encouragement of sexual immorality. The Syrian Law of Personal Status, 1953, merely reasserts this traditional doctrine when it enacts (article 209): "It is a condition of the validity of a bequest that it should not be made in favour of something forbidden by the law."

5.4.2. Improper motive

The Egyptian Law of Testamentary Dispositions, 1946, however, also declares to be null and void a bequest inspired by a motive which is contrary to the purposes of the lawgiver. Under this law, for example, a bequest in favour of the testator's mistress might be held to be null and void on the ground that it was designed to reward her for, or to encourage her to continue, her immoral (and, of course, in the eyes of Islamic law, criminal) behaviour. So, too, a bequest in favour of a perfectly legitimate object might be declared null and void on the ground that the testator's primary intention was to deprive his legal heirs of the property. Once again the Egyptian legislation could claim juristic support in the individualistic views of such Ḥanbalī scholars as Ibn al-Qayyim, who maintained that the validity of bequests, as indeed that of other contracts and transactions, was dependent upon the absence of any improper or wrongful motive. Traditional Sharī'a doctrine generally refused to enquire into the motive that a testator might have in bequeathing property to someone who was legally capable of owning it.

6. Failure of bequests

A valid declaration or offer of bequest becomes binding only upon the death of the testator. During the lifetime of the testator the offer may be deemed to have lapsed, so that the bequest fails and its subject matter, if still in existence at the time of decease, forms part of the testator's general estate. The circumstances in which a bequest so fails may be subsumed under four principal heads.

6.1. Revocation by the testator: express revocation

Provided the words used are clear and unambiguous, traditional Sharī'a doctrine does not require the observance of any particular formalities for the effective revocation of a bequest. Modern legislation, however, invariably requires for the revocation of a bequest the same formalities as are necessary for its effective constitution or declaration. Thus, the Iraqi Law of Personal Status, 1959, enacts (article 72): "A bequest is nullified...by the testator's revocation of his bequest. But no legal recognition is to be afforded to revocation unless it is established by evidence at least as strong as that which established the bequest itself." Accordingly, under this law, revocation of a bequest of immoveable property can be validly effected only by a written document authenticated by a public notary (p. 216 above).

6.2. Loss of the subject matter of the bequest: implied revocation

A bequest fails when the property bequeathed is so affected by subsequent events, whether by the testator's own act or otherwise, that it can no longer pass to the legatee in the state envisaged by the testator at the time he made the bequest. In these circumstances the law holds that the bequest is impliedly revoked. Three principal cases of failure of this type, which, of course, can apply only to specific as opposed to general bequests, may be distinguished.

(i) Loss, destruction or consumption of the property bequeathed, either by the act of the testator or otherwise.

(ii) Alienation of the property by the testator through sale, gift or any other means. To this most authorities would add any attempted alienation of the property by the testator, such as an offer to sell it or give it away, since even if this does not actually result in the testator losing ownership of the property, it is a clear indication that he no longer intends it to pass to the legatee on his death. For the same reason a bequest fails if the testator subsequently bequeathes the same property to another person.

(iii) Substantial change in the character of the property bequeathed, whether instigated by the testator or otherwise. A bequest of a roll of cloth, for example, will fail if it is subsequently tailored into garments, and a bequest of a block of stables will fail if it is subsequently converted into dwelling flats. On the other hand, the normal maintenance of property or minor improvements of it, such as redecorating a house or installing a new heating system, do not constitute an implied revocation of the bequest since the essential character of the property remains unchanged.

6.3. Testator's subsequent loss of capacity: lunacy

In the contemplation of the Ḥanafī jurists, the testator's right to revoke his bequest is so much of the essence of the transaction that if he loses the capacity of revocation for a substantial time the bequest will fail. Accordingly, the rule of Ḥanafī law is that a bequest is nullified by the subsequent lunacy or mental derangement of the testator which lasts for one month or more, even if he recovers sanity before death. Although the other schools do not subscribe to this doctrine, the current law in Egypt, Syria, Tunisia and Iraq is that a bequest fails through the subsequent lunacy of the testator unless he recovers his sanity before death and thereby has the opportunity of revocation.

6.4. Legatee predeceasing testator

The Sunnī schools are unanimous in the view that a bequest lapses if the legatee predeceases the testator, whether the latter knew of the death or not. Since the transaction of bequest can only be completed by the legatee's acceptance after the testator's death, it must fail when such acceptance becomes impossible.

Although some Shī'ī jurists subscribe to the same view, the most authoritative Shī'ī doctrine is that the predecease of the legatee does not *ipso facto* nullify the bequest. If the testator does not revoke the bequest, the right to accept or refuse it passes to the legatee's heirs. Only where the legatee has no heirs will the bequest fail. This is one of a number of details of Shī'ī law which indicate that a *spes successionis* – here the expectation that a legatee has from the declaration of a bequest – is a far more substantial right than it is in Sunnī law, substantial enough, in this context, to be inheritable.[1]

6.4.1. Uncertainty of legatee's death or survival

Where it is uncertain whether or not the legatee predeceased the testator – because, for example, the legatee is a missing person at the time of the testator's death or because the testator and legatee die together in the same accident – the same principles apply as in the case of intestate succession (pp. 198–204 above). As a general rule, therefore, the bequest will fail in

[1] The other related details of Shī'ī law are as follows: (i) the rule that a legatee may validly accept a bequest before the testator's death (p. 232); (ii) the rule that a legal heir may validly ratify an *ultra vires* bequest during the testator's lifetime (p. 246); (iii) the rule that bequests take priority according to the time at which they were made (p. 252).

such circumstances because there is no evidence that the basic condition of succession, namely, the survival of the testator by the legatee, has been fulfilled. According to Shīʿī law, however, in all these cases, and according to Ḥanbalī law in the case of the death of the testator and the legatee in the same calamity, the legal presumption will be that the legatee survived the testator. Hence, in this minority doctrine, the bequest will not fail on the ground of the legatee's predecease, but it will be treated as a case of the legatee dying after the testator without having accepted or refused the bequest, so that the option to accept or refuse it will pass to the legatee's heirs (pp. 233–4 below).

7. Conditions relating to the legatee

Property, or the usufruct thereof, may as a general rule be validly bequeathed to any person capable of owning property, or to an institution, or for a religious or charitable purpose not opposed to the tenets of Islam.

7.1. Existence of the legatee

7.1.1. Actual or legal existence of the legatee at the time of the testator's death

It is, in general, a fundamental condition of the validity of a bequest that the legatee must be in existence at the time of the testator's decease. Basically this rule rests upon the ground that the transaction of bequest is a transfer of property from the dead to the living which requires acceptance by the legatee for its completion, and must therefore fail if such acceptance by the designated beneficiary is impossible at the time of the testator's death.

"Existence", however, in this context, means that the legatee may be alive either in fact or in law at the time of the testator's death. A child in the womb has a legal existence and is therefore entitled to take a bequest. Such legal existence is determined by the application of the legal presumptions relating to the gestation period in precisely the same manner as they are applied to determine whether or not an alleged child in embryo has a right of inheritance (pp. 204–12 above). Where, however, a testator makes a bequest to a child in embryo whose existence he expressly acknowledges, the bequest will be effective if the child is born within the maximum period of gestation from the date of the acknowledgment, even if the child's mother is married. Such a child would only have a right of inheritance if it was born within the minimum, or at most the normal, period of gestation after the death of the praepositus. The recent reforms of traditional Sharī'a law in the matter of the gestation period and paternity in general have, of course, precisely the same relevance in testate as in intestate succession.

There are two exceptions to the general rule that the legatee must be alive in fact or in law at the time of the testator's decease. The first is the obvious case of bequests for a general and continuing charitable purpose like "the poor" or "the sick". The second is confined to the Mālikī school and to certain Shāfi'ī authorities, who recognise as valid bequests in favour of legatees, described as members of a restricted class or group, who may come into existence after the testator's decease – e.g. a bequest in favour of "any children that Zaid may have before he dies".

7.1.2. Specific legatees must be in existence at the time of the bequest

A bequest in favour of a legatee individually named or otherwise described by the testator fails, on the broad ground of fundamental mistake, if the legatee was not in existence at the time the bequest was made. The Iraqi Law of 1959, for example, preserves traditional Sharī'a doctrine in this regard when it enacts (article 68): "The legatee must be alive in fact or in law at the time of the bequest and at the time of the testator's decease." On the other hand, a bequest in favour of a class or group of persons only generally described is held to refer to the time of the testator's death, so that those who fall within the description at that time qualify as beneficiaries. For example, a bequest to "the children of Zaid" goes not only to those children alive in fact or in law at the time of the bequest but also to those born subsequently and alive in fact or in law at the time of the testator's decease. This distinction is precisely parallel to that which obtains in relation to the subject matter of a bequest between property specifically identified and that generally described, the former being held to refer to the testator's property at the time of the bequest and the latter to his property at the time of death (pp. 218–19 above).

7.2. Impediments to testamentary succession: the distinction between testate and intestate succession

Traditional Sharī'a law takes a very different view of impediments to testate and impediments to intestate succession. The distinction is most obvious, perhaps, in the case of a difference of religion. Since the compulsory rules of inheritance are designed to ensure the proper devolution of property to the family group within the broader community of Islam, a non-

Muslim relative is totally debarred from inheriting from a Muslim praepositus. A bequest, on the other hand, as a discretionary transmission of property at death and a personal transaction between the testator and the legatee, lies outside such considerations of religious allegiance. Hence, a legatee who is a non-Muslim is not thereby disqualified from taking a bequest from a Muslim testator. There are also significant variations in the circumstances in which homicide constitutes a bar to testate, as opposed to intestate, succession – variations which again reflect the essentially different nature of the two modes of devolution of property. Recent legislation in this branch of the law in the Middle East displays two notable trends. First, it treats homicide as a bar to both testate and intestate succession on the same footing, and second, where a legatee has a different nationality from that of the testator, it goes some way towards establishing parity between Muslim and non-Muslim legatees.

7.2.1. Homicide

The circumstances in which, according to the different schools, the killing of the praepositus by the heir constitutes an impediment to inheritance have been explained above (pp. 176–85). In that context the schools are agreed upon the basic principle that homicide creates an absolute bar to inheritance and differ only as to the type of homicide which creates the bar. Towards the question of homicide as a bar to testamentary succession, however, no less than three fundamentally different approaches are adopted.

7.2.1.1. Shīʿī and Ḥanafī law

The first approach is to equate bequests and inheritance on the ground that they are both rights of succession. Then, since a right of inheritance, as a compulsory right, is stronger than a right to a bequest, it follows that a legatee will be disqualified, *a fortiori*, in the same circumstances as an heir is disqualified. This is the basis of Shīʿī law, under which a legatee is debarred from taking a bequest if he is guilty of the deliberate homicide of the testator, and of Ḥanafī law, where any direct killing of the testator by the legatee is a bar to his taking the bequest. In Ḥanafī law, however, the bar is not absolute as it is in the case of inheritance, but the bequest is valid if ratified by the testator's heirs, and is therefore, in effect, treated not as a void but as an *ultra vires* disposition.

7.2.1.2. Mālikī and Shāfiʿī law

The second approach is to distinguish between inheritance and bequests as essentially different modes of transfer of property, and to regard the transaction of bequest as being most closely parallel to that of gift. Hence, since a killer as such is not debarred from taking a gift from his victim, a legatee is not debarred by his homicide of the testator. This is the view of Mālikī and Shāfi'ī law, where even a murderer may take a legacy, but may not of course inherit, from his victim.

7.2.1.3 Ḥanbalī law

The final approach, which clearly expresses the distinction between compulsory and discretionary succession, is that of the Ḥanbalīs, who consider the issue in terms of the personal wishes of the testator rather than in terms of the presence or absence of a technical impediment in the legatee. The normal presumption is that a testator would not wish to benefit his killer and that he would, given the opportunity, revoke the bequest. Accordingly, a bequest made to one who causes the death of the testator by any form of actionable homicide fails, unless, where there is an interval between the act which caused his death and death itself, the testator expressly confirms the bequest. It follows that a bequest made for the first time during this interval to the killer is perfectly valid.

7.2.1.4. Modern legislation in the Middle East

In Egypt and Syria homicide is now a bar to testamentary succession in the same circumstances as it is a bar to inheritance (pp. 182–3 above). The Tunisian Code of 1956 follows the Egyptian and Syrian Laws very closely, except for the age of criminal liability, when it enacts (article 198):

> A bequest, voluntary or obligatory, fails if the legatee has deliberately caused the death of the testator, directly or indirectly, whether he acted as principal, accomplice or accessory, or was a false witness whose testimony led to a sentence of the testator's death being executed, provided the killing was without lawful excuse and the killer was sane and at least thirteen years of age.

There seems, therefore, to be some variation under current Tunisian law between the circumstances in which homicide is a bar to testate and to intestate succession, since the final proviso concerning the age and sanity of the legatee does not apparently apply to a legal heir (p. 184 above).

It is doubtful whether the Iraqi legislation of 1959 has changed the traditional Sharī'a law at all in this regard. Article 68 of the Law simply enacts: "It is a condition in relation to the legatee...that he should not have killed the testator." This brief provision seems to admit of interpretation according to the traditional tenets of either Ḥanafī or Shī'ī law, except that the legal heirs, perhaps, no longer have the option to ratify the bequest as they have according to Ḥanafī law.

7.2.2. Difference of religion and nationality: the criterion of reciprocity in modern law

Under traditional Sharī'a doctrine the only bar to testamentary succession on the ground of a difference of nationality arises in Ḥanafī and Shī'ī law, where a bequest made by a Muslim testator to a non-Muslim subject of a non-Muslim state is invalid. But even such a bequest, void in the eyes of the Ḥanafīs and the Shī'a on the ground that it is contrary to the public interest to benefit an alien enemy, is valid for the other schools.

Modern legislation in this respect, as is the case with difference of nationality as an impediment to intestate succession, is based on the principle of reciprocity. Thus, the Egyptian Law of 1946 provides that a bequest made by a Muslim testator of a Muslim state in favour of a non-Muslim subject of a non-Muslim state is valid if the law of the non-Muslim state concerned would allow reciprocal treatment. The principle is carried much further by the Syrian Law of 1953 (article 215) and the Tunisian Law of 1956 (article 175), which both provide: "Where the legatee is a foreigner, reciprocity of treatment is a condition of validity"; for this clearly includes Muslim as well as non-Muslim legatees and subjects of a foreign Muslim as well as a non-Muslim state.

Finally, the Iraqi Law of 1959, apart from following the principle of reciprocity in these cases, introduces a novel element by restricting bequests in favour of legatees whose religion differs from that of the testator to bequests of moveable property. Article 71 of the Law enacts: "Where there is a difference of religion between the testator and the legatee, only a bequest of moveables is valid, while if there is a difference of nationality as well, the bequest is valid only if there is reciprocity of treatment."

8. Acceptance of bequests

8.1. When acceptance is required

Acceptance is required to complete bequests in favour of specific individuals. Where the legatee is adult and sane, his personal acceptance is necessary, while bequests to minors, children in embryo and other interdicted persons are completed by the acceptance of their proper guardian, who is not, as a matter of law, allowed to refuse a bequest which is clearly advantageous to his ward. Traditional Ḥanafī law allows a minor who has reached the age of seven, or the age of "discrimination", to accept a bequest personally, and does not require any acceptance, by the guardian or otherwise, in the case of bequests to children in embryo. Here the bequest becomes fully effective upon the testator's death. According to all the schools no acceptance is necessary in the case of bequests for pious or charitable purposes, bequests in favour of a general class of persons, or bequests in favour of institutions, unless the institution has a recognised legal representative, in which case his acceptance is necessary.

8.1.1. No formalities are necessary

No formalities attach to the acceptance of a bequest. Any words or actions indicative of consent suffice, the notion of implied acceptance being particularly strong in Ḥanafī law, where the bequest in effect becomes complete by the failure of the legatee to reject it. A legatee may accept a bequest in part only and, of course, in the case of bequests to a number of legatees, some may accept and others refuse.

8.1.2. The time of acceptance

In the contemplation of Sunnī law a declaration of bequest becomes binding only upon the testator's death, and therefore any purported acceptance or refusal by the legatee during the testator's lifetime is premature and devoid of legal effect. A legatee may validly accept or reject a bequest only after the testator's decease. According to Shī'ī law, however, a declaration of bequest, notwithstanding the testator's right to revoke it, creates a right substantial enough to be accepted (p. 226, n. 1 above). Accordingly, in Shī'ī law, a legatee's acceptance during the testator's lifetime is valid and binding, although the refusal of a bequest during the testator's lifetime may be withdrawn by the legatee and replaced by acceptance after the testator's death.

8.1.3. Acceptance or refusal is generally irrevocable

Acceptance or refusal of a bequest after the testator's death is final, in the sense that a subsequent change of heart on the part of a legatee cannot *per se* operate to revive a bequest which has lapsed through his refusal, or to nullify his ownership of the property bequeathed which vested in him upon his acceptance. A limited exception to the rule exists in Ḥanbalī and Shāfi'ī law where a legatee who has accepted a bequest of fungible goods may validly refuse it before he takes delivery of the goods. The exception rests on the ground that ownership becomes established in property of this type only when it is taken into possession by the transferee. Mālikī law, it is true, holds that subsequent acceptance following prior refusal, and vice versa, is effective if the testator's legal heirs consent thereto. But the consent of the legal heirs here does not revive a bequest which has lapsed through the legatee's refusal or nullify one which has become effective through his acceptance. The heirs' consent is either an offer or an acceptance of a new and distinct transaction of gift between themselves and the legatee, and the effective transfer of the property requires the observance of all the particular rules of gift. This is precisely the same way in which the Mālikīs treat the consent of the legal heirs in the context of *ultra vires* bequests (pp. 244–50 below). The Tunisian Law of 1956 preserves this Mālikī rule intact, while the Egyptian Law of 1946 partially adopts it by enacting (article 24) that an acceptance of a bequest after the testator's death is only nullified by a subsequent rejection if his rejection is accepted by one of the testator's legal heirs. It is clear from the terms of the Egyptian Law, however, that such subsequent rejection does not constitute a new transaction of gift between the legatee and the legal heirs.

8.2. Failure of the legatee to accept or refuse

Where a legatee dies without having accepted or rejected the bequest, the doctrine of the Sunnī majority and the Shī'a is that the option to accept or refuse the bequest passes to the legatee's heirs. Ḥanafī law, on the other hand, holds that the bequest forms part of the legatee's estate and passes to his heirs, since the legatee's failure to refuse the bequest during his lifetime amounts, in the Ḥanafī view, to an implied acceptance of it. On this particular issue the terms of modernist legislation in the Middle East, involving both the process of selection from among the variant opinions of traditional doctrine and the introduction of novel elements, provide a good example of the growing diversity of contemporary Islamic legal practice.

Thus, the Iraqi Law of 1959 simply preserves traditional Ḥanafī doctrine. The Egyptian Law of 1946 adopts the general Sunnī rule that where a legatee dies without either accepting or refusing, the option passes to his heirs. But the same Law then goes on to provide that a bequest lapses if the legatee fails, without adequate excuse, to respond within thirty days to official notice of the bequest and a request for his acceptance or refusal from the testator's heirs. Under the Syrian Law of 1953 it is expressly declared to be a condition of the refusal of a bequest that it should take place within thirty days of the testator's death or of the legatee learning of the bequest if he did not know of it at the time of the testator's death. Failure to refuse the bequest within this time, or the death of the legatee during the period before he has refused it, constitutes an implied acceptance of the bequest. Finally, the Tunisian Law of 1956 requires the legatee to refuse the bequest after the testator's death and within two months of his learning of it; otherwise he is presumed to have accepted it. But if the legatee dies within the two month period without having accepted or refused the bequest, the option passes to his heirs.

9. Ownership of property bequeathed: the time at which it passes

Following the death of the testator, the ownership of property he has bequeathed is generally held to be in suspense until the wishes of the legatee become known. Refusal of the bequest clearly establishes the fact that the property was owned by the testator's heirs from the time of his death. But the schools are divided on the question of ownership when the legatee accepts the bequest. According to Mālikī and Ḥanbalī law, ownership passes from the testator's heirs to the legatee upon the latter's acceptance and not before. But in Ḥanafī, Shāfi'ī and Shī'ī law acceptance by the legatee is deemed to establish his ownership of the property from the time of the testator's death. For these latter three schools the further question then arises of the legal position with regard to any separable income or produce of the bequest arising between the time of the testator's death and the legatee's acceptance. Shī'ī and Shāfi'ī law regard such produce or income as a simple addition to the legatee's property, and this is the rule adopted by the Egyptian Law of 1946. But traditional Ḥanafī law regards the increase as an integral part of the bequest, a rule which affects, as will be seen (pp. 238–9 below), the application of the *ultra vires* doctrine.

14. THE LIMITS OF TESTAMENTARY POWER

1. The scope of the *ultra vires* doctrine

In the context of succession law, an act or transaction of the praepositus which offends against the interests of the legal heirs established by the laws of inheritance may properly be termed *ultra vires* since it exceeds the permitted limits of the discretionary transmission of property at death. The interests of the legal heirs become, of course, fully mature at the time of the praepositus' death, so that any testamentary disposition of property, becoming effective only after the testator's death, is potentially *ultra vires.* But the law goes further and regards the rights of the legal heirs as crystallising at the moment when it can be established that the process of the praepositus' dying had irrevocably begun. Accordingly, acts of the praepositus performed during what is termed his death-sickness may be caught by the *ultra vires* doctrine insofar as they are deemed to constitute an infringement of the interests of the legal heirs. Two concluding chapters will consider both these limbs of the *ultra vires* doctrine in some detail.

2. The one-third rule

Bequests which, singly or collectively, exceed in value one-third of the testator's net estate – i.e. the assets available for distribution after the payment of funeral expenses and debts – are *ultra vires* to the extent of the excess portion.

2.1. The time for calculation of the bequeathable third

As thus stated, the rule is common to all the schools of law. But since the value of an estate may increase or decrease between the time of the testator's death and its actual distribution, the effect of the rule depends to a large extent upon the time at which the valuation of the net estate is to take place: and on this point the schools adopted three distinct criteria.

Shāfi'ī, Ḥanbalī and Shī'ī law hold rigidly to the principle that the bequeathable third is to be calculated solely by reference to the value of the net estate at the time of the testator's death, on the ground that this is the time when the rights of the legal heirs mature.

Mālikī and Ḥanafī law, on the other hand, hold that the proper time for calculating whether a bequest is *ultra vires* or not is when the transaction itself is complete and binding; and bequests, in this context, are regarded as parallel with gifts *inter vivos*. A gift is complete and binding in Mālikī law upon acceptance by the donee, but in Ḥanafī law only upon delivery to the donee. Hence, the proper time for calculation of the bequeathable third is, in Mālikī law, the time of the legatee's acceptance and, in Ḥanafī law, the time of the actual distribution of the estate.

2.2. Ownership of the bequest is not relevant to the calculation of the third

As has been observed above (p. 234), the schools are divided on the question of when ownership of property bequeathed ceases to belong to the testator or his heirs and vests in the legatee. In Mālikī, Shāfi'ī and Shī'ī law, the time at which ownership passes coincides with the proper time for the calculation of the bequeathable third. But in Ḥanafī law ownership passes on the testator's death, while the proper time for calculation is the time of the distribution of the estate; and in Ḥanbalī law ownership passes on the legatee's acceptance, while the proper time for calculation is the time of the testator's death. Hence, ownership of property bequeathed may be regarded as an issue quite separate from that of the proper time for calculating whether a bequest is *ultra vires* or not.

2.3. General bequests

General bequests, then, may or may not be affected, under the law of the different schools, by an appreciation or a depreciation in the value of the estate which occurs after the death of the testator and prior to distribution.

> T's will contains a bequest of £1,000 in favour of L. At the time of his death T's estate is valued at £5,000. A fire then destroys most of his property, and at the time of L's acceptance and the distribution the total net estate is valued at £1,500.

In Shāfi'ī, Ḥanbalī and Shī'ī law, the time of calculation being T's death, L will be entitled to the full sum of £1,000, since this was within the bequeathable third at the time of T's death, and the subsequent loss to the estate will fall exclusively upon T's legal heirs.

On the other hand, under the criteria adopted by Mālikī and Ḥanafī law – namely that the proper time for calculation of the bequeathable third is the time of acceptance by the legatee or distribution of the estate – the loss will fall upon both the legatee and the legal heirs. T's bequest will be good only as to £500 and *ultra vires* as to the remaining £500.

Conversely, a general legatee may benefit from an appreciation in the value of an estate subsequent to the testator's death under Mālikī and Ḥanafī law, but will not do so under the law of the Shāfi'ī, Ḥanbalī and Shī'ī schools.

T bequeathes "a new car" of a specified make (price £6,000) to L. At the time of T's death his total assets are valued at £12,000, but due to the discovery of oil on his land soar to many times this value prior to L's acceptance and distribution of the estate.

Under Mālikī and Ḥanafī law, L will be entitled to the car as specified. According to the other schools the bequest will be good only to the extent of £4,000.

2.4. Specific bequests

Specific bequests may be similarly affected by a rise or fall in the value of the testator's estate subsequent to his death. But they differ from general bequests inasmuch as the application of the *ultra vires* rule may also be affected by any increase or decrease in the value of the bequeathed property itself. Here the common ground of all the schools is the principle that a legatee is entitled to the property bequeathed, or such part of it as constitutes the bequeathable third, as it stands at the proper time for calculation. Thereafter the legatee naturally enjoys or suffers any appreciation or depreciation in its value.

2.4.1. Fall in the value of the bequest

T bequeaths to L a specific herd of cattle. On T's death the herd is worth £9,000 and the remainder of his estate £9,000. Before L's acceptance and the distribution of the estate, disease strikes the herd and reduces its value to £4,500.

(*a*) Mālikī and Ḥanafī law: L is entitled to the whole herd as it does not exceed in value one-third of the estate at the time of acceptance and distribution.

(*b*) Shāfi'ī, Ḥanbalī and Shī'ī law: L is entitled only to an interest of two-thirds in the herd, since the bequest was good only to the extent of two-thirds of its value at the time of death.

The subsequent loss in the value of the herd is to be borne by the legatee and the legal heirs of the testator *pro rata* their established interests therein at the time of death.

2.4.2. Rise in the value of the bequest

T bequeathes "one-half of my lands" to L. T's lands are valued at £20,000 on his death and the remainder of his property at £20,000. Because of development schemes the lands are worth £100,000 at the time of L's acceptance and the distribution of the estate.

(*a*) Shāfiʿī, Ḥanbalī and Shīʿī law: L takes a half interest, worth £50,000 in the lands. This example, in conjunction with the previous one, makes it quite clear that for these schools a specific bequest is valued at the time of the testator's death *solely* to determine whether or not it is *ultra vires*, and not to fix the precise value of the legatee's entitlement. The legatee will benefit from an increase in the value of the property just as he will suffer from a decrease in its value.

(*b*) Mālikī and Ḥanafī law: The bequest is *ultra vires* since it exceeds the bequeathable third at the time of acceptance and distribution. L will be entitled only to such an interest in the lands as constitutes one-third of the value of the net estate – i.e. £40,000.

2.5. The right to income or produce is generally determined by ownership

Where, after the death of the testator and before distribution of the estate, separable produce or income arises from a specific bequest (such as the young of animals or the fruits of orchards), all schools except the Ḥanafīs hold that such income belongs to the owner of the property. The Ḥanafīs, for their part, ignore the question of ownership and maintain that the income or produce attaches itself to the bequest so as to form an integral part of it and must therefore be taken into account in calculating the one-third.

T bequeathes his farm, Wadī Ḥimār, valued at £5,000 and occupied by tenants, to L. Between T's death and the time that L formally accepts the bequest, rentals from Wadī Ḥimār of £300 accumulate. Between L's acceptance and distribution of T's estate further rentals of £300 accumulate. The value of T's other assets remains constant throughout this period at £10,000.

2.5.1. Shāfiʿī and Shīʿī law

Wadī Ḥimār is within the bequeathable third on T's death and is owned by L from that time. Therefore L alone is entitled to all the subsequent income from his property.

2.5.2. Ḥanbalī and Mālikī law

The bequest of Wadī Ḥimār itself is perfectly valid. But since ownership of it does not vest in L until his acceptance, the legal heirs of T take the first £300 rentals, while L takes the second £300.

2.5.3. Ḥanafī law

The bequest comprised of Wadī Ḥimār and its income together will be good only to the extent of one-third of the estate at the time of distribution. L will therefore be entitled to £200 in all of the rentals.

2.6. Usufructory bequests

Difficulties may obviously arise in the valuation of usufructory bequests for the purposes of the *ultra vires* rule. Sunnī law generally regards the value of the usufructory right, whether it is in perpetuity or for a limited period, as equivalent to the value of the corpus of the property to which it attaches. Should this exceed the bequeathable third, then the usufructory right of the legatee attaches only to such a portion of the property as constitutes the bequeathable third. Shī'ī and Ḥanbalī law, however, attempt a more systematic valuation of usufructory bequests, particularly those limited in point of time, by calculating both (*a*) the value of the property denuded of the usufructory right and (*b*) the value of the usufructory right itself, and then setting the former off against the latter.

3. "No bequest in favour of a legal heir"

3.1. The rule confined to the Sunnī schools

In the view of Sunnī jurisprudence, the purpose of this ruling by the Prophet is to prevent interference with the precise balance between the claims of the various relatives established by the laws of inheritance. Practically, the Sunnīs argue, the rule avoids the emnity which might arise among the heirs as a result of the preferential treatment of one of their number by the deceased in his will. A number of dicta attributed to the Prophet condemn parents who show partiality towards any of their children through gifts *inter vivos*; and the case against preferential treatment through testamentary gifts is even stronger since there is no possibility of subsequent readjustment.

Considerations of this kind, however, had little appeal for the Shī'ī jurists who did not recognise this second limb of the *ultra vires* doctrine.

According to the Shī'a, the ruling of the Prophet is to be interpreted as abrogating the *duty* to make bequests to near relatives (as enjoined in the Qur'anic verse of bequests) but not the *right* to do so. In sum, the words are held to mean "it is not obligatory to make a bequest", rather than "it is not permissible to make a bequest". Alternatively, the Shī'īs claim, the most authentic version of the Prophet's statement ends with the additional words "except within the (bequeathable) third". Bequests to legal heirs, therefore, stand on exactly the same footing in Shī'ī law as bequests to non-heirs. This constitutes the supreme difference between the Sunnī and the Shī'ī laws of testate succession and is the outstanding example of the generally more permissive Shī'ī attitude to bequests.

3.2. Dispositions caught by the rule

Apart from bequests *stricto sensu* the rule covers all testamentary dispositions which are directly and necessarily beneficial to a legal heir of the testator. Accordingly, the release of an heir from a debt owed by him to the testator, such as a wife's relinquishment of her claim to the unpaid portion of the dower due from her husband, or a direction to the executor to pay off the debts owed by an heir to a third party are caught by the ban. Even the apportionment by a testator of specific items of his estate to one or more of his legal heirs strictly in accordance with the value of their prescribed shares in the inheritance constitutes undue favouritism in the eyes of Sunnī law and therefore an *ultra vires* disposition, since the right of an heir is not merely a right to a fractional part of the value of the estate but attaches to the various properties of the estate *in specie*.

Most schools, however, accept the validity of testamentary dispositions under which a legal heir in fact acquires a benefit but not directly from the testator. One example given by a Shāfi'ī text is where the testator bequeathes a sum of money to L on condition that L makes a gift of a specified sum of money to H, an heir of the testator.[1] This is specifically termed a *ḥīla*, or device, to circumvent the *ultra vires* doctrine, and therefore would not, presumably, be effective in Ḥanbalī law, which pays particular attention to the motives underlying transactions and consistently refuses to countenance any obvious legal trickery of this kind.

Even the Ḥanbalīs, however, admit the validity of bequests which do not *necessarily* benefit a legal heir, however strong the presumption may be that the testator intended and expected that his legal heir would in fact benefit therefrom. Such is the case, for example, where a testator leaves a

[1] *Fatḥ al-mu'īn* of Zain al-Dīn al-Malībārī (Cairo, 1925), p. 96.

legacy to his son's creditor or to his son's wife or minor child, where it is reasonable to assume that the son himself will benefit therefrom. In all such cases the bequest is good in law, although Ibn Qudāma comments (*al-Mughnī*, VI, 7) that if the testator's purpose was in fact to benefit his heir, the bequest "is not valid as between himself and God Almighty".

3.3. The meaning of "legal heir"

Because a will speaks from the time of death, the ban operates only against one who is a legal heir of the testator at the time of the latter's decease.[1] Accordingly, a bequest in favour of a person who is an "heir" of the testator at the time the bequest is made, but due to supervening circumstances is not his heir at the time of decease, does not constitute an *ultra vires* disposition. This is the case, for example, where a husband bequeathes property to his wife and subsequently the couple are effectively divorced before the husband's death. Conversely, a bequest made to a woman whom the testator subsequently married would fall within the *ultra vires* rule.

In regard to the one-third rule, as has been seen, the schools differ as to whether the proper time for calculation of the one-third is the death of the testator, the time of the legatee's acceptance or the time of the distribution of the estate. But the time of the legatee's acceptance or the time of the distribution of the estate can have no relevance to the decision whether or not a legatee is a legal heir. Although the value of the testator's estate may change after his death, entitlement to it by way of inheritance cannot. Once an heir, always an heir. A person's status as heir or non-heir is finally and irrevocably established at the moment of the praepositus' death, even though actual knowledge of that status is sometimes of necessity delayed. This is the case, for example, when one of the deceased's relatives is a missing person, or when the determination of entitlement must await the birth of a child which is in embryo at the time of decease.

> T, who is married but has no children, makes three bequests in favour of his three brothers: A, his germane brother; B, his consanguine brother, and C, his uterine brother. At the time of T's death his wife is pregnant.

If the child is stillborn, the bequests to A (the residuary heir) and to C (a Qur'anic heir) will be *ultra vires*. Only the bequest to B will be good since B is not an heir, being excluded from inheritance by A.

[1] Logically, perhaps, a person cannot by definition be "an heir" until he is made such by the death of the praepositus. But the language of the law here follows popular usage and uses the term "heir" of someone who is in fact only a potential heir – i.e. one who would be an heir if the praepositus died at that moment or without any further change in the *status quo* of the family.

If the child is born alive and is male, the bequests to all three brothers will be good since they are all excluded from inheritance.

If the child is born alive and is female, the bequest to A (the residuary heir) will be *ultra vires*, while the bequests to B (excluded from inheritance by A) and to C (excluded from inheritance by the daughter) will be good.

For the purpose of the *ultra vires* rule those relatives of the deceased who are not excluded from inheritance under the rules of priority but are debarred therefrom by the existence of some impediment in themselves are not counted as legal heirs. Bequests to relatives disqualified from inheritance solely through their difference of religion with the praepositus are not *ultra vires* under this rule. Similarly, a bequest made by the deceased to his son, who is barred from inheritance because he caused his father's death, is not *ultra vires* on the ground that it is made to a legal heir. A killer, of course, as such may be barred from taking a legacy from his victim, but cases may arise, particularly in Mālikī and Shāfi'ī law, where a relative who has caused the testator's death and is thereby disqualified from inheritance is nevertheless entitled to take a bequest made to him by the deceased (pp. 229–30 above).

For the purposes of the *ultra vires* doctrine, therefore, "heir" clearly means "entitled heir", that is to say, a relative who is not excluded from inheritance by any superior heir and is not disqualified by any impediment. But what of the case of a relative who is such an entitled heir but in fact receives no share of the inheritance?

> T makes a bequest in favour of L, her consanguine brother. T is survived by her husband, mother and two uterine brothers in addition to L.

Here L is the residuary heir, but because the Qur'anic portions of the other relatives (husband one-half, mother one-sixth, uterine brothers one-third) exhaust the estate, he in fact receives nothing. Is the bequest in his favour *ultra vires* as being made to a legal heir or not?

There does not appear to be any precise authority in the legal manuals on this point. But while legal and popular usage would doubtless describe the consanguine brother in these circumstances as a "legal heir", it would perhaps be wholly contrary to the spirit of the law to consider the bequest in his favour as falling within the ambit of the *ultra vires* rule.

The essential purpose of this limb of the *ultra vires* doctrine is to preserve the balance between the claims of the various relatives which was established by the rules of inheritance. And from this standpoint a relative who is *prima facie* entitled to inherit but in fact receives nothing is in exactly the same position as a relative who is altogether excluded or debarred from inheritance. A final and precise formulation of the rule would therefore seem to be: A bequest is *ultra vires* if it is made in favour of a person who actually inherits part of the testator's estate.

4. The legal effect of *ultra vires* bequests

4.1. Consent or refusal of the heirs is decisive

Since the law is here designed to protect the position of the legal heirs, *ultra vires* dispositions are not necessarily devoid of any effect. Their effect depends simply upon the wishes of the heirs and the extent to which they are prepared, individually, to waive or forgo their established interests.

4.2. The relevance of the doctrine concerning the Treasury

It is necessary to consider at this point the effect upon the *ultra vires* doctrine of the role allotted to the Public Treasury (*bait al-māl*) in the scheme of succession. According to the Sunnī majority and to the Shī'a, the Treasury is entitled only by way of escheat to the estate of a person who dies intestate without any surviving blood relative. The Mālikīs, on the other hand, hold that the Treasury is a residuary heir and succeeds as such in the absence of any agnatic residuary heir by blood.

In the majority view, therefore, a person who dies without any surviving relative has no heirs whose interests need protection. Accordingly he is not subject to the *ultra vires* doctrine and may dispose of the whole of his estate by will. Where the sole surviving heir is the spouse relict, there is complete testamentary liberty as regards the residue of the estate (one-half or three-quarters as the case may be) after the deduction of the spouse relict's portion: for a spouse relict is not entitled to any surplus by way of *radd* and therefore has no interest requiring protection beyond the fixed portion. This principle is not affected by the rule now adopted in certain countries that the spouse relict is entitled to *radd*, because the spouse relict is so entitled solely in preference to escheat to the State (pp. 139–40 above).

Under Mālikī law, however, a person who dies without any surviving relative can never effectively bequeath more than one-third of his estate. For in these circumstances the Treasury is the residuary heir, and neither the ruler nor any other representative body has the power to consent to any *ultra vires* disposition on its behalf. Furthermore, this principle applies wherever a deceased is survived only by Qur'anic heirs whose fixed portions do not exhaust the estate, so that any *ultra vires* bequest will necessarily be void to the extent of the Treasury's interest, as residuary heir, therein.

4.3. Modern law in Tunisia and Iraq

Two details of modern legislation are noteworthy in this regard. In Tunisia the traditional Mālikī law has now been abandoned. Article 188 of the Code of Personal Status, 1956, enacts: "A person who...leaves no heir may effectively bequeath even the whole of his estate notwithstanding the succession rights of the Treasury." To precisely the opposite effect, the Iraqi Law of Personal Status, 1959, departs from the Ḥanafī doctrine traditionally applied when it enacts (article 70): "The State is to be considered the legal heir of one who has no heirs by blood." The law then goes on to provide that the validity of any bequest made by such a person in excess of the bequeathable third is dependent upon ratification by the Ministry of Finance, and one commentator observes that "the Ministry of Finance will not, as a general rule, ratify the bequest unless it is for a charitable purpose or for the public welfare and the Ministry considers its ratification would be conducive to the public interest".[1]

Passing now to those cases of *ultra vires* bequests which do not involve the Public Treasury in any way, three principal situations are to be considered. The heirs may unanimously ratify the *ultra vires* disposition; they may unanimously repudiate it; or the bequest may be partially ratified.

5. Ratification of *ultra vires* bequests

There is a fundamental divergence of view between the generality of Muslim jurists on the one hand and the Mālikī school on the other as to the legal nature of an heir's consent to an *ultra vires* bequest. The majority hold that the bequest is *ab initio* valid but subject to subsequent annulment by the legal heirs. Their assent, when given, operates simply as the removal of this bar, and the legatee takes the property directly from the testator. Mālikī law, on the other hand, holds that an *ultra vires* bequest is *ab initio* void. The consent of the heirs to its taking effect, therefore, constitutes a new and distinct act of transfer, and the legatee takes the property as a gift from the legal heirs. In other words, while the majority regard the formal expression of consent by the legal heir as a waiver of his claim to the property of another, the Mālikīs regard it as a declaration of a gift of his own property. This fundamental distinction causes the respective doctrines of the two groups regarding the conditions and effect of ratification to vary considerably; and for this reason it will be best to deal with them separately.

[1] Muḥsin Nājī, *Sharḥ Qānūn al-Aḥwāl al-Shakhṣiyya* (Baghdad, 1962), pp. 462 ff.

5.1.1. Ḥanafī, Ḥanbalī, Shāfiʿī and Shīʿī law: conditions of ratification

5.1.1.1. Capacity: heirs must not be under interdiction

A full legal capacity to engage in transactions belongs only to adult persons who are sane and have the quality of normal prudent judgment (*rushd*). Accordingly, persons under interdiction on account of either minority, lunacy or prodigality cannot validly ratify an *ultra vires* bequest.

Where, then, an *ultra vires* bequest has been made by a testator whose legal heirs include one or more such interdicted persons, the bequest cannot be immediately effective to the extent of that person's interest therein. Since it is a fundamental rule of the law of guardianship that no guardian has the power to dispose of his ward's property gratuitously, any purported consent to the bequest given by the guardian on behalf of the interdicted person is void. Neither, however, is the bequest, to the extent of the interdicted heir's interest therein, *ipso facto* void: it is deemed to be "suspended" (*mauqūf*) until the heir does acquire capacity and his consent or otherwise can be validly obtained. Certain texts state the general principle to be that "where the heir is expected to acquire capacity within a short period, the bequest is suspended until this event; otherwise it is void".[1] But the weight of authority seems to hold that the bequest will be *pro tanto* void only where the interdicted heir is an insane person or a prodigal and there is no reasonable prospect of his recovering sanity or prudent judgment. Where the heir is a minor, the bequest must, apparently, remain in suspense, at least to the extent of the minor's interest therein, until he attains majority.

5.1.1.2. Partial incapacity through death-sickness

In addition to these cases of total incapacity, where persons are placed under interdiction to protect their own interests, the law recognises in this context one case of defective capacity where persons are subject to partial or qualified interdiction in order to protect the interests of others. This is the case of persons who are in their death-sickness. As will be seen in the following chapter, in order to protect the interests of his legal heirs, gifts made by a person in his death-sickness are subject to precisely the same *ultra vires* doctrine as bequests: and as far as the legal heirs are concerned the dying person's waiver of a right of inheritance ranks as a gift. Where, therefore, the legal heir of a testator who has made an *ultra vires* bequest is in his death-sickness, his consent to this bequest will be effective only where the extent of his interest in the bequest amounts to less than one-

[1] *Fatḥ al-Muʿīn* of Zain al-Dīn al-Malībārī, p. 97.

third of his total assets and where, in Sunnī law, the legatee is not his own legal heir. Otherwise his consent will be effective only upon ratification by his own legal heirs.

5.1.1.3. Time of assent: after the testator's death

Since the heir's right to his share in the inheritance does not come into existence until the death of the praepositus, any purported waiver of this right at any time prior to the death of the praepositus is premature and devoid of legal effect. Assent to an *ultra vires* bequest, just as a rejection thereof, is valid only when given after the testator's death.

Although certain authoritative Ithnā 'Asharī texts endorse the above rule,[1] Shī'ī law as applied in the Indian sub-continent is that the heir's consent is effective whether given before or after the death of the praepositus.[2] Here the heir's right of succession, although subject to variation and even total lapse prior to the praepositus' death, is yet deemed sufficiently real to be the subject of a valid waiver. This rule is therefore in line with those other distinctive features of Shī'ī law which are based on the recognition of a *spes successionis* as a substantial right.[3]

5.1.1.4. Knowledge: reasonable mistake of fact nullifies the heir's consent

It is an accepted principle that the assenting heir must have knowledge of the extent of the right that he waives by his assent. If the heir satisfies the court that he ratified the bequest because he believed that its value was less than it actually was, or because he believed that his own share in the inheritance was greater than it actually was, he will not be bound by his assent.

There must, however, be reasonable grounds for such misapprehension. Where, for example, the property bequeathed has valuable hidden assets, or where the heir's share in the estate turns out to be far less than anticipated because of the appearance of an additional heir who was generally believed to be dead, the heir's statement upon oath that he was ignorant of these facts will be accepted and, failing proof to the contrary, will render his ratification inoperative. But where the circumstances of the estate are ascertainable after normally prudent enquiry, the law imputes knowledge of them to the heir, and such constructive knowledge precludes any claim of ignorance.

[1] See, for example, A. Querry, *Droit Musulman* (Paris, 1872), I, 613.

[2] See Baillie, Imameea Code (London, 1869), p. 233, and A. Fyzee, *Outlines of Muhammadan Law* (Oxford, 1964), p. 307.

[3] Above, p. 226 and footnote.

5.1.1.5. Absence of duress

The heir must give his assent freely and he will not be bound by any assent obtained under duress – as a result, for example, of intimidation by the legatee.

5.1.2. The effect of ratification

Where the assent of all the legal heirs has been given in accordance with the above conditions, the *ultra vires* bequest becomes immediately and fully effective. The assent is binding and irrevocable and the legatee may demand delivery of the bequest, which he takes directly, as a bequest, from the testator.

5.2.1. Mālikī law: conditions of ratification

5.2.1.1. Capacity

Since, in Mālikī law, the assent of the heir constitutes a declaration of gift, it will be valid only when the assenting heir has the capacity to make a gift of his property. In addition, therefore, to the four classes of interdicted persons recognised by the majority doctrine in this regard – minors, lunatics, prodigals and persons in death-sickness – there are three further cases in Mālikī law of total or partial incapacity to ratify an *ultra vires* bequest.

5.2.1.2. Three additional grounds of incapacity

First, it is a rule peculiar to Mālikī law that a woman does not acquire a legal capacity to deal with her property until she has consummated her marriage and two qualified witnesses have testified that she is a prudent person capable of managing her own affairs.

Secondly, because it is pre-eminently patriarchal in outlook, Mālikī law allows a husband a limited measure of control over his wife's dealings with her property. A Mālikī wife may not dispose gratuitously of more than one-third of her property without the consent of her husband. Thus, in appropriate circumstances, the validity of her consent to an *ultra vires* bequest will be dependent upon ratification by her husband.

Thirdly, bankruptcy is, of course, a ground for interdiction according to all schools of law, and any transaction by a bankrupt with his own property, particularly any purported gift thereof, is a nullity unless his creditors agree to it. It follows that under Mālikī law the assent of a bankrupt heir to an *ultra vires* bequest is void failing ratification by the creditors. In the majority view, where the heirs' assent is not regarded as a transfer of their own property, bankruptcy is not a ground of incapacity.

Under Mālikī law, where one or more of the legal heirs is an interdicted person, there is no question of the bequest being "suspended", to the extent of his interest therein, until he has the capacity of assent or otherwise. Since an *ultra vires* bequest is *ab initio* void, and becomes effective only when a new act of transfer is initiated by the heir, ownership of the property bequeathed passes to the interdicted heir in accordance with the normal principles of intestacy.

5.2.1.3. Time of assent: assent during the death-sickness of the testator is valid

Mālikī law holds that the heir's assent is valid when given either after the testator's death or during his death-sickness, on the ground that with the death-sickness of the testator the rights of his legal heirs have matured and are therefore a proper subject of transfer by gift.

5.2.1.4. Knowledge: mistake of fact or law nullifies consent

In addition to a reasonable mistake of fact, a reasonable mistake of law will also nullify the heir's consent. If the heir swears upon oath that he was ignorant of his right to refuse to ratify an *ultra vires* bequest, and if such ignorance appears to the court reasonable in the circumstances, the assent will not be effective.

5.2.1.5. Absence of duress: undue influence by the testator

Since Mālikī law holds that assent may be validly given during the testator's death-sickness, it includes under this head any undue influence exercised over the heir by the testator. An heir will not be bound by his assent if he swears upon oath that he gave it in fear of the testator, because, for example, he was in his debt or dependent upon him for maintenance.

5.2.2. Effect of ratification: transaction not complete until delivery

In Mālikī law a declaration of gift, whether oral or written, is binding and enforceable, and at the suit of the donee the donor will be compelled to deliver the gift to him. But the transaction of gift is only complete when the donee has accepted and taken delivery of the property given; and the transaction must be completed while the donor still has a legal capacity to make a gift of the property concerned.

Precisely the same principles apply to the assent of the heirs to an *ultra vires* bequest. Their assent is binding and the legatee, having duly accepted the "gift", may then demand delivery of it. But the bequest will fail if, before such delivery is taken, any of the following circumstances occur:

(*a*) Interdiction of the assenting heir on the ground of lunacy, prodigality, bankruptcy or death-sickness.

(*b*) Death of the heir or legatee.

(*c*) Loss or destruction of the property bequeathed.

(*d*) Gift, completed by delivery, of the property bequeathed to a third party. Alienation of the property bequeathed other than by way of gift does not extinguish the legatee's right. If such alienation occurs before the legatee knew of the assent by the heirs, he may opt either to confirm the transfer and take the consideration paid to the heirs by the transferee, or to annul the transfer and take the property bequeathed. If the alienation takes place after the legatee knew of the heirs' assent, he cannot recover the property bequeathed but may claim the consideration paid therefor to the heirs.

5.2.2.1. The transaction is complete without delivery in two cases

There are two principal circumstances in which the assent of an heir, like a declaration of gift, is fully effective without delivery and in which, therefore, the bequest is not subject to lapse on any of the grounds mentioned above:

(*a*) Where the legatee is already, at the time of assent, in possession of the property bequeathed.

(*b*) Where the assenting heir is the legal guardian of the property of the legatee. In this case, however, the guardian must formally make a declaration of the gift before two witnesses and the gift must be a specifically identifiable chattel or piece of property. Where the guardian-heir is assenting to a pecuniary legacy or a bequest of fungibles, there must be delivery to a third party appointed as an *ad hoc* guardian of the ward-legatee.

5.2.2.2. The parents of a legatee may revoke the ratification after delivery of the bequest

Delivery of the bequest perfects the legatee's title in all cases except where the assenting heir is the parent of the legatee; for parents, in Mālikī law, have the power to revoke a gift made and delivered to their children. But this power of revocation is lost in the following circumstances:

(*a*) Where the parent loses legal capacity through lunacy or death-sickness.

(*b*) Where the child is in death-sickness, and therefore the rights of the child's legal heirs have matured.

(*c*) Where a substantial change has taken place in the property given.

(*d*) Where the child has undertaken legal obligations – has married, for example – relying on the gift as part of his assets.

(*e*) Where, in the case of attempted revocation of a gift by a mother, the child's father has died, whether before or after the gift was made.

6. Rejection of *ultra vires* bequests

6.1. The problem of priorities and abatement

An *ultra vires* bequest fails when there is no ratification by the legal heirs, a situation which may arise either from express rejection of the bequest by all the legal heirs after the testator's death, or from their failure to fulfil the conditions of ratification, or from a combination of both circumstances.

In default of ratification, a bequest which is *ultra vires* solely on the ground that it is in favour of a legal heir fails completely, while a bequest or series of bequests which are *ultra vires* because they exceed the bequeathable third will be valid only to the extent of the bequeathable third. Where there is only one bequest, this is simply reduced to the value of the bequeathable third. A specific bequest, therefore, of property which exceeds in value the bequeathable third does not effectively pass ownership of the property concerned to the legatee. The legatee's specific entitlement in this case is transformed into a general one to the bequeathable third, and he may only take the specified property with the consent of the legal heirs and subject to his reimbursing the estate to the extent that the value of the bequest in fact exceeds the bequeathable third. The only problem of substance in cases of repudiation of *ultra vires* bequests by the legal heirs arises when there are a number of different bequests which *in toto* exceed the bequeathable third. The question which then falls to be answered is that of the priorities, if any, which are to be observed in the necessary process of abatement.

6.2. The Sunnī rule of *pro rata* abatement

A testator may validly specify the order in which several bequests he has made are to be executed, in which case the bequests take effect in the order specified until the bequeathable third is exhausted. Otherwise, the strict rule of Sunnī law is that all bequests must be abated proportionately, on the broad ground that wills speak from the time of death and therefore the rights of the several legatees all mature at the same point of time. No priority is given to one bequest over another on the ground of either the time at which it was made, or the type of the bequest (a specific, say, as opposed to a general bequest), or its purpose (whether, for example, it is for the benefit of an individual or a religious or charitable object). For the Sunnīs here "equity is equality", as it is with creditors' claims against a bankrupt and, more pertinently to the law of succession, with the procedure of '*awl*, the proportionate reduction of the heirs' portions.

6.3. The Ḥanafī variant

For the Sunnī majority the rule of proportionate abatement is absolute. But Ḥanafī law, following the view of Abū Ḥanīfa as opposed to that of other early authorities of the school, holds that a bequest which is itself in excess of the bequeathable third must first be reduced to one-third before being subject to *pro rata* abatement with other bequests. Pecuniary legacies are exempt from this rule on the ground that at the time the legacy was made it could not definitely be known that it would in fact exceed the bequeathable third. It is difficult, however, to rationalise this exception. It is equally uncertain, at the time it is made, whether a specific bequest will in fact exceed the bequeathable third or not. But specific bequests are certainly caught by the rule, along with bequests which expressly exceed one-third, i.e. bequests of a fraction of the estate in excess of this.

T leaves a net estate valued at £210. His will contains three bequests: (i) to Zaid his library, which is valued at £140; (ii) to 'Umar the sum of £70; (iii) to the local mosque "one-ninth of my estate". T's legal heirs unanimously reject the bequests insofar as they are *ultra vires*.

6.3.1. Mālikī, Shāfi'ī and Ḥanbalī law

Expressed as fractions of the estate, the value of the bequests is (i) two-thirds, (ii) one-third and (iii) one-ninth. Proportionate abatement of the bequests to the total amount of the bequeathable third reduces them to (i) six-thirtieths, (ii) three-thirtieths and (iii) one-thirtieth. Zaid is therefore entitled to an interest in the estate worth £42, 'Umar to £21, and the local mosque to £7.

6.3.2. Ḥanafī law

Preliminary reduction of Zaid's bequest to one-third of the estate makes the ratio value of the three bequests (i) 3: (ii) 3: (iii) 1. Zaid is accordingly entitled to an interest in the estate worth three-sevenths of the bequeathable third – i.e. £30. 'Umar is similarly entitled to £30, and the mosque to £10 (one-seventh of the bequeathable third).

6.4. The Shīʿī rule of precedence by chronological order

Under Shīʿī law, the necessary reduction of a number of bequests to the maximum of the bequeathable third is achieved by giving priority to the first bequest in point of time and then to subsequent bequests in strict chronological sequence until the bequeathable third is exhausted. In the circumstances of the case above, for example, and assuming that the bequests appeared in the will in that order, Zaid would be entitled to the whole of the bequeathable third and the bequests to ʿUmar and to the mosque would fail. This rule stems from the Shīʿī view that a declaration of bequest itself creates a substantial right, so that the time at which the right was created naturally determines priority. Sunnī law, by contrast, rests its doctrine of proportionate abatement on the ground that a legatee has no substantial right until the death of the testator, and that therefore the rights of the different legatees come into being simultaneously.

6.5. The Shīʿī view of bequests for the performance of a religious duty

Finally, Shīʿī law gives a special status, in the context of the *ultra vires* doctrine, to bequests for the performance, on behalf of the testator, of some religious duty like the pilgrimage which he did not fulfil during his lifetime. Where a testator has bequeathed a fixed sum for such a purpose, and this sum, in conjunction with other bequests he has made, exceeds the bequeathable third, then, if the legal heirs fail to ratify the bequest, it will take effect as a first charge upon the whole estate, while the bequeathable third will go to satisfy, as far as possible, the remaining bequests. In effect, this is to remove bequests for the performance of a religious duty from the ambit of the *ultra vires* doctrine and treat them as though they were civil debts of the deceased. There is no parallel to this rule in Sunnī law, where a bequest of a fixed amount for the performance of a religious duty would, if necessary, suffer *pro rata* abatement along with any other type of bequest.

7. Partial ratification of *ultra vires* bequests

Partial ratification of an *ultra vires* bequest occurs when either (*a*) some of the testator's heirs ratify the bequest and others reject it, or (*b*) the heirs ratify part only of the bequest, or (*c*) there is a combination of these two situations.

7.1. The rule of the anticipated share

In all three circumstances the principle is the same. The power of each individual heir to ratify or reject is proportional to his share of the inheritance, so that an *ultra vires* bequest will be effective only to the extent that it is ratified and only against those heirs who do so ratify. Although views may vary as to the most appropriate arithmetical method of implementing this principle and calculating the entitlement of the heirs and legatees concerned, the method adopted here may be called the method of the anticipated share. Each heir is given such a share of the inheritance as he may properly anticipate as a result of his ratification or rejection. The remainder of the estate then goes to the legatees.[1]

In the following illustrations the bequests are all expressed as fractional parts of the deceased's net estate, because any bequest, general or specific, must be reduced into these terms for the purpose of the necessary calculation. Accordingly, the fractional part of the estate which is ultimately allotted to the legatee merely represents the value of the interest that he acquires from the bequest.

7.1.1. Some heirs ratify, others reject

P's only surviving relatives are his wife, son and daughter. He has bequeathed one-quarter of his estate to his wife. His son ratifies this bequest but the daughter does not.

Here the son may anticipate as his share two-thirds of the residue left after the deduction of the bequest of one-quarter and the wife's Qur'anic portion of one-eighth – i.e. $2/3 \times 5/8 = 10/24$. The daughter, having rejected the bequest, anticipates a share of one-third of the residue left after deduc-

[1] This is not, however, the method expounded in the traditional Arabic legal authorities. Basically, the method of the classical jurists is to ascertain what the fractional shares of heirs and legatees would be in the event of both total ratification and total rejection of the *ultra vires* bequest. Then, if the share of an heir or legatee is $\frac{a}{b}$ in the case of total ratification and $\frac{y}{z}$ in the case of total rejection, his share where he personally ratifies, or where his bequest is ratified, will be $\frac{a \times z}{b \times z}$, and where he personally rejects, or his bequest is rejected, $\frac{y \times b}{z \times b}$. This approach is typical of the emphasis that traditional Muslim jurisprudence is inclined to place upon the means rather than the end result, one instance of which has been noted in the doctrine of *'awl* (p. 47 above). The end result in each case of partial ratification is simply that the heir or legatee receives the share he may properly anticipate.

tion of the wife's Qur'anic portion only – i.e. $1/3 \times 7/8 = 7/24$. Taking into account the wife's Qur'anic portion, this leaves 4/24 of the estate as the amount to which the wife is entitled by way of bequest.

7.1.2. Heirs ratify part only of the disposition

P's sole surviving heirs are his son and daughter. He bequeathes one-half of his estate to Zaid and one-quarter of it to 'Umar. His son and daughter ratify the bequest to 'Umar but reject the bequest to Zaid.

Here the heirs agree that 'Umar is entitled to a bequest of one-quarter. It is not, however, within the power of the legal heirs to nullify the bequest to Zaid completely. Had the heirs rejected the *ultra vires* disposition *in toto*, the normal Sunnī rule of proportional abatement would have resulted in Zaid being entitled to two-ninths (and 'Umar one-ninth) of the estate. Zaid remains entitled to this two-ninths, which, added to 'Umar's bequest of one-quarter, leaves as the amount of the estate which the heirs may properly anticipate as available for inheritance, 19/36. This will be apportioned between the son and the daughter in accordance with the normal rule of double share to the male.

Under the particular Ḥanafī rule of proportional abatement (where Zaid's bequest would first be reduced to one-third), Zaid would have been entitled to 4/21 (and 'Umar to 3/21) had the heirs rejected the *ultra vires* disposition *in toto*. Therefore Zaid's bequest of 4/21, added to 'Umar's of one-quarter, leaves 47/84 of the estate as inheritance for the son and daughter.

Under Shī'ī law, assuming that the bequest to Zaid was first in point of time, Zaid remains entitled to one-third, notwithstanding the rejection by the legal heirs. Hence, the amount of the estate available for inheritance in Shī'ī law will be five-twelfths.

7.1.3. Varying extent of ratification by different heirs

P bequeathes one-third of his estate to 'Alī and one-sixth to Ḥasan. His heirs are (i) his germane sister, who ratifies the bequest to 'Alī but not that to Ḥasan; (ii) his mother, who ratifies the bequest to Ḥasan but not that to 'Alī; (iii) his consanguine sister, who rejects both bequests; and (iv) his uterine sister, who ratifies both bequests.

Here, each heir is given her anticipated share – i.e. her Qur'anic portion of the residue of the estate left after deduction of the amount of bequests that she has personally ratified – and the remainder of the estate is then divided among the legatees *pro rata* the value of their original bequests. This may be expressed in tabulated form as follows:

	Value of bequests ratified		Anticipated share
	'Alī	Ḥasan	Residue × Qur'anic portion
Germane sister	$\frac{1}{3}$	$\frac{1}{9}$	$\frac{5}{9} \times \frac{1}{2} = \frac{90}{324}$
Mother	$\frac{2}{9}$	$\frac{1}{6}$	$\frac{11}{18} \times \frac{1}{6} = \frac{33}{324}$
Consanguine sister	$\frac{2}{9}$	$\frac{1}{9}$	$\frac{2}{3} \times \frac{1}{6} = \frac{36}{324}$
Uterine sister	$\frac{1}{3}$	$\frac{1}{6}$	$\frac{1}{2} \times \frac{1}{6} = \frac{27}{324}$
			Total $\frac{186}{324}$

This leaves for the legatees 138/324, of which 'Alī is entitled to 92/324 and Ḥasan to 46/324.

8. Modern reform

8.1. A bequest to an heir no longer *ultra vires* in the Sudan, Egypt and Iraq

Experience has shown that people are in need of a certain relaxation of the rules regarding bequests at present in force... Seeing that heirs normally differ between themselves in poverty and wealth, in majority and minority, or in their need or freedom therefrom, testators feel inclined to distinguish between them in favour of those most in need of their property... It is (also) a matter of concern to a man who has property of which to dispose, to put his estate in order and effectually to distribute it by will among his heirs, item by item, as seems most beneficial. In this way he obviates the quarrelling which would otherwise arise among his heirs regarding the distribution of his estate after his death...

Thus runs the preamble to the Sudanese Judical Circular no. 53 of 1945 which abolished the traditional ban on bequests in favour of legal heirs, a reform subsequently adopted by the Egyptian Law of 1946 and the Iraqi Law of 1959.

In these three countries, therefore, a bequest in favour of an heir now stands on precisely the same footing as a bequest in favour of a non-heir and will be *ultra vires* only if, and to the extent that, it exceeds the bequeathable third. And it is, of course, a natural corollary of this major innovation that a distribution by the testator of the items comprising his estate among his legal heirs is valid and effective, unless the allotment to any heir represents an increase upon his share of the inheritance of more than one third of the net estate, in which case the validity of the allotment will be dependent upon ratification by the other heirs.

8.2. The juristic basis of reform

While respectable authority may be derived from certain Shāfi'ī and Ḥanbalī jurists for the rule that a testator may validly allot particular items of his estate to individual heirs, provided the value of the allotment does not exceed the heir's share of the inheritance, there is no support at all in traditional Sunnī jurisprudence for the validity *per se* of a bequest to a legal heir. In the preamble to the Sudanese Circular and the Explanatory Memorandum of the Egyptian Law, juristic justification of the reform is confined to a reference to the Qur'anic "verse of bequests", which enjoins testamentary provision for close relatives, and to the opinion of "certain jurists outside the four schools", which means, of course, the Ithnā 'Asharī Shī'īs. It is, therefore, hardly surprising that such further juristic considerations as have been put forward in support of the reform – particularly by commentators upon the Egyptian Law – have a distinctly Shī'ī flavour. Thus it is argued, *inter alia*, that there is no evidence that the Qur'anic verse of bequests was wholly abrogated by the subsequent rules of inheritance; that one version, at least, of the Prophet's alleged statement "No bequest in favour of an heir" continues with the additional words "in excess of one third", and that the Prophet's dictum, in any event, might be construed as abolishing the duty, but not the right, to make bequests in favour of heirs.

Such juristic arguments are, of course, in themselves sound enough, though naturally much more at home in Iraq, with its strong Shī'ī tradition and a new codified law of inheritance which is based on the Shī'ī system of priorities, than in the Sunnī countries of Egypt and the Sudan. But in the process of modern reform of Sharī'a law juristic considerations invariably play only the secondary and supporting role of justifying changes for which the primary impetus comes from social need or purpose. And in this case the Sudanese Judicial Circular makes it perfectly plain what the social purpose which inspired the reform was. It is true that the circular lays particular emphasis upon the criterion of the greater need of one heir as justifying an additional provision for him by bequest, but it is clear that a testator may use his new freedom simply on grounds of affection or to benefit those relatives he feels are closer to him. Since, therefore, bequests may now be used to increase the share of the estate that goes to, say, a wife or daughter, and to diminish that which goes to male agnate residuaries, the reform falls into line with those recent changes in the law of intestacy which are designed to strengthen the position of the nuclear as opposed to the extended tribal family.

8.3. The significance of the reform

In this instance, however, the implementation of this broad social purpose has meant a break with past legal tradition of a far more radical nature than that occasioned by the changes in the traditional system of priorities in inheritance. What is involved here is a much deeper issue than that of what precedence one relative should have over another. It is the fundamental issue, which goes to the root philosophy of succession law, of the relative value that is to be set upon, and the respective scope that is to be given to, the compulsory and the discretionary transmission of property at death. Sunnī jurisprudence, with its consistent orientation to the needs of the tribal group, regarded the duty of the deceased as ideally performed, and the rights of his surviving relatives as ideally provided for, by the compulsory rules of succession. This system of inheritance was self-sufficient and totally independent of the power of testamentary disposition, which, whatever other purposes it might legitimately fulfil, was not to be used to supplement or to disturb the balance of the system of inheritance by right. The rule of no bequest to a legal heir was not merely, for the Sunnīs, a restriction on testamentary liberty; it was an emphatic assertion of the quite separate roles of the mandatory rules of inheritance and the testator's discretion in succession law, a declaration of the final, comprehensive and inviolable nature of the divinely ordained shares of the legal heirs. Shī'ī jurisprudence, by contrast, adopts an essentially different philosophy of succession law. With their more individualistic approach, their more permissive attitude towards testamentary dispositions generally and their less rigid attitude towards the fixed shares of inheritance, the Shī'īs regard the shares of the legal heirs not as a final and maximum, but rather as a minimal, entitlement, and maintain that proper provision for surviving relatives might be achieved by a combination of the mandatory rules of inheritance and discretionary testamentary dispositions. This, in brief, is the position to which Egypt and the Sudan have now moved.

Seen, therefore, in this way as a departure from the basic Sunnī philosophy of succession, the removal of the ban on bequests to heirs must constitute one of the most significant reforms in succession law that has taken place to date in Sunnī Islam. And it is perhaps precisely because the reform is so fundamentally contrary to past Sunnī tradition that it has not as yet been adopted elsewhere than in the Sudan or Egypt. Countries like Tunisia and Syria, and more recently Pakistan, are very much in the van of the reform movement and in certain respects have shown a more adventurous spirit of legal reform than Egypt or the Sudan. But in these countries such social or juristic arguments as might be advanced in favour of removing the ban on bequests in favour of heirs have not proved strong enough to break the attachment to the basic philosophy of Sunnī succession law. Tunisia and Pakistan, therefore, remain firmly committed to the traditional rule that any bequest in favour of an heir is *ultra vires*, while Syria has merely adopted the rule, for which there is some Sunnī authority, that a testator may validly apportion particular items of his estate to his heirs, provided these items do not exceed in value the heir's share of inheritance.

15. DEATH-SICKNESS

The doctrine of death-sickness (*marḍ al-maut*) is concerned with the legal effect of transactions entered into by persons in their death-sickness, persons who are termed in Arabic *marīḍ* and who may be alternatively called here, for the sake of convenience, "dying persons".

As the second major branch of the *ultra vires* doctrine, the law of death-sickness basically extends the limitations imposed upon bequests to cover gifts made by a dying person. But here the law is also concerned with those other acts and transactions of a dying person which may affect the substance and the devolution of his estate, such as sales, acknowledgments of debt, marriage and divorce. Because these are acts of immediate effect which are not, like bequests, postponed until death and which therefore may affect the gross, as opposed to the net, estate, the doctrine of death-sickness has the broader purpose of protecting the interests of the dying person's creditors just as much as those of his legal heirs.

1. Rationale of the doctrine

Although a dying person may, in terms of sanity and prudent judgment, be perfectly competent to engage in transactions, he is placed under interdiction in order to protect the interests of his creditors and his heirs, to the extent, basically, that any transaction which offends their interests will be effective only if they ratify it. The law aims only to protect mature interests, that is to say, in the case of an heir, when his right to succeed to part of the estate has crystallised, and in the case of a creditor, when his right has become attached to the estate. These rights are held to be so mature not only with death itself but with the advent of the immediate and effective cause of death, be it a physical disease or some other fatal circumstance. In other words, the law antedates the maturity of the heirs' and creditors' rights to the time at which it can be established that the process of dying had irrevocably begun.

1.1. Interdiction is not grounded upon personal contemplation of death

It must be emphasised, therefore, that determination of the initial issue as to whether or not a person is a dying person for the purposes of the *ultra vires* doctrine is essentially an objective process which has little to do with the state of mind of the person concerned or the possible motives that might have inspired his transactions. Unless and until the law is satisfied that a person is in fact dying, he is not subject to any form of restraint in his dealings with his property, however clear it may be that he was acting in contemplation of his death or with the manifest intention of circumventing the laws of succession, and however closely death in fact followed his transactions. On the other hand, once the law is satisfied that a person is dying, then he is subject to interdiction, however proper the motives behind his transactions might be and however convinced he may personally have been that he was not dying. In short, it is the physical fact of impending death and not the mental contemplation of it that is the basis of the interdiction. The purpose of the law is primarily to control the acts of dying persons rather than acts done in contemplation of death.

1.2. Gifts in death-sickness are not *donationes mortis causa*

Certain statements by modern writers on the subject of death-sickness, particularly with regard to gifts made therein, tend to confuse and complicate the issue simply because they are based on the false assumption that the doctrine is primarily concerned with questions of motivation. Fyzee,[1] for example, draws a parallel between a gift made during *marḍ al-maut* and the Western institution of *donatio mortis causa* – a gift which is made in contemplation of the donor's impending death and which may be revoked if the donor recovers from the illness or survives the circumstances from which he apprehended death. A *donatio mortis causa*, asserts Fyzee, is

> a gift of an amphibious nature; not exactly a gift, not exactly a legacy, but partaking of the nature of both. It is impossible to describe a Muslim gift during mortal illness in terms more apt, for in Muhammadan law such a gift is governed by rules deduced from a combination of two branches of the law, the law of gifts and the law of wills.

Fyzee does not, of course, imply that the *donatio mortis causa* as such is a recognised institution of Sharīʿa law, because any contingent gift, including one suspended upon the contingency of the donor's death, is null and void under Sharīʿa law.[2] But the notion of a gift made in contemplation of death

[1] A. Fyzee, *Outlines of Muhammadan Law* (Oxford, 1964), p. 363.

[2] A *donatio mortis causa* could in effect be achieved under Sharīʿa law, at least according to those schools which accept the validity of legal devices or *ḥiyal*, by the device of a sale with the option of inspection. The donor "pays" his gift to the donee as consideration for a wrapped or packaged object which he "buys" from the donee. Such a sale is not binding until the object has been declared satisfactory after inspection by the transferee.

suggests the parallel with *donatio mortis causa,* which in turn leads to the statement that a gift made by a dying person under Islamic law is a hybrid institution, partaking at once of the nature of both a gift and a legacy. And this is definitely misleading. For under the doctrine of *maraḍ al-maut* a gift made by a dying person is simply a gift *inter vivos* which is subject to the *ultra vires* rule: and it is so subject to the *ultra vires* rule not because it was made in contemplation of death but because it is a gift of property to which the rights of others, namely the donor's creditors and heirs, have now become attached.

Linant de Bellefonds also suggests[1] that the basic reason for placing a dying person under interdiction is the presumption that he is acting in contemplation of his death. He then notes the settled Sharīʿa rule of the validity of any transactions, particularly gifts, effected by a person who is so seriously ill as to apprehend death but subsequently recovers, and confesses it "difficult to understand this doctrine since (the transactions) were undertaken in contemplation of death". The rule would, of course, be totally illogical if the purpose of Sharīʿa law, like the law of *donationes mortis causa,* was to regulate acts done in contemplation of death. But that is not the rationale of the doctrine of *maraḍ al-maut.* The law is concerned only with the acts of a dying person; and a person who recovers from an illness, however serious, is not a dying person. Hence there is no ground for the nullification of any gifts such a person may have made during his sickness. In essence, the distinction between the law of *donationes mortis causa* and the Sharīʿa law of gifts made during death-sickness is that the former is designed to protect the donor in the event of his apprehension of death being unfounded, while the latter is designed to protect the matured interests of the creditors and the heirs of the donor.

Death-sickness is not, however, a purely objective doctrine of the causation of death. It does involve the subjective element of contemplation of death in a way which is systematically somewhat untidy and can be, admittedly, confusing. Basically, in traditional Sharīʿa law, a person's state of mind is irrelevant to the initial question of whether or not he is to be placed under interdiction on account of death-sickness, but his state of mind becomes decidedly relevant once it has been determined that he is in fact a dying person. For then the legal effect of the various transactions that he has undertaken during his death-sickness is governed by the basic

If, therefore, the donor does not die from the circumstances contemplated, he may nullify the gift by exercising his option of repudiating the "sale" after inspection. If he does die, his option lapses so that the gift will be binding.

[1] In his most valuable *Traité de droit Musulman Comparé* (Paris, 1965), I, 262–77.

presumption that he has acted in contemplation of his death. In short, therefore, death-sickness means both that the praepositus was in fact a dying person and that there is reason to presume that he acted in contemplation of his death.

It seems best, accordingly, to deal with the incidents of the doctrine of *marḍ al-maut* under two separate heads. It must first be established what circumstances, precisely, constitute death-sickness; for it is only during the period that a person may be technically described as *marīḍ*, or a dying person, that his transactions are subject to review. The second head of enquiry will then be concerned with the extent of the interdiction to which a dying person is subject in order to protect the interests of his creditors and legal heirs. On the first issue the various schools of Sharī'a law are broadly in agreement, but on the second they differ considerably.

2. Circumstances constituting death-sickness

Because the doctrine of death-sickness is primarily an objective theory of the causation of death and only secondarily a subjective theory of the personal apprehension of death, its starting point is necessarily the actual death of the praepositus. To ascertain the existence or otherwise of death-sickness is then a retrospective process of tracing events back from the time of death to the point of time in the past at which it can be established that the praepositus was a dying person. Those who are concerned to establish this are, of course, the creditors and heirs of the praepositus, whose purpose will be to challenge transactions undertaken by the deceased prior to his death as contrary to their matured interests. And they will do this successfully (for the purposes of a working definition) if they can show that, at the time of the transaction challenged, the circumstances of the praepositus were such as created a reasonable and settled apprehension of, and were in fact the cause of, his impending death.

For a person to be deemed *marīḍ*, therefore, four principal conditions must be met.

2.1. Reasonable grounds for apprehending death

The Mālikī jurist al-Ṣāwī speaks for most authorities when he describes death-sickness, basically, as "circumstances in which death comes as no surprise". In more detail the text runs:

Interdiction falls upon the person sick with a disease which normally, though not necessarily, causes death, such as one suffering from consumption or colic or raging fever, or a woman who is six months or more pregnant, or a person who is imprisoned for murder, or a soldier in the fighting ranks of battle. But there is no interdiction in the case of minor ailments such as ophthalmia or the scab... however afraid of death the sufferer may be.[1]

The requirement that there should be apparent and reasonable grounds for apprehending death is clearly the result of the combination of the objective and subjective elements of the doctrine. If it were solely a case of establishing when the praepositus became a dying person, the existence or otherwise of obvious grounds for apprehending death would be immaterial. If, on the other hand, the doctrine were a purely subjective one going only to the state of mind of the praepositus, the only requirement would be that the praepositus in fact apprehended death, whatever the grounds of such apprehension might be. The necessity, therefore, that the circumstances should be such as give rise to a reasonable apprehension of death (and in fact cause death) serves two purposes. First, it provides clear evidence to the world at large that the praepositus was a dying person; second, it enables the conclusion to be drawn that the praepositus must have known that he was a dying person and was acting in contemplation of his death.

While the settled principle recognised by all schools is that the circumstances constituting death-sickness must be, in the Arabic terminology, *mukhawwif* – i.e. "causing a fear" of death in the mind of a reasonable person – there is some controversy as to precisely what circumstances fall under this head. While most authorities, for example, freely admit that a variety of circumstances other than physical disease might amount to death-sickness – such as travellers at sea during violent storms, criminals sentenced to death, apostates in some circumstances (pp. 188-90 above), or persons resident in an area struck by an epidemic of a fatal disease – some Shīʿī jurists limit cases of death-sickness specifically to persons suffering from physical disease. An example of a more minor divergence of view is that concerning pregnant women. Some authorities hold that pregnancy can never be regarded as death-sickness because women normally survive it; others that all pregnant women are to be accounted *marīḍ* when delivery is imminent – i.e. after six months of pregnancy; and others, like the Ḥanbalī Ibn Qudāma (*al-Mughnī*, VI, 86), that pregnant women only become *marīḍ* when birth-pangs begin, "because this is a severe pain which causes an apprehension of death".

Clearly the existence or otherwise of a reasonable apprehension of death is a question of fact for each individual case, but there is general agreement upon the following evidential criteria:

[1] al-Sāwī, *Bulghat al-Sālik* (Cairo, 1952), II, 144.

(*a*) Minor ailments such as headaches can never constitute death-sickness however apprehensive of death the sufferer may in fact be, while manifestly fatal diseases or wounds always constitute death-sickness however optimistic of recovery the victim may be.

(*b*) To qualify as death-sickness an ailment need not necessarily be one which is invariably fatal; it is sufficient that there is reasonable probability of death.

(*c*) Physical pain, debility or incapacity is not a necessary condition of death-sickness, except in the case of chronic diseases such as tuberculosis or elephantiasis, or of simple senility, where it is only when the sufferer becomes incapacitated or bed-ridden that a reasonable apprehension of imminent death can be deemed to exist.

(*d*) Whether or not certain ailments constitute death sickness will often be a matter of the degree of their seriousness. Spasmodic dysentery, for example, will not normally qualify as death-sickness, but constant and uncontrollable dysentery will. Cases of doubt in this respect are to be resolved by expert medical evidence.

2.1.1. Traditional Sharī'a doctrine

According to traditional Sharī'a doctrine, therefore, the test of whether an ailment or condition gives rise to an apprehension of death is a purely objective one, which is based on the gravity of the condition itself and ignores any evidence of the personal state of mind of the sufferer.

2.1.2. Anglo-Muhammadan law: personal apprehension of death is necessary

Judicial practice in India and Pakistan, however, insists that a personal and subjective apprehension of death is an essential ingredient of death-sickness, and that no ailment or condition will constitute death-sickness unless there is acceptable evidence that the victim did in fact believe that his death was imminent. But this requirement of Anglo-Muhammadan law is additional, and not alternative, to the criteria of Sharī'a doctrine. In other words, no circumstances will constitute death-sickness under Anglo-Muhammadan law unless they amount to death-sickness under Sharī'a doctrine, but what is death-sickness according to Sharī'a doctrine is not necessarily so in Anglo-Muhammadan law. Where, for example, a person is informed after medical tests that he has a fatal form of heart disease, but nevertheless demonstrates an absolute conviction in his eventual recovery, be will be a dying person according to Sharī'a doctrine but not according to Anglo-Muhammadan law.

2.2. Apprehension of impending death: criterion of imminent death

An apprehension of death, however reasonable, is not in itself a sufficient foundation for death-sickness: the apprehension must also be one of imminent death. From the standpoint of the subjective aspect of the doctrine, this means that the law must be able to conclude that the praepositus acted under a sense of urgency stemming from a belief that his death was close at hand. From the standpoint of the objective aspect of the doctrine, it means that the circumstances must be the immediate cause of death, and this, of course, is a matter which can only be determined retrospectively, when death has in fact occurred within such a time from the advent of certain circumstances as enables the law to conclude that those circumstances were the proximate cause of death.

In any theory of causation, the decision as to whether given circumstances constitute either a proximate or a too remote cause must inevitably be to some degree arbitrary. In the event Sharīʿa doctrine settled upon the period of one year as fulfilling the necessary criterion of imminence. An ailment or condition, therefore, may only be deemed, retrospectively, to give rise to an apprehension of impending death if it in fact resulted in death within the outside limit of one year. This means that protracted diseases, however serious at their inception and however strong the apprehension of impending death at that time, will only rank as death-sickness in their terminal stages and never for longer than one year prior to death. Here it is clear that it was objective considerations of causation, rather than subjective considerations of the praepositus' state of mind, which conditioned the thought of the jurists and determined the scope of the *ultra vires* doctrine.

2.3. Settled apprehension of death

The apprehension of death must be settled in the sense that it must continue uninterrupted until the time of death. In fixing, retrospectively, the time at which the process of dying may be said to have irrevocably begun, the law will not go back beyond any time when there was a reasonable prospect of survival, even if there had been good cause before this to apprehend death. The strict notion of death-sickness in Sharīʿa doctrine is that of a progressive decline and steady deterioration in the dying person's condition. Accordingly, any improvement in the condition of a sick person which is substantial enough to remove the apprehension of imminent death means that the person will not be *marīḍ* in the eyes of the law for the period prior to this recovery, even if a subsequent relapse results in his death. He will be *marīḍ* only from the time of the relapse.

2.4. Death from the cause anticipated

The final condition of death-sickness is that death should in fact result from the circumstances which created an apprehension of it. The theory of causation requires strict and absolute proof that the praepositus was a dying person, and there is no such proof that any given circumstances are death-sickness unless and until they actually cause death. It is this settled rule of the law which finally dispels any notion that the doctrine is primarily concerned with acts done in contemplation of death.

P, for example, is informed by his doctors that he is suffering from an incurable form of cancer and has no more than six months to live. P thereupon gives away the whole of his property to his mistress. Two months later, when his condition has progressively deteriorated, P is involved in a road accident and dies two days afterwards from the injuries he sustained. His wife and family dependents are left penniless.

Here, P's act of gift is not *ultra vires* because he cannot be deemed technically a dying person at the time he made it. Although he had a reasonable and settled apprehension of impending death, and although death did in fact follow, his cancer was not the effective cause of death. Despite the clear intention of P, in contemplation of his impending death, to provide for his mistress instead of his family dependents, the *ultra vires* doctrine cannot be invoked to protect the interests of the legal heirs. P would in fact be deemed *marīḍ* only for the period of two days between the road accident and his death.

To summarise, then, the four criteria of death-sickness, a court which is asked to declare an act of the praepositus *ultra vires* because it was the act of a dying person must be able to answer the following question in the affirmative. Can it be established that (i) at the time of the relevant act there was good and obvious reason to conclude that the death of the praepositus was imminent, and (ii) nothing subsequently occurred, such as recovery, survival for more than a year or death by some other intervening cause, to affect the validity of that conclusion?

3. The extent of the interdiction of dying persons

Where the disease or condition from which a dying person is suffering affects his rational appreciation of events, his acts or transactions may be devoid of effect on the general ground of a lack of legal capacity. The *ultra vires* doctrine is not concerned with such circumstances but only with the transactions of a dying person whose rational appreciation and legal capacity as such are unimpaired. Following his death the concern of the law is to review his transactions and regulate their effect in a manner which protects the established interests of his creditors and heirs. Considerable divergence exists among the different schools on the particular issues involved, but it may be observed, as a general guide-line, that the Mālikīs adopt the most restrictive, and the Shāfi'īs the least restrictive, approach towards the acts of a dying person, with the other schools falling midway between these two extremes. The doctrine is best considered under the five separate heads of the principal transactions of gift, sale, acknowledgment of debt, marriage and divorce.

3.1. Gifts

3.1.1. The *ultra vires* rule applicable to gifts is basically identical with that applicable to bequests

The origin of the limitations imposed upon gifts made during death-sickness, which themselves provide the basis for the regulation of other acts and transactions of a dying person, is traditionally ascribed by Muslim jurisprudence to a precedent of the Prophet. When a man on his death-bed manumitted the six slaves which were his only property, the Prophet ruled that lots should be cast between them and only the winning two set free, the other four passing as inheritance to the legal heirs.

From this basis arises the systematic doctrine that a gift made by a dying person is *ultra vires* for precisely the same reasons and to precisely the same extent as a bequest. Hence, a gift is *ultra vires* insofar as it exceeds the bequeathable third or, in Sunnī law, if it is made to an heir, and the effect of the gift is determined by precisely the same conditions of ratification by the legal heirs, due account taken of the differences between the schools, as obtain in regard to bequests.[1]

[1] Only certain Shī'ī authorities depart from this settled doctrine and do not impose any restrictions upon gifts made during death-sickness. It is noteworthy, however, that the current Civil Code of Iran follows this minority view. Under the terms of the code the gratuitous dispositions of a dying person are governed by the general law, except that a

3.1.2. The donee as an "heir"

A gift to an "heir", however, means a gift to one who (*a*) actually succeeds to part of the estate of the donor, and (*b*) also was, by relationship, potentially the heir of the donor at the time the gift was made. In the case of a bequest the only time relevant to the question of whether the legatee is an heir or not is the time of the praepositus' death, because the bequest only becomes effective at that time. A gift in death-sickness, on the other hand, is a transaction with immediate effect and systematically can only be said to be in favour of an heir if the donee was at least potentially an heir at the time the gift was made and delivered.

Accordingly, just as is the case with a bequest, a gift will be *ultra vires* if it is made in favour of the donor's brother, even though at that time the donor had a son, if the subsequent decease of the son lets in the brother to inheritance. So, too, neither a gift nor a bequest will be *ultra vires* if it is made in favour of the dying person's brother, when the subsequent birth of a son excludes the brother from inheritance. But a gift in favour of a woman whom the dying person subsequently marries will not be *ultra vires*, whereas a bequest in her favour would be *ultra vires*.

3.1.3. Dispositions covered by the doctrine

A gift in death-sickness means, of course, a gift which is completed before the dying person's death. If the transfer of ownership is not immediate, but is in some way postponed until after the donor's death, the transaction will constitute a bequest for all purposes. Again, a gift lapses if it is not completed by delivery of possession to the donee before the dying person's death. Should the heirs in this case wish the donee to have the property concerned, he can take it only by a new transaction of gift between himself and the heirs.

The term gift in this context also covers any gratuitous disposition of property by the dying person, such as the release of a debtor from his debt, the provision of a guarantee, a charitable or family settlement by way of *waqf*,[1]

transaction to avoid the payment of debts is null and void, and a charitable or family settlement under the *waqf* system which is to the detriment of the dying person's creditors is valid only upon ratification by the creditors.

[1] The divergence of view between the schools as to the legal nature of the heirs' ratification of *ultra vires* dispositions (pp. 244–50 above) has an interesting result where the *ultra vires* disposition concerned is a *waqf* settlement by a dying person in favour of his heirs. Where the heirs ratify the *waqf*, it is valid for the Sunnī majority, who regard ratification as being in the nature of a waiver of the heirs' rights. But the *waqf* must fail in Mālikī law, where the heirs' ratification is regarded as a new gratuitous disposition of their own property, because no person can validly make a *waqf* in his own favour.

or even, according to some schools, payment by the dying person of a debt due to one of his creditors.

3.1.4. Preferential payment of a debt ranking as a gift

This last point is a controversial one which goes to the limits of the *ultra vires* doctrine as applied to dying persons. All the schools agree that a dying person may validly pay a debt which he incurred, from a sale or loan for example, during his death-sickness; for this is merely the completion of a transaction for reasonable consideration. The problem arises if a *marīḍ* person pays off a debt which arose before his death-sickness, when he has other creditors whose debts were also incurred before his death-sickness and his estate, upon death, proves to be insolvent. Is this preferential payment valid, or does it rank as an *ultra vires* disposition, so that the unpaid creditors may insist that it is reckoned as part of the estate available for the proportionate satisfaction of all the debts?

According to the majority, which includes the Ḥanafī and the Mālikī schools, payment of a debt in these circumstances is an *ultra vires* act. With death-sickness, they argue, as with bankruptcy, the rights of all creditors become attached to the dying person's estate, and the dying person is not allowed to act in a manner prejudicial to any of those rights. In the case of an insolvent estate, it is settled law that any instruction by the deceased in his will that one particular debt should be paid before others is invalid without the consent of the other creditors. The same rule must therefore apply to actual payment of the debt during death-sickness.

The alternative view, which finds particular support in the Shāfiʿī school, is that the preferential payment is perfectly valid *per se*. On this side it is argued that the dying person has merely paid what he was obliged to pay, just as if he were paying the price for an object bought; and further that the law recognises that a person may achieve by an act *inter vivos* what he could not validly achieve by a testamentary disposition. He may, for example, validly purchase an excessively elaborate and costly shroud, while instructions in his will that such a shroud should be purchased for him would not be binding upon his heirs, whose duty is to provide only a suitable shroud.

Whatever the merits of these various arguments – and perhaps those in support of the majority view are intrinsically more sound – they clearly reflect a different approach to the fundamental question of the extent to which the interdiction of a dying person should be carried. The view of the majority, and particularly the Mālikīs, is that an estate crystallises upon death-sickness and the dying person should not be allowed to disturb the *status quo* as regards the rights of the creditors and the heirs in any way. Shāfiʿī law is much less restrictive. A dying person is still a living person, and subject to the basic limitations imposed upon gratuitous dispositions as such, still has the right to order his affairs – a view which, as will be seen in what follows, conditions the Shāfiʿī law regarding acknowledgments of debt, marriage and divorce during death-sickness.

3.1.5. Priorities affecting gifts in death-sickness

Any gratuitous disposition of property during death-sickness, then, failing ratification in appropriate circumstances by the creditors or the heirs, is effective only after payment of the deceased's debts and only out of one-third of the net estate. Where a dying person has made two or more gifts which *in toto* exceed one-third of the net estate, the gifts take effect in order of chronological precedence until the third is exhausted. Where a gift or gifts made during death-sickness and bequests together exceed the third, the gifts have total priority over the bequests, simply because, as transactions *inter vivos*, they precede the bequests in point of time.

3.2. Sales

3.2.1. *Muḥābāt* transactions subject to the *ultra vires* rule

A normal sale or purchase contracted by a dying person for reasonable consideration is fully valid and effective. After the decease, however, the legal heirs may challenge a transaction of purchase or sale on the ground that it was a disguised gift – i.e. that the price paid by the deceased was greatly in excess of, or the price he received was greatly below, the true value of the object he bought or sold. The onus of proving that the consideration was reasonable falls upon the person who contracted with the deceased. If he fails to provide this proof, the transaction will be regarded as a *muḥābāt* – i.e. a contract for consideration with part of the consideration being waived or released. The difference between the real value of the object and the actual price paid will then be treated as a gift and as such subject to all the normal incidents of the *ultra vires* doctrine. If the person who contracted with the deceased is his legal heir, the whole of the gratuitous element in the *muḥābāt* will be *ultra vires* in Sunnī law, while if he is not a legal heir it will be *ultra vires* to the extent that it exceeds, by itself or along with other gifts and bequests, one-third of the net estate.

3.2.2. Controversy as to the legal effect of *muḥābāt* transactions

But while these general principles are clear and settled enough, the practical effect of *muḥābāt* transactions, particularly as regards ownership of the property concerned, is a controversial issue, as may be seen from the following example.

> During his death-sickness 'Umar sells his house, which represents the whole of his property and is worth £3,000, to his friend Zaid for £1,000. 'Umar's heirs object to the sale.

Here the court must determine precisely what the respective rights of the purchaser and the heirs are, not, of course, as being necessarily the final solution, but as the basis from which the parties may proceed to a more convenient settlement. Because of the variety of views within each school it is impossible to be dogmatic about the solution that any given court would adopt, but the general position is as follows.

3.2.2.1. Ḥanbalī law

Zaid is the owner of a two-thirds share in the property (one-third by way of sale and one-third by way of gift), and the heirs own a one-third share.

3.2.2.2. Ḥanafī law

Zaid must opt between (*a*) rescinding the sale altogether, and (*b*) keeping the property by paying its full price less the maximum gratuitous element – i.e. a further £1,000.

3.2.2.3. Shī'ī law

Zaid must opt between rescinding the sale altogether or confirming it. If he confirms it, the heirs then have the right to demand from him a further sum of £1,000 or to retain ownership of a one-third share in the property.

3.2.2.4. Mālikī law

Zaid may confirm the purchase, in which case he is the owner of a two-thirds share, and the heirs are the owners of a one-third share, in the property, or he may rescind it, in which case he is still entitled to a one-third share in the property as a gift.

3.2.2.5. Shāfi'ī law

Zaid must opt between (*a*) rescinding the sale altogether, or (*b*) taking a one-half share in the property by paying a further £500 to the heirs.

Ibn Qudāma (*al-Mughnī*, VI, 92–4) argues for the validity of this last solution by an elaborate algebraic equation. What it represents, briefly, is an attempt to enforce the contract which may be said to have been closest to the minds of the parties. The sale is seen as falling into three parts. One-third of it was clearly effective and one-third of it clearly ineffective. The final, potentially *ultra vires*, third is split between the purchaser and the heirs, being deemed half effective and half ineffective, so that the purchaser takes a further one-sixth share in the property for a further one-sixth of the true price.

3.3. Acknowledgments of debt

It is a settled principle of the Sharī'a law of evidence that a formal acknowledgment, or *iqrār*, of a debt owed by the acknowledgor to the acknowledgee is binding and irrevocable, in the sense that it establishes the existence of the debt, unless and until the contrary is proved: and proof of the non-existence of a debt is, for all practical purposes, impossible. Acknowledgments of debt by dying persons, therefore, created a particular problem. On the one hand, acknowledgment might be the only means by which a dying person could establish a debt which he in fact owed and thus avoid the serious sin of failing to provide for payment of his debts. "Even martyrdom thrice repeated", runs an alleged dictum of the Prophet, "would not atone for a debt undischarged." On the other hand, a false acknowledgment was obviously a simple and effective way of evading the laws of succession, particularly since payment of the deceased's debts would be the first charge, prior to gifts, bequests or inheritance, upon his estate.

3.3.1. The meaning of an acknowledgment of debt

The acknowledgments which are the concern of the law in this context are not only acknowledgments of debt arising from a loan or sale but also any other acknowledgment of financial responsibility – by way of guarantee, for example, or for the loss of a deposit held on trust by the acknowledgor for the acknowledgee. They also include acknowledgments in the nature of a release by the acknowledgor – for example, that a debt owed to him has been paid or that property held on trust for him by someone has been delivered to him. But in all these cases the acknowledgment itself is the only evidence that the dying person owes a debt or that a debt he was owed has been paid. Where a debt is established by other evidence, then, with or without acknowledgment by the dying person, it must rank as a true debt in the administration of his estate.

3.3.2. Shāfiʿī law: no special rules for the *iqrār* of a dying person

Shāfiʿī law, following its principle of minimal interference with the acts of a dying person, maintains that there is no reason for treating acknowledgments of debt during death-sickness any differently from acknowledgments made during normal health, particularly as, the Shāfiʿī jurists argue, a person who apprehends imminent death is most likely to tell the truth. Accordingly, debts established only by acknowledgment during death-sickness stand on a parity with all other debts in every respect. And this applies whether the acknowledgment is declaratory of a debt which arose before or during the death-sickness.

All the other schools, however, agree that an acknowledgment by a dying person that he has contracted a debt, or has been paid a debt which arose, during his death-sickness must be treated as a gift for the purposes of the *ultra vires* doctrine. But there are two views as to the regulation and effect of a dying person's acknowledgment of debt which purports to refer to a transaction concluded prior to the death-sickness of the acknowledgor.

3.3.3. Mālikī and Shīʿī law: suspect *iqrār* treated as a gift

Under Mālikī and Shīʿī law, where an acknowledgment made by a dying person is challenged by his creditors or heirs, the duty of the court is to investigate all the circumstances relevant to the acknowledgment. If, as a result of this, there is a reasonable suspicion that the acknowledgment was false, the sum of money or property involved will be treated in every respect as a gift for the purposes of the *ultra vires* doctrine. Where there is no such suspicion, the debt is established.

3.3.4. Ḥanafī and Ḥanbalī law: *iqrār ultra vires* only when it is in favour of an heir

Ḥanafī and Ḥanbalī law rests upon a clear distinction between cases in which the acknowledgee is a legal heir of the dying acknowledgor and those in which he is not.

Where the acknowledgee is a legal heir, the acknowledgment is *ultra vires*. This rule rests upon an extended version of the Prophet's statement concerning bequests which runs: "No bequest in favour of an heir and no acknowledgment of a debt in favour of an heir." Only with the consent, therefore, of the legal heirs, or some of them, will the acknowledgment be fully or partially effective. But with such consent the debt may be claimed by the acknowledgee as a debt, and will be paid out of the estate before any gifts made by the dying person or any bequests.

But, again, the *ultra vires* rule applies only where there is no other evidence for the origin or the existence of the debt than the acknowledgment. An example of a valid acknowledgment in favour of an heir would be where the dying person acknowledges the destruction of property entrusted to him as a deposit by one of his heirs, when there are witnesses to the fact of the deposit.[1]

"Heir", for the purposes of this rule, just as for the rule relating to gifts made in death-sickness, means one who was potentially the heir of the acknowledgor at the time of the acknowledgment and who actually succeeds to part of his estate.

Where the dying person's acknowledgment is made in favour of a non-heir, it is just as effective as an acknowledgment made in health, even though it should bind the whole estate. In Ḥanafī law, however, but not in Ḥanbalī law, the payment of debts established only by the acknowledgment of a dying person is postponed until after the payment of the debts established by other means, because, it is said, of the "suspicion" that attaches to them.

3.3.5. Acknowledgment of paternity is effective

Finally, no school lays down any special provisions for the case of an acknowledgment of paternity made by a dying person. Such an acknowledgment, which may, of course, have the effect of entitling the acknowledgee to the bulk of the dying person's estate, is governed entirely by the general law.

3.4. Marriage

A valid marriage contracted by a dying person, male or female, may clearly affect the amount of the estate which passes to the creditors or the heirs. Where the dying person is a male, he is obliged to pay dower and the wife, provided she is Muslim, becomes a legal heir with an indefeasible entitlement to a basic portion of at least one-eighth of the inheritance. Where the dying person is a female, the dower she receives may augment her estate but her husband, as her legal heir, will be entitled to a minimum portion of one-quarter of the net estate.

3.4.1. Majority view: marriage is valid for proper dower

With the exception of the Shī'a and the Mālikīs, however, the schools refuse to interfere with the freedom of dying persons to contract a valid

[1] See the translation of the Ḥanafī text *Hedaya* by C. Hamilton (Lahore, 1957), p. 437.

marriage or with the rights of inheritance which are the necessary result of marriage. The only limitation imposed is that a woman who marries a man during his death-sickness is entitled to claim as consideration for the marriage no more than her proper dower. If the dower agreed by the husband exceeds this, the excess is treated as a gift, or *muḥābāt*. Accordingly, the wife, as a legal heir, will not be entitled to the excess unless the other heirs agree; while if the wife is not a legal heir (because she is non-Muslim), the excess will be subject to the one-third rule. No such limitation applies, of course, where a *marīḍ* woman marries; for then any dower she receives in excess of the proper dower can only be to the benefit of her creditors or heirs. Nor is there, apparently, any rule that a *marīḍ* woman who marries must do so for at least her proper dower.

3.4.2. Shīʿī law: marriage is valid only if consummated

In Shīʿī law, a dying person who contracts a marriage is presumed to do so with the primary intention of creating a right of inheritance for the "spouse", and the purported marriage will be wholly null and void on the ground of improper motive. The presumption, however, is rebuttable by evidence that the dying person intended a *bona fide* marriage, and such evidence is held to be provided by the consummation of the marriage. With consummation, therefore, the marriage becomes valid for all purposes, including inheritance and dower.

With some hesitation the Shīʿī authorities rule that a dying person, male or female, who marries someone who is not *marīḍ*, will inherit from the other spouse, in the case of the latter's predecease, even if the marriage has not been consummated. In these circumstances the marriage is held to be valid because the only reason for holding that a marriage by a dying person is invalid – namely, that it adds to the number of the dying person's heirs – does not in fact apply. On the contrary, the heirs of the *marīḍ* person will benefit from the augmentation of the estate by the inheritance received from the deceased spouse.

3.4.3. Mālikī law: marriage is null and void

Under Mālikī law, any marriage contracted by a man or woman during death-sickness is null and void on the ground that it would introduce a new heir. The rule is absolute, no account being taken of the wishes of the legal heirs, or of the motive for the marriage, or of the predecease of the other partner. But where the union has been consummated the woman is entitled to dower. If she is herself the dying person, she is entitled to the proper or stipulated dower, whichever is less. If the man is the dying person, she is entitled to the proper or stipulated dower or one-third of the dying man's estate, whichever is less.

3.5. Divorce

If the normal rule that a final form of divorce terminates the mutual rights of inheritance between spouses were to apply to divorces during death-sickness, the devolution of the *marīḍ* person's estate would necessarily be affected. The divorced spouse could no longer claim any share of the inheritance but might, as a non-heir, take up to one-third of the net estate by way of gift or bequest. The *ultra vires* doctrine is directed only to this one question of whether a right of inheritance still belongs to a spouse who has been divorced during the death-sickness of the other spouse. Assuming the conditions of the general law to be satisfied, the divorce will be valid and effective for all other purposes, including that of extinguishing the *marīḍ* spouse's right of inheritance in the event of the predecease of the other spouse. Furthermore, the doctrine is not concerned with any judicial decree of divorce which happens to be granted during the death-sickness of one of the spouses, whether the ground for such a divorce arose during the death-sickness or before it. The scrutiny of the court is attracted only by the extra-judicial forms of divorce, effected either by unilateral repudiation from the husband or by the mutual consent of the spouses, which might have the primary purpose of destroying or improving the surviving spouse's rights of succession.

3.5.1. Divorce by *ṭalāq*: the wife's right to inherit is not extinguished

A *ṭalāq* which is pronounced in a final form during the husband's death-sickness has the normal effect of immediate extinction of the wife's right to inherit only in Shāfi'ī law. According to all the other schools the presumption will be that the husband's repudiation had the improper motive of interfering with the laws of succession, and therefore the wife's right of inheritance will not be extinguished. Only where the circumstances clearly rebut this presumption, as, for example, where the repudiation is occasioned by the flagrantly immoral conduct of the wife, will her right of inheritance be lost.

The improper interference with the laws of succession which is presumed by the law may take one of two forms. The repudiation may be designed to cut the wife off from succession altogether; in which case it is her rights which the law seeks to protect. Alternatively, in Sunnī law at any rate, the repudiation may be designed to allow the wife, as a non-heir, to take a gift or bequest of up to one-third of the net estate, instead of, say, a share as a co-wife in one-eighth of the inheritance; in which case the law seeks to protect the interests of the other heirs. In either event the rule is the same: the divorced wife remains an heir, entitled to her appropriate portion of the inheritance, and any gift or bequest in her favour is *ultra vires*.[1]

The duration of the divorced wife's right of inheritance varies according to the different schools. Under Ḥanafī law it continues only for the period of the wife's *'idda*, so that the divorce is in effect treated, but only for the purposes of succession by the wife, as a revocable divorce. In normal circumstances, perhaps, a *marīḍ* husband would die before the expiry of the *'idda*, but this is not necessarily so since death-sickness may last for one year. According to the other schools, the wife's right of inheritance continues for one year, which means that she must inherit if the husband is in fact *marīḍ*. She loses the right, however, in Shī'ī and Ḥanbalī but not in Mālikī law, if she remarries after the completion of her *'idda* within the one year period.

3.5.2. Divorce by mutual consent (*khul'*)

It is obvious that a spouse who agrees to a divorce by *khul'* during the death-sickness of the other spouse accepts the loss of his or her right of inheritance. Accordingly, in this context, the law is not concerned with the protection of the interests of the surviving spouse. The principal question that arises is whether the consideration paid by the wife to the husband in respect of the *khul'* divorce can be regarded as a disguised benefit, designed to give him in fact a greater share of the estate than he would receive as a legal heir – in other words a transaction which is prejudicial to the interests of the other surviving relatives. There is then the further allied question, in Sunnī law, of whether a gift or bequest made in favour of the divorced spouse constitutes improper interference with the rules of succession.

[1] Certain writers, including Linant de Bellefonds (*Traité de droit Musulman Comparé*, Paris, 1965, II, 334–9), state that where a husband repudiates his wife and then makes a gift or a bequest in her favour, her collusion in the divorce is presumed and the rule is that she takes her share of the inheritance or the gift/bequest, whichever is less. But could the collusion of the wife reasonably be presumed if, after repudiation which deprived her of, say, a Qur'anic portion of one-quarter of the inheritance, the husband left her a bequest of £1? If the wife in this case *must* take either her share of the inheritance or the bequest, whichever is less, the whole purpose of the *ultra vires* doctrine in protecting her interests is easily defeated.

3.5.2.1. *Khul'* during a husband's death-sickness extinguishes a wife's right to inherit except in Mālikī law

When the *khul'* divorce takes place during the death-sickness of the husband it is perfectly valid, in the majority view, in all respects and the wife loses her right of inheritance. The basis of this view is that the position of the husband's heirs can only be improved by his receipt of financial consideration from the wife in respect of the divorce.

Mālikī law, however, pursues its consistent policy of refusing to countenance any disturbance of the *status quo* as regards succession rights during death-sickness, and holds that the wife continues to be a legal heir. It is only in Mālikī law, therefore, that a gift or bequest in favour of a wife divorced by *khul'* during the husband's death-sickness will be *ultra vires* – and such a gift or bequest may, of course, far exceed the consideration paid by the wife for *khul'*.

3.5.2.2. *Khul'* during a wife's death-sickness: the husband remains the heir except in Shāfi'ī and Shī'ī law

When the *khul'* divorce takes place during the death-sickness of the wife, all the schools recognise that the consideration paid to the husband may constitute a disguised and beneficial right of succession, but vary in the extent to which they are prepared, in this event, to protect the interests of the other heirs.

The least restrictive doctrine is that of the Shāfi'īs and the Shī'a. Following the principle that there is no cause for interfering with any contract concluded by a *marīḍ* person for reasonable consideration, and taking the standard of the proper dower as the normal and reasonable consideration for a *khul'* contract, a *khul'* divorce is valid in all respects if the consideration paid to the husband is not greater than the wife's proper dower. Any amount in excess of this is treated simply as a gift to a non-heir during death-sickness and therefore attracts only the one-third rule, as does any further gift or bequest made to the husband. Certain Shī'ī authorities, in fact, set no limit at all upon the consideration paid for *khul'* during the wife's death-sickness.

Mālikī and Ḥanbalī law regard the husband in these circumstances as still the legal heir of his divorced wife. Accordingly, on the death of the wife, the husband is entitled only to the agreed consideration for the *khul'* or to his share of the inheritance, whichever is less. The amount by which the consideration exceeds his share of the inheritance, or any further gift or bequest made to him, will be *ultra vires* as being in favour of an heir.

Ḥanafī law similarly holds that the husband continues to be the legal heir of his divorced wife, but only for the duration of the wife's *'idda* – a rule parallel to that regarding inheritance by the wife following *ṭalāq*. Further, it introduces the criterion of one-third of the net estate as the maximum entitlement of the husband in these circumstances. In detail, then, the rule of Ḥanafī law is that where the wife dies during her *'idda*, the husband is entitled to either the agreed consideration or his share of the inheritance or one-third of the net estate, whichever is less; and that where the wife dies after her *'idda*, the husband is entitled to either the agreed consideration or one-third of the net estate, whichever is less. Any excess in the agreed consideration over these amounts attracts the *ultra vires* rule.

4. Modern law

With the two principal exceptions of (*a*) the insistence of Anglo-Muhammadan case law upon evidence that the dying person in fact apprehended death (p. 264 above), and (*b*) the apparent abandonment of the whole doctrine of death-sickness by the current Civil Code of Iran (p. 267, n. 1 above), this is a sphere of succession law in which virtually no changes of substance have been introduced, by legislation or otherwise, in modern times. Despite the widespread codification and reform of the law in the countries of the Middle East, the peculiarly Islamic doctrine of death-sickness remains the exclusive province of the mediaeval legal manuals.

INDEX OF ARABIC TERMS

INDEX OF CASES

"Analogy with Mālik's Rule", 87–8
Bafatun v. *Bilaiti Khanum* (1903), 30 Cal. 683, 174
Beguman v. *Saroo*, P.L.D. (1964), Lah. 451, 185
Chandrashekharappa v. *Government of Mysore*, A.I.R. (1955), Mysore 26, 187
"Computation", 85–6
"Confounding Rule", 88–90
"Deceit", 88
"Divided Inheritance", 74
"Donkey", 73–7, 127
"Hen and her Chicks", 69
Khurshid Bibi v. *Mohammed Amin*, P.L.D. (1967), S.C. 97, 20
"Lucky and Unlucky Kinsman", 55–7, 69–71
"Mālik's Rule", 87, 158
Narantakath v. *Parakkal* (1922), 45 Mad. 986, 190
"Pulpit", 47–8
Rahmatullah v. *Maqsood Ahmad*, 1950 I.L.R. All. 713, 174
"Restricted Female", 86
"Sa'd's Estate", 29–30, 130, 132
"Tatters", 79–80
"Two Deceivers", 46
"Two Decisions of 'Umar", 45–6, 127, 131–2

INDEX OF COUNTRIES

ALGERIA, 5
CEYLON, 5
EGYPT, 5
  bequests: acceptance of, 233; capacity of testator, 217–8, 226; conditional, 223; improper motive for, 224; proof of, 216; to heirs, 255–8; usufructory, 221
  daughter's right of inheritance, 7
  difference of domicile as bar to succession, 193–4, 231
  divorce, 21
  embryos, determination of rights of inheritance of, 212
  grandchildren as obligatory legatees, 143–57
  grandfather inheriting with collaterals, 158–61
  homicide as impediment to succession, 182–3, 230
  legitimacy, 27
  marriageable age, 12
  missing persons, judicial decree of death of, 211
  registration of marriage, 12
  "return" to spouse relict, 139–40
  succession in a dual title, 171
INDIA
  bequests, capacity to make, 217
  capacity to marry, 13
  death-sickness, 264, 279
  grandfather inheriting with collaterals, 158
  homicide as impediment to inheritance, 184
  illegitimate persons, inheritance by, 174
  legitimacy, 28
  marriageable age, 13
  missing persons, judicial decree of death of, 211
  "return" to spouse relict, 139
IRAN
  childless wife's right of inheritance, 114
  daughter's right of inheritance, 7
  death-sickness, 267, 279
  missing persons, judicial decree of death of, 211
  school of law applied, 5
  temporary marriage, succession rights in, 17
IRAQ
  bequests: acceptance of, 233; capacity of testator, 217, 226; existence of legatee, 228; proof of, 216; revocation of, 225; to heirs, 255–8
  daughter's right of inheritance, 140–3

INDEX OF LEGISLATION

INDEX OF NAMES

INDEX OF SUBJECTS